REAL WEALTH

Without Risk

**Escape the "Artificial Wealth Trap"
in 48 Hours...Or Less!**

J.J. CHILDERS

New York

Real Wealth Without Risk

©2009 J.J. Childers

Hardcover ISBN: 978-1-60037-469-2
Paperback ISBN: 978-1-60037-590-3

Published by:

MORGAN · JAMES
THE ENTREPRENEURIAL PUBLISHER™
www.morganjamespublishing.com

Morgan James Publishing, LLC
1225 Franklin Ave. Ste 325
Garden City, NY 11530-1693
Toll Free 800-485-4943
www.MorganJamesPublishing.com

Front Cover Design by
Kevin Berry
www.adworksinternet.com

Layout & Typesetting
Deborah Fields

DEDICATION

To my wife, Jill,
and my daughters,
Mary Katherine and Annabelle,
my inspiration
and my greatest supporters.

FOREWORD

by Robert G. Allen
Best-Selling Author
Nothing Down, Creating Wealth and
Multiple Streams of Income

Writing the foreword to anyone's book is an honor. To be able to write the foreword to a book by someone who you've had the pleasure of knowing and working with for over a decade makes it even more special. That is exactly the opportunity that I've been given by my friend, J.J. Childers. I'm honored to be able to make this contribution to his incredible book and I'm excited for all those who take the time to read it and apply the strategies that it contains. I know that it is something that will pay you back many times over.

For over twenty years, I've worked with countless people helping them to learn the art of creating wealth. I've had the great fortune to have written some of the best-selling financial books of all time. Through these books, my audio programs, and the educational companies that I've created, I've helped tens of thousands of people to generate hundreds of millions of dollars. I mention this not to boast but to let you know that I've got a sufficient background when it comes to recognizing good, valuable financial information. This is how I know the enormous value of the information in the book that you now hold in your hands.

I first met J.J. Childers through his father, John. John has served as a trusted friend, advisor, and mentor to me over the years and has been someone whose opinion I've greatly respected. John has always had an amazing grasp on financial strategies that anyone can use to build lasting wealth. It's no surprise that his son would have learned these strategies but it has been surprising at how well he has been able to articulate them in a way that can make a difference in people's lives. He is one of those rare individuals who not only listens to the strategies that he's exposed to, but absorbs them, studies them, and does what it takes to master them. This is why I chose to work with him both personally as well as through my companies. In this book, he shows us the strategies that he has learned from the many financial geniuses that he has worked with over the years as well as many others that he mastered on his own.

This book contains the type of hard-hitting, money-making, no-nonsense financial knowledge that you would have to spend years of study in order to find, if you were to ever find it. It is full of common-sense strategies that are unfortunately, not so common. While I'm honored to write this foreword, I'm also honored to have had a part in shaping the knowledge and philosophy that made it possible. This book will change your life.

ACKNOWLEDGEMENTS

I read a book one time that included the quote, "Writers should be careful with the pronoun I." Since writing a book is one of the most challenging endeavors you could undertake, it's virtually impossible to do it by yourself. While I may get a lot of the credit, there is no way that I could do it without the assistance and teamwork of some great people.

First, I've got to thank David Hancock and his team at Morgan James Publishing. Their dedication to publishing entrepreneurial books is something that I know makes a tremendous impact on their readers. Also, my friends Mark Dove, Steve Carlson, and Scott Bell who challenged me to put this book together. The three of you know the power of the "motivation through obligation" strategy and I thank you for pushing me to get it done. I've also got to thank David Early and Johnny Tollett for their assistance with managing my operations so that I could make this book a reality. My good friend, Ragnar Danneskjold, as always, did what he does best and helped me to knock down obstacles and make things happen.

This book would certainly not be complete without the tireless efforts of my book writing team. Attorney D. Bryce Finley made a major impact with his assembly and review of many of the concepts contained throughout the book. Without his work, you wouldn't be reading this right now. Additionally, Deborah Fields helped immensely with managing the book project and keeping the rest of the team on target. Kevin Berry did a great job with the cover design and does an outstanding job with all of my graphic design. My friends David and Wanda Phillips and Jeff Herb helped by providing a lot of the content for the insurance and investment strategies and continue to assist us, as well as our clients, with their wealth of knowledge. Marinda Bean and Michele Hunter did a great job in helping to compile and formulate the material on developing the "millionaire mindset." Dennis Depositario and Katrina Cristel Pineda were also invaluable to the overall project and continue to assist in the creation of our written materials. Without the assistance of these professionals, this book would not exist.

My wife Jill, and my daughters, Mary Katherine and Annabelle, demonstrate tremendous patience and understanding in putting up with my work schedule and provide me with the inspiration to do everything I do. I'd also like to thank my parents, John and Brenda Childers, for teaching me the importance of financial education and providing me with common sense knowledge that has reaped enormous rewards.

Finally, I'd like to thank all those who have written, assembled, distributed, taught, or in any way produced solid, time-tested, and proven financial strategies that have influenced me either directly or indirectly throughout my life and career. Without these resources, I wouldn't have been able to formulate the strategies that I use personally and included in this book. I'm forever indebted to two of my greatest mentors, Charles J. Givens, for designing the blueprint for financial education, and Francisco d'Anconia for his speech on money that has helped shape my beliefs. I'm also tremendously grateful for all those believers in the American Dream. Small business, entrepreneurs, and capitalists are what keep the engine running. If this book helps more people to join their ranks, my work has made the impact I've intended.

REAL WEALTH WITHOUT RISK

MY STORY

If there be any truer measure of a man than by what he does,
it must be by what he gives.

Robert South

I f you're looking for a story of someone who overcame insurmountable odds to create a once-in-a-million success story for themselves, this book is probably not for you. That's not to say that the strategies that you will learn throughout this book cannot make that happen. However, what I have found is that these types of stories can often be difficult, if not impossible, to duplicate. If, on the other hand, you are looking for a story of someone who has learned a set of strategies that, when properly followed, can enable virtually anyone to attain enormous success for themselves, you've picked up the right book.

My name is J.J. Childers and for the past twenty plus years, I have spent my life looking for ways to make and keep more money. In the course of this search, like many other people, I have found a lot of ways that didn't work. Despite this experience with ineffective methods, I have also been fortunate enough to find a set of strategies that work extraordinarily well. Even better, it has been my experience that these strategies can work, not just for those who have the proper experience, education, family background, etc., but for anyone who takes the time to learn them and more importantly, apply them.

In my life, I have had the privilege of generating enough income and building up enough assets to provide an amazing lifestyle for myself and my family. We've been able to do things that many people only dream about. We've been blessed with abundance that for many people would seem like something out of a fairy tale. In short, I have the life that I always dreamed of as a child. But it wasn't always like this.

To give you a little background on myself, I am an attorney. You may be thinking to yourself, "No wonder he's been able to create a great lifestyle, he's a lawyer." Well, what you may be surprised to find out is that very little of what I've been able to accomplish is a result of applying my legal skills. I must confess, however, that a lot of what I've been able to do is a direct result of what I've learned *from my clients*. That's right. I've learned more from my clients than they could ever hope to learn from me as their attorney.

You see, over the course of my career, I've had the opportunity to work with literally thousands of people. As an attorney, I work with people to help them implement legal strategies that enable them to protect their assets. Whether the threats to their assets come from lawsuits, taxes, estate issues, or any other type of source, I have assisted these clients in keeping their hard-earned wealth as safe as possible from these dangers. In doing so, I've been entrusted with sensitive, personal information about these clients that they would never dream of sharing with anyone outside of their inner circle. As a member of that inner circle, I was granted VIP access into the finer details of their financial lives. What I observed through this access was nothing short of amazing.

I've got to tell you, one of the things that has truly opened my eyes in working with people and their finances is the discovery that what I always thought to be true was completely wrong. Let me tell you what I mean. Like most people, I had a general impression of wealth that involved making an assumption of how much money someone had based on their appearance. If someone drove a nice car, lived in a big house, wore fancy clothes, and had a lot of "stuff," I presumed that they must be rich. What I have since found is that the saying, "you can't judge a book by its cover" is very true.

The reason that I know how true this saying is deals more with my personal situation than in merely dealing with clients. When I first got started in my career, I followed the path that seemed to be what everyone ought to be following. I wanted the big house, the nice car, the fancy clothes, and all of the "stuff." I found out that all of that was pretty easy to get, as long as you would sign up for the necessary credit. Even worse, I found out how easy it could be to acquire loads of real estate if I would only sign off on a big mortgage. Before I was thirty years old, I had become a millionaire. I had a great income, was building several new luxury homes that I intended to sell for profit, and had all of the "things" that I thought would make me happy. What I learned, the hard way, was that all of this could be taken away in the blink of an eye.

After I'd lost nearly everything that I'd worked so hard to accumulate, I was dumbfounded as to why all of these bad things had happened to me. I couldn't understand why the world was out to get me. What had I done that would cause the universe to go against me? What I found was that the "universe" hadn't gone against me, I'd gone against the universe.

What I didn't tell you earlier was how I had been able to achieve the things that I'd been able to accomplish. I hadn't won the lottery, received an enormous inheritance, or created an internet wonder company. The way that I had built up my fortune was by applying the strategies that I had learned from my clients.

In working with so many clients from so many different walks of life, I was exposed to a variety of differing approaches to wealth and wealth-building. I was able to see who really was wealthy and who only looked wealthy. In seeing their vital financial information, including financial statements, income tax returns, and other important financial documents, I saw those who "walked the walk" and those who merely "talked the talk." In my discussions with them, I did something different from the other professionals that they dealt with, I asked *them* for advice.

Many of these clients that I spoke with were almost caught off guard by the fact that I would actually ask them for advice. They explained to me that they were accustomed to having professionals talk down to them and position themselves as the ultimate authority without ever giving a second thought to the fact that their clients might have something worth their knowing. Because they sensed that there was something different about me, they were more than happy to share their wisdom.

In talking with dozens of the most successful clients at length, I soon discovered that many of their stories were very similar. In fact, I noticed that many of them followed similar, if not the same, strategies and principles. Every one of them gave credit to the strategies for their success rather than to themselves. I found this so interesting because the way I looked at it, if the strategies were responsible for their success, if I followed the strategies, I could follow their results.

Once I began implementing these strategies, I was blown away by the results I began to experience. Even better, I was struck by how quickly I began seeing a difference in my life. It was as if I had discovered a magic formula that worked miracles. The world was mine for the taking, until it all came crashing down.

After the crash, I spent more than my fair share of time making excuses for why things had gone wrong. I blamed everyone but myself. When I would talk with the people who taught me the strategies, I would tell them that the strategies didn't work. The funny thing is, they all gave me the same explanation. To summarize their responses, they said, "the strategies worked, you didn't." While I didn't understand what they meant at the time, I have since developed a great appreciation for the lesson that they taught me.

In looking back over the entire episode, it became increasingly apparent to me what had happened. *It wasn't that the strategies had stopped working, it was that had I stopped working the strategies*. I began thinking that I was the reason for my success rather than the strategies. As is so often the case, success started going to my head and I believed that I was responsible for all of my accomplishments. It was when I stopped following the strategies that I found out how much I was responsible for my success, or more specifically, my lack of success.

Once I came to the realization that I had indeed stopped working the strategies rather than that the strategies had stopped working, I knew what must be done. Since then, I have implemented a plan in my life of following the strategies and have been able to build my financial situation stronger than it ever was before things crumbled. Even better, I've worked with thousands of people who have been able to achieve the same type of success, and in some cases, even more than I have had personally.

The truth is that there are universal laws of success that can help you to attain whatever you set your mind to attaining. The key is that you have to know what these laws are and how they can be implemented. I have done this for myself, but more importantly, I have been able to help others to do it too. Through the teaching of these strategies, I have helped thousands of people build and save millions of dollars. Because of my success in sharing the strategies and helping others, I know that I can help you as well.

Through the financial education group that I've started, I am now able to share this message of financial hope with thousands of people. It was my goal when I started this endeavor to begin something that could truly make an impact on the lives of those around me so that they could experience the types of success that they were truly capable. The only thing that kept these people from seeing their dreams come true was a lack of knowledge. I've built an organization, as well as a career, on the foundation of that vision of seeing others prosper through the implementation of their own financial planning systems. We've seen success greater than anything we imagined when we began.

You can have this same type of success. While I haven't had the opportunity to personally meet you, I know that your life can be better. You deserve to have the type of life that you've always dreamed about. By following the strategies contained in this book, you can have it. A better life awaits you if you will simply take the time to learn how to get it. I look forward to hearing your success story and adding it to those of others who've learned the art of creating real wealth for themselves and their families.

To Your Success-

THE ARTIFICIAL WEALTH TRAP

*More people should learn to tell their dollars where to go
instead of asking them where they went.*

Roger W. Babson

We should have seen it coming. The signs were there. We knew what would happen. We'd been warned repeatedly. Even so, we fell in and have found ourselves in some serious trouble.

What am I talking about? The "Artificial Wealth Trap." Basically, we've fallen victim to a serious trap that has been set for us and our money. Even worse, the trap has been set not only for the money we currently have, but also for the money that we must make in the future. We've pledged not only the assets that we currently have but also many of the assets that we will work so hard to accumulate in the future. We've mortgaged more than just our houses, we've mortgaged our futures as well. And for what? All so we can live what we've been sold as the so-called "American Dream."

In working with people on their asset, estate, and financial planning for years, I've seen it happen. I've seen people fall prey to these "creditor predators" who flash images of the lifestyles of the rich and famous only to lead the unwary astray and off the road to prosperity. They are tricky in their methods. They are incredibly good at what

What has happened to the American Dream? Really, what has it become?

Today, we live in a society that has taught us that the key to happiness is to live "the good life." This "good life," is all about getting the things that we've been taught come with living that life. To live it, you need to wear the right clothes, drive the right luxury car (or monster SUV), live in the right neighborhood of houses with the latest decor, have the latest, greatest technology gadget(s), eat at the right restaurants, vacation at the right resorts, and so on and so on.

Now don't get me wrong. I'm all in favor of being able to have all of these things and more. As you'll see, I am not only in favor of these things, I believe that we should go after them with vigor. I believe that we should drive ourselves to get all of the things that we want, as long as we can afford them. This is where the challenge comes into play.

You see, years ago, these were the things that distinguished the wealthy from others. With their vast fortunes, they were able to afford things that most people only dreamed about. For them, this was the way of life that came as a reward for their years of hard work building and amassing their millions of dollars. These were the ways that most people used to determine if one was rich. After all, isn't that the primary goal of the American Dream for many?

Today, things have changed drastically. This is the essence of the "Artificial Wealth Trap." If you were to ask most people how to go about determining if someone was rich, they would probably list off all of the things that I just mentioned: nice clothes, luxury car, big house, exotic vacations, and a whole lot of other "stuff." The truth is, in today's society, you don't have to be rich to gain access to all of this "stuff," you just have to be willing to go into debt. The problem is that society has found our weakness.

Society, along with all of the products and services that it provides, has identified the human need to live the rich life and has made it accessible to virtually everyone. This is the carrot that they've dangled before us. What makes it so bad is that they've brainwashed us into thinking that life is simply not worth living if we don't have all of this "stuff."

Do you doubt me on this? Take a look around you sometime if you want proof. People are doing everything they can, everything within their power, to get as much of the right stuff as possible to prove their "success" and "prosperity" to everyone else. They get bullied into buying their kids the latest video games and the latest "it" electronic items so that they can have the things that their friends have. Look around at how many kids, let alone adults, have their own iPods and cell phones. Once again, I'm not against these things, I have plenty of these gadgets myself.

The biggest problem is that people are spending all of their money on these things (overconsumption) without setting aside anything for savings or retirement (under-saving). My point is not that we should live a life of deprivation, but that we've fallen into the trap of building "artificial wealth" rather than "real wealth." We've got to break this cycle before this cycle breaks us.

The effects of this trap are astounding. According to statistics provided by the *American Bankruptcy Institute*, the *Federal Reserve*, and the *National Endowment for Financial Education*:

- More young people filed for bankruptcy than graduated college in 2001.

- The U.S. has the lowest personal savings rate of any major industrialized nation.

- Half of American households have a savings of less than $1,200.

- From 1992-2000, disposable personal income rose 47% but personal spending climbed 61%. At the same time, the overall personal savings rate fell from 8.7% of disposable income in 1992 to zero in 2000.

- The personal saving rate went negative for the first time ever in 1998. Americans are spending $100.20 for $100.00 they bring home.

- Today's average 50 year old has only $2,300 saved toward retirement.

- 2 out of 3 households will probably not be able to accomplish one of their major life goals because they did not plan for the future.

On top of all of this, house foreclosures are at an all-time high with over two million foreclosure filings in 2007. According to an article in *Kiplinger* magazine, America is the richest country in the world, yet, ironically, we have the highest percentage of people living paycheck to paycheck.

The darkest part of this picture is that we have been lulled into a false sense of success in digging ourselves into a hole. Even worse, the more trouble that we get ourselves into, the better we look like we're doing. The banks and credit card companies are making millions off of us and our desire to live the life of "artificial wealth." We've gone from a life of living paycheck to paycheck to living paycheck to credit card to minimum payment debt slavery. This isn't the way life was meant to be lived. I mean, really, is this what they had in mind when they came up with the concept of the American Dream?

The harsh reality is that this "American Dream" is becoming more of an "American Nightmare." People today are working more and more and getting less and less. We find our nation, and ourselves, on an endless treadmill of despair striving to keep up only to find ourselves failing to make any progress. The economic outlook is brutal and seems to be getting worse.

The picture isn't pretty, but we have to realize, *it is what it is*. Right now, America is neck-deep in credit card debt, facing all-time foreclosure records, and on the wrong side of a trade imbalance. In other words, America is not going to bail you out. The government is every bit as much of a part of causing you to fall into the "Artificial Wealth Trap" as any other group. Think about it. Recently, the U.S. government outlined an economic stimulus plan to jump-start the economy. As part of that plan, the government stated that they would issue rebates to taxpayers so that they would have more money to spend. You see, the government knows that when people get money in their hands, they spend it. Make no mistake, the government is not going to come to your rescue.

The situation out there is scary. People are in trouble. They are in way over their heads with no way out. The bad news is that things are only getting worse. Those members of our society who benefit by others' falling into the "Artificial Wealth Trap" are getting better at what they do. They've got enough money to finance their message and begin spreading their affluenza- inducing propaganda out there to an extent that it infects everyone.

Consider the way that they are getting their hooks into us, even from a very early age:

- In 2000, credit card companies mailed 3.54 billion solicitations to consumers; this corresponds with an average of 3 credit card offers per month per household.

- More than three-fourths of college undergraduate students have credit cards; most have multiple credit cards with an average total balance of $2,748. Ninety-five percent of college graduate students have cards; each has an average of four cards with an average total balance of $4,776.

- Seventy percent of college undergraduates have at least one credit card, and 20 percent of students who carry balances on their cards have debts of more than $10,000.

- Approximately 35 million Americans pay only the required minimum-as low as 2%- of their balance each month.

- The average credit card debt among 25-to-34 year olds was $5,200 in 2004, 98% higher than in 1992. (*Business Week*)

I spoke with a friend of mine the other day who told me that he counted up how much money in credit offers that his son (who was still in college) received and the total came up to over $90,000. He couldn't understand how someone so young with no job and no credit experience could be offered so much credit.

The answer is simple. The credit card companies recognize that this affluenza is a disease that is contracted through learned behavior. They recognize that young people are especially susceptible to the message of instant gratification and that the way to get it is through credit cards. They understand that if they can get them started early in this pattern of overconsumption and under-saving that they will most likely have them for life. They've paid psychologists and behavioral scientists millions of dollars to teach them the methods for essentially hypnotizing people into doing whatever it is that they want them to do.

This is the way things are out there. You've gotten yourself in trouble. It's not your fault. How could you possibly expect to survive when there are legions of highly educated people out there working together to take your money from you. The worst part of it all is that they convinced you into voluntarily and willingly giving them your money. Just like a drug dealer starts out by giving a prospective junkie a "free sample," we've been lured down the same type of destructive pathway. Now you've found yourself caught up in the trap.

Do you want out? Are you tired of paying out more than you take in? Are you fed up with worrying? Are you sick and tired of being sick and tired? Are you looking for a way to make your escape? If so, you've done the right thing by getting your hands on this book. To get out of this mess, this "Artificial Wealth Trap," you're going to need an escape plan. That's what this book is all about.

The good news is that breaking free from the clutches of those "creditor predators" and making your escape to real wealth is also a learned behavior. If you'll take the time to educate yourself on the strategies needed, you can find yourself one of the truly prosperous members of your generation.

There's only one chance for you to reclaim your own personal American Dream, and it begins right now, right here, with this book. This book was written to help you to learn how you can make your own American Dream become a reality for yourself and your family. You may be in trouble right now. Realize that it's not your fault. The forces out there have set a trap for you that you didn't know how to avoid. By following a plan for building real wealth, you can get out and stay out. You can have anything you want. *You can do it*.

CHAPTER 1

THE ARTIFICIAL WEALTH E.S.C.A.P.E. PLAN

A man with a surplus can control circumstances,
but a man without a surplus is controlled by them,
and often he has no opportunity to exercise judgment.

Harvey S. Firestone

The "Artificial Wealth Trap" is very real and very disastrous. If you fail to take the steps necessary to get yourself out of this trap, or steer clear of it from the very start, you will end up like so many of those less fortunate souls who wonder what happened to them. That's why I've written this book, to make sure that you can take control over your finances rather than having your finances take control over you.

For years I've thought of writing a book on wealth. I've always thought of a book as a detailed description of the results or secrets obtained through in-depth study of a particular subject. As such, a book on wealth seemed only natural for me. You see, throughout my life, I've been greatly intrigued with the reasons why there aren't more people in our country who are able to become truly wealthy. Really, it is sometimes downright perplexing to try to determine why it is that some people are phenomenally wealthy while others seem to struggle just to make ends meet. This, in a country where we are literally surrounded by more opportunities than we can possibly take advantage of that could produce more wealth than we've ever dreamed attainable. Yet amidst all of this opportunity, the vast majority of people seem to just drift along through life like a ship without a rudder.

When I say that I've been greatly intrigued by this study, let me tell you that it is something that has somewhat consumed me and has driven me in everything that I now do or have ever been involved with professionally as well as personally. In fact, I've spent most of my life working with individuals who were striving to acquire wealth. As an attorney, I devoted my practice to dealing primarily with wealth preservation issues focusing on the areas of asset protection, estate planning, and tax reduction. In that capacity, I've worked with countless clients who were engaged in all sorts of businesses at every stage from start-up to family succession planning. I've even worked with organizations and companies whose primary objective was to educate students on the nuts and bolts of making money. Through this experience, I've been fascinated with my observations on how some prosper while others seem to fail time and time again. It has been an eye-opening, and in many instances, shockingly surprising study.

I've seen examples of individuals who had no formal education, training, experience or any of the other so-called necessary ingredients for success achieve far more than those who had all of the appropriate traits that we've always been taught were essential to achieving success. I've been thoroughly surprised to see some people who were seemingly doomed to fail from the beginning go on to attain extraordinary results while those who had everything in their favor attain little or no real or meaningful results. This was something that always surprised me until I came to one of the most important realizations in my life. *I realized that there were certain key characteristics that those who achieved their goals all possessed that those who were not successful failed to possess.* In every single situation, there was a plan that was followed that gave those who followed it no choice but to succeed. It was as if they had eliminated the risks and were simply destined to reap the benefits of following their dreams.

Would you like to know some of those components? Would you like to *learn* how to master the concepts required to envision, strategize, create, accumulate, preserve, and execute plans for unlimited amounts of wealth? Would you like to *learn* the "secret" recipe for making everything that you've always wanted to accomplish become reality?

These may seem like rhetorical questions but let me assure you, not everyone will answer these questions in the same way. There are plenty of people who will say that they would like to master the methods for building wealth but they just aren't willing to do it. Let me assure you of something right now. I will make you a promise if you are willing to make one to me. It's simple. It's fool-proof. It's risk-free.

Here's my promise.

> *I will show you in clear, concise, easy to understand terms the secret formula for envisioning, strategizing, creating, accumulating, preserving, and executing wealth in such extraordinary amounts that anything you wish to acquire can be yours.*

Is that a bold statement? You better believe it. Is it too good to be true? For many people, yes it is.

The fact is, most of the people who read that statement may not have the wherewithal to truly comprehend the magnitude of that incredible assertion. There are many people who simply don't truly want to succeed. That may sound crazy to you right now but let me assure you that it is one of the most accurate statements you will ever encounter. Sure, everyone wants the results of success but very few people are willing to *do what it takes to make it happen.*

Over the course of this book, I will lay out a plan for you that, when properly implemented, will change your life in ways that you never dreamed, much less believed, were possible. Even better, once put into place, the steps involved in this plan will work in your life in a manner that almost seems too easy. Have you ever known someone who seemed to have the so-called Midas touch, where everything they touched turned to gold? Chances are, they were following the concepts outlined in this book. I'd be willing to bet that they were following them whether they realized it or not.

The simple fact is, *if you follow these steps, you will get the same results.* There is indeed a recipe for success and you have it in your hands right now. The question is, are you willing to follow it? I made you a promise but now I'll tell you what you must promise in return.

You must be willing to follow the steps outlined in this book and commit to following a new way of life. It is a way of life that will enable you to accomplish anything you set out to accomplish, acquire anything you set your mind to acquire, and to achieve any goal you set out to accomplish. The most difficult part is to determine what it is that you want most. If you can do that, I can do my part.

The introduction to this book explained the concept of the "Artificial Wealth Trap." People find themselves in a situation where they simply don't know what to do to get out of this trap. The answer is that they must find a way to escape. This book outlines the way for them to do that by following the "Artificial Wealth Trap E.S.C.A.P.E. Plan."

E.S.C.A.P.E. is an acronym for the six essential steps that must be followed in order to free one's self from the financial bondage that results from falling into the "Artificial Wealth Trap." These steps make up the plan that I have learned from working with clients and others who have attained vast levels of success. Even better, I've seen it work in my own personal life as well. But best of all, I've seen it work exceedingly well in the lives of those who I've helped to implement a plan of their own. What that means is that it can work for anyone who takes the time to learn and apply these strategies in their own personal lives.

The truth is, you can do this. You can have anything that you set your mind to if you first learn how to go about doing it. My six step plan can help you do it. Over the course of this book, these six steps are explained in greater detail with dozens and dozens of strategies showing you exactly how to make your dreams a reality starting from Day One. But before we get to the specifics, we've first got to take a look at an overview of the various steps involved in this plan.

The six steps that make up this plan include:

Envision – If you can't see yourself becoming financially free, you most likely will fail. The first step you will need to take to achieve your own E.S.C.A.P.E. is to envision exactly what you want out of life, and get used to what that life looks, sounds, and feels like. One of the most powerful concepts that I've ever learned in my studies on wealth is the power of the following statement: *you must be able to conceive it and believe it if you are to achieve it.*

Strategize – This is the planning stage of the E.S.C.A.P.E. plan. You'll take the future you envisioned for yourself in Step 1, and lay the groundwork for achieving the real wealth you desire and need.

This is where you formulate your plan for accomplishing what you set for yourself in the envisioning process. This is the process that most people overlook and the key reason why they tend to go about life aimlessly without ever accomplishing anything of true value. You can do whatever it is that you want to do if you will first take the time to map out the way to reaching your desired destination. This book will take you through the process of doing that.

Create – The next step is to create streams of income that can help you build your wealth. This step is all about making money. Some might say that this is the most important step: I would suggest that it is certainly the most exciting, but not necessarily the most important, at least in the long run. After envisioning and strategizing comes the time to actually create the cash flow that can help you to start building real wealth. Most people get started on this part but never become wealthy because they never make it past this step. Remember, there is no amount of money that you can make that you can't outspend. Money is the fuel that powers our lives but just as an engine eventually runs out of gas, our lives will run out of money if we don't set in motion the other steps involved in creating real, long-term wealth.

Accumulate – This is the step that makes the biggest difference between those who make a lot of money and those who become wealthy. Believe me, there is a difference. I've worked with countless individuals who have made really good incomes only to find themselves living paycheck to paycheck. Granted, these paychecks are bigger than most people's, but they still find themselves on the same treadmill. There are many people who generate a lot of income only to find themselves stuck in an undesirable situation when it comes time to retire or to take a break from their frenzied work lives. Unfortunately, they're not able to leave their work behind because they haven't built any wealth. To become wealthy, you've got to have your assets working for you. Many people are their only income-producing assets. Once they produce income, all that income goes out for various expenses. To become wealthy, that income must be put to work as an income-producing asset as well. This step is critical to your success and will make all the difference between living a great short-term lifestyle and living a long-term life of real wealth.

Preserve – You can't create real wealth without knowing all of the best ways to protect assets, plan your estate, limit your taxes, defeat devastating debt, and control health care expenses. If you fail to implement this step, you will end up losing a substantial portion of all that you've worked to accumulate. This situation is similar to pouring water into a bucket. If the bucket has a bunch of leaks in it, it doesn't matter how much water you pour into the top, it will never fill up. It's the same way with stopping the loss that results from improperly safeguarding our assets from those unnecessary distractions. Keep in mind that there will be some initial investment to get your plan properly structured. However, this is a step that begins paying for itself immediately. The wealthy know the secrets to legally paying less in taxes than others by employing certain strategies. You need to learn to apply those strategies in your life as well if you plan on becoming wealthy.

Execute – Nothing happens in life without action. We can have the best plan imaginable but if we don't implement the plan, there is no point. This is the time in your E.S.C.A.P.E. plan to turn the key, step on the gas, and make things happen. The bottom line in this last step is that you must stop talking the talk and start walking the walk. This is the part of the plan that makes all the difference between those who achieve their dreams and those who simply dream of achieving. This book will unveil strategies that will help you to make things happen.

As you begin to delve into the process of envisioning, strategizing, creating, accumulating, preserving, and executing wealth, there is something that you must understand. *There is nothing difficult about becoming wealthy. It's just different.* The sad truth of the matter is that most people aren't wealthy because they never decided to become wealthy. Because they never decided to become wealthy, they never took the time to learn what it takes to become wealthy. As such, they were not, or have not been, engaged in the activities that will create the wealth that they wish to acquire. I want you to understand one important principle that must be put into place before you go any further. *You must be willing to do what it takes to make your dreams possible.* There will be times that you don't want to do certain things. There will be times when you would rather follow a different set of rules. You must realize that it is in these times that following the principles in this book can make the difference between someone who is wealthy and someone who is not.

If you will do for a few years what most people won't do, you can do for the rest of your life what most people can't do.

It is with this thought in mind, that I welcome you to one of the most important, life-changing books that you will ever read. Are you up for the challenge? Let's make our escape from the "Artificial Wealth Trap" and begin building real wealth.

Chapter 2

Taking Control Over Your Own Financial Matters

Never stand begging for that which you have the power to earn.

Miguel de Cervantes

I never cease to be amazed at the way that many financial professionals act and how they treat people. In fact, sometimes I find it downright incredible that they are able to make a living for themselves when so much of their income is dependent on working with others. For a profession that relies on generating income from people who willingly turn over the control of their money to them, many of these people seem pompous, ungrateful and downright inconsiderate in dealing with their clients. I would even go so far as to say that they often treat their clients like idiots. The worst part about it is that the clients not only put up with it, they keep coming back for more.

This whole relationship is one that I find rather baffling. Why on earth would a financial professional treat their "customers" in a way that most businesses would never dream of? Considering that the people that they are dealing with had to have some sort of sense in order to generate the dollars that they bring in for these financial "professionals" to invest for them, it stands to reason that these clients just might have some sense when it comes to understanding their finances as well. Nonetheless, they end up treating their clients in some of the most condescending manners imaginable. Rest assured, not all professionals are like this but it's far too prevalent.

While the industry provides "equal access for all" in dishing out their courses of condescension, the treatment seems to be worse when dealing with some people than others. I often find it humorous when I'm with my wife to observe how certain members of the financial services industry treat her. By "financial services industry," I'm referring not only to bankers, stock brokers, and other types of money managers, but also to lawyers, accountants, insurance agents, real estate professionals, and others. It has almost become a hobby of mine to let her do the talking when we go into a meeting with these groups. I get an enormous kick out of seeing them talk to her as if she's a child only to have her respond back to them in terms that are above their heads.

You see, my wife is one of those super-smart overachievers who has never received less than an "A" in any course that she's ever taken. Not only that, she graduated at the top of her class when she got her accounting degree from college, went on to pass the C.P.A. exam, and then graduated at the top of her graduate school class with a Masters of Business Administration in Finance. Suffice it to say that she can hold her own when it comes to financial matters. As you can probably imagine, she doesn't particularly appreciate it when the so-called "financial professionals" talk down to her. But you know what? Regardless of her credentials, knowledge, or experience, the primary reason that she doesn't appreciate it is because it's just not acceptable.

I certainly agree with her that it's unacceptable for people to treat others this way no matter what their level of knowledge. I guess the thing that baffles me the most is that the "customers" are so often willing to put up with it. Why is that? I think that the primary reason for it is that people find financial matters to be rather confusing and even downright scary. There's good reason for this since we're simply not taught a whole lot about the matter. Think about it. Do you remember that course in school called, *How to Make Money* 101? Of course you don't, it wasn't there.

I learned a very valuable point from one of my mentors many years ago in studying the process of building wealth. The point was that there are essentially three things that we were never taught in school:

1. How to have a successful marriage;

2. How to raise children; and

3. How to successfully handle our finances to become wealthy.

These are some of the most important things in life yet no one teaches us much about them. Since we've never been taught a whole lot about these things, we end up going to others who are supposed to have the proper expertise on these matters for assistance. Unfortunately, many people often find themselves asking someone who may not be any better suited to tackle the issue than they are. This book is designed to keep that from happening.

The purpose of this book is to help you to gain better control over one of those issues on which we've received no real training. As you should probably realize by now, this is not a book on successful marriages or raising children. It is, however, a book that can make an enormous difference in your life by preparing you to take control over your personal finances and get you on the path to prosperity.

An essential step in that process is to make the decision to become your own financial expert. From the beginning, I want you to understand that I am not implying that you will end up handling every aspect of every tax, legal and financial issue that you ever face all by yourself. There will undoubtedly be circumstances and times where you will want to employ the services of some qualified professionals with areas that are above your level of expertise or that you simply don't want to handle for yourself. This book will enable you to significantly limit those times to only the ones where advanced help is truly necessary or warranted.

I often compare the process of dealing with finances to the process of dealing with one's automobile. A basic understanding of automobiles is necessary for anyone who operates one. We all know that it won't operate if we fail to put gasoline in it, but there's more to it than that. Additionally, we've got to put oil in the engine and keep the tires in good condition so that it will operate properly. While there's certainly a lot more than that, let's stick to these for now. There are many people who could probably change their own oil and tires if they had to, but they choose to have someone else do it since it is something that they don't particularly want to deal with. On more complicated issues, it may be necessary to hire a specialist to assist with things. We

While each of these groups can certainly provide their own types of assistance, and should definitely be relied on for certain services, none of them should be viewed exclusively as your sole financial advisor. These are merely members of your team who serve in "utility" roles, each one has a part but none of them is the "Director" of your overall financial "picture." Who then should serve as the Director of your finances? The answer is *you*.

Many people feel ill-equipped to function in this role. They often feel like they lack the knowledge to manage their finances or make the decisions that must be made to ensure that their finances are handled safely, securely, and in a manner that will ensure their ability to retire comfortably. This is a legitimate concern but one that can easily be handled by obtaining the knowledge to make it happen. This book will serve as your guide.

In working with people over the years, I've encountered my fair share of people who seemed almost petrified at the thought of being their own financial director. What I always tell these people is that they already have experience in the role. When they give me that strange look, I remind them that whenever they turn things over to someone else, this is an act of them serving as their financial director. The difference is that I want them to develop a better understanding of financial issues so that they will be better equipped when they make that decision in the future.

This book will help you to gain the confidence necessary to become your own financial expert and to eliminate two of the undesirable elements that often accompany the handling of money. Those two elements are *risk* and *fear*. If we can learn to reduce the risk involved, we can essentially eliminate any fear associated with taking care of our finances ourselves. To reduce the risk, you must increase your knowledge. By increasing your knowledge, you greatly reduce the level of risk involved in any activity.

One of the things that I work with my clients on is a formula for building what I refer to as "real wealth without risk." If you're like most of them, I'd imagine that the concept seems somewhat appealing. But what does it mean to be "without risk?" As you can probably imagine, there's no such thing in life as being truly "without risk." There are risks involved in everything we do. There's even risk involved by *not* doing things. Actually, that's not a bad thing.

First of all, let's decide whether or not we would truly want to be "without risk" even if we could. Some of you reading this right now might be asking yourself, "why on earth would anyone *not* want to be without risk?" Well, that is exactly how many people feel, so much so that they never accomplish anything because of their absolute paralyzing fear of risk. To overcome this fear, we need to take a closer look at the whole concept of risk and see how it can be effectively managed. When you develop an understanding of risk management, taking the first step to learning how to become your own financial expert is a snap.

When it comes to risk, you've probably heard at some point in your life the saying that *along with greater risk can come the prospect of a greater reward.* While that well-known axiom can hold the potential to make you an enormous amount of money, it can also serve as a recipe for disaster. That statement can make or break you in your quest for wealth. The secret is in finding a proper balance. If you are to become your own financial expert, you've got to understand the balance associated with walking the fine line of risk-taking.

You see, throughout my business life and in my work as a lawyer with countless other business men and women, I've struggled with finding the proper balance of risk. I like to consider myself personally as somewhat of a risk-taker. I actually pride myself on the fact that I am willing to move forward in many situations where others may have had the same opportunity but were simply unwilling to take the risk. This has made me a lot of money over the years but it is not a concept that you can blindly follow. There is a process that you must follow.

One thing that you must understand is that *there is a big difference between taking reckless, imprudent risks and taking methodically calculated risks.* The ability to assess a situation and determine the proper amount of risk involved can mean the difference between getting involved in something that can make you a fortune or leave you high and dry. This ability is increased by obtaining a greater level of knowledge. Increasing your level of knowledge on financial matters is critical. The information contained in this book will help you do it.

One of the areas that will prove especially critical in operating your financial affairs is determining the risk associated with various financial moves. While I am certainly not what one would refer to as "risk averse," I try to steer clear from involving myself in activities that carry an unacceptably high level of risk. The reason for this is that I have learned some valuable lessons from the most expensive school in this or any other country, the School of Hard Knocks. Through the "classes" taught in this school, I've learned that it is the times where I took those uncalculated risks where I got myself into trouble. By learning from the experience of myself and others who've attended this school, you can borrow this experience without having to pay the high tuition for the lessons yourself.

There is an important part of getting involved in any type of arrangement, business or otherwise, and that is what is referred to as *due diligence*. I am a firm believer that one must look before one leaps. Due diligence is the process of doing just that. By simply taking a little time to look into a situation, you can save yourself a lot of potential problems and reduce the amount of risk involved significantly. This is where knowledge comes into play. The process of reading this book is now part of your own due diligence. Through the process, you will build the confidence necessary to take control over your finances.

Do not allow the existence of risk to keep you from getting involved in an activity. Risk will always exist no matter what you do in life.

If you plan on becoming wealthy, you must understand that there is both good risk and bad risk. There are certain situations where risk may be rather beneficial and other situations where it should be avoided, or at least managed quite closely. The ability to accurately assess and maintain a proper risk balance is an ability that must be mastered. Throughout this book, I provide you with strategies for minimizing risks and maximizing profits. You will find that there will be risks that you take that will mark turning points that make the difference for you between a mediocre life and an incredible one.

One of the most important principles that you could ever learn when it comes to building wealth is that *the activity itself does not determine the level of risk involved.* To illustrate this point, I'll use a gentleman who has been referred to as the "World's Greatest Investor," and who was recently listed in *Forbes* magazine as the richest man in the world,

Warren Buffett. Considering his success, we could certainly assume that he knows a thing or two about wealth. Even more important for our current discussion is that he made his money by investing so we can also presume that he knows a few things about the stock market. With that understanding, my question for you is this: who has the greatest amount of risk involved when trading in the stock market, Warren Buffett or the new investor just getting started? Needless to say, the greater risk goes to the new investor just getting started by a wide margin.

That's not to say that there is no risk involved when Mr. Buffett is involved, it's just that the level of risk has decreased exponentially. For Mr. Buffett, investing in the stock market is not an overly risky endeavor. It is something that he's been actively involved in for a number of years and he has been able to learn a great deal about it over that time period. One of the things that he's learned is how to assess the level of risk involved in making certain financial moves. He recognizes that there are always risks involved and he applies enough due diligence to minimize the risk to a point of virtually assuring that, *over the long run*, he will not lose money.

One of my favorite investment quotes of all-time is from Mr. Buffett regarding the "rules" of money: *"Rule #1: Never lose money. Rule #2: Never forget Rule #1."*

The difference between Warren Buffett and the new investor in this example is knowledge. This leads us to another of the most important lessons you must learn if you ever plan to accumulate any significant wealth: As your knowledge in an activity increases, the risk involved in that activity decreases.

Once again, it is important to understand that there is still some risk involved in Mr. Buffett's investments. As a matter of fact, the risk involved in his investments is part of what makes them so profitable. But it's equally, if not more, important to understand that Mr. Buffett is engaged in taking methodically calculated risks rather than those taken by those chasing after speculative profits. Similarly, when we seek to create wealth for ourselves, we should only take these same types of risks.

"Real Wealth Without Risk" can be attained by significantly reducing, if not eliminating, the risk involved in our activities. This is accomplished by increasing our knowledge level. By doing that, you will be well-equipped to serve as the Director of your financial picture. After all, who cares more about you and your money than you do? By following the strategies laid out in the E.S.C.A.P.E. Plan, you will be well on your way to building your own wealth, and with much less risk. Let's get started in making our "escape".

Part I:

ENVISION

CHAPTER 3

ENVISIONING WEALTH FOR YOUR LIFE

A rock pile ceases to be a rock pile the moment a single man contemplates it, bearing within him the image of a cathedral.

Antoine de Saint-Exupery

No matter what it is that one sets out to accomplish, regardless of the size, scope, magnitude, or enormity of the task, it all begins with an idea. Many people never create the lives that they want, never become wealthy, and never escape the "Artificial Wealth Trap" because they have never taken the time to picture themselves in a position of financial independence. This is especially disheartening considering the fact that people could accomplish so much more for themselves if they would only come to the realization that they can control their lives by controlling their thoughts.

One of the keys to achieving anything in life is to visualize the dream as a reality. In working with extraordinarily successful people over the years, I've found it especially significant that every one of them has had a clear vision of what they wanted. This is referred to as the "Millionaire Mindset." It is the foundation upon which all things are built.

In my life, one of the success principles that has had the greatest impact on me is that *all seeds of success must first be planted in the mind.* All that we have to do is determine what type of success that we'd like to achieve and then we can figure out the type of seeds to plant. The biggest challenge that people face is that they never take the time to think about exactly what it is that they most want for their lives. If they can't come up with a target to shoot for, it is highly unlikely that they will ever strike it.

Even worse, many people mistakenly believe that their dreams are nothing more than fairy tales that will never come true. The truth is that all things that have ever been accomplished first began as a thought in someone's mind. It can work the same way for you but you must first determine what it is that you want to accomplish.

STRATEGY 1: Determine exactly where it is that you are going.

In order to achieve your goals, you must know what they are and you must believe that they are attainable. Belief in one's self is absolutely critical to success, especially in a world full of skeptics, cynics, pessimists, and worse. Being able to know where you are going, and really seeing yourself in that position with your goals fully realized, is essential to being able to achieve that life. Having a picture in your mind of where you want to go in life and what kind of lifestyle you want to have, is critical to your being able to reach that pinnacle.

Because this is so important to your success, it is the first step in the overall E.S.C.A.P.E. Plan from the "Artificial Wealth Trap." That first step is what I refer to as ENVISION. You must picture yourself where you want to be and the life that you would like to create for yourself.

STRATEGY 2: Use your mind as a computer by following the "G.I.G.O." (Garbage In Garbage Out) principle.

From a very early age, my father required my brother and me to listen to personal development audio cassettes. Early on, as you can probably imagine, this was not something we looked forward to doing. Not only that, he would make us do things such as looking into a mirror and telling ourselves, "To be enthusiastic, you've got to feel enthusiastic." We would have to repeat this saying over and over again, with increasing excitement and volume, until we convinced him that we were indeed enthusiastic. I remember hating this ritual. As I've gotten older, however, I can't thank him enough for making us do it. He knew the importance of a positive mental attitude and the greater importance of passing this trait on to his children.

You see, the audio cassettes and these motivational exercises began to shape our minds. Although we didn't particularly like going through this ritual, one of the things that ended up happening was that we would laugh at ourselves which put smiles on our faces. When you start your day out with a big smile on your face, good things seem to happen to you.

We also began to think differently than other people. We didn't know that we were different. As far as we were concerned, everyone did these things. How wrong we were. We thought that since we had to do these things that everyone else must be doing them as well and that everyone else must be looking at the world in the same manner. What we didn't realize at the time was that we were developing a vision for our lives that we have since implemented and seen become realities. This has been far more valuable than any amount of money that my dad could have given us.

In dealing with people from all walks of life, I am dumbfounded by the lack of vision that most people have for their lives. Strangely enough, at least to my way of thinking, they've never listened to positive messages or gone through exercises for helping them to envision a life of abundance. Even worse, they may have been taught by their parents or others that the exercise was worthless and they've since developed that belief themselves. For them, the thought of ever becoming wealthy is nothing more than a pipe dream that is for someone else but certainly not for them.

STRATEGY 3: Create a "Dreams List" for what you most want to accomplish for your life.

It is sad, but true, that most people never take the time to sit down and think about what it is that they truly want out of life. Because they never formulate their vision, they never achieve the results that they are capable of achieving. This is a major challenge that holds the vast majority of people back.

In my lifetime and over the course of my business career, I have worked with literally tens of thousands of people, either directly or through the readership of my articles and attendance at my educational seminars. I never cease to be amazed at the lack of understanding of the importance of a positive mindset. Many people even go so far as to call it "fluff." This "fluff" has helped create fortunes for many, many people and can do the same for you once you apply it.

To begin the process of creating the life that you've always wanted, create a "dreams list" for yourself. Sit down and write out a list of all the things that you'd like to accomplish in your life. Your dreams list is simply a compilation of your completions to this statement:

"If I had unlimited time, money, talent, and the support of my family, I would..."

Take the time to sit down and write out your ideas for how you would like to complete this statement. Go somewhere that you know you won't be bothered so that you can focus. Once you've found your spot, relax and let your imagination flow. Let the ideas pour out. Your ideas and dreams may come slowly at first, but as your imagination takes over, you may have trouble writing fast enough to keep up with the flow.

Don't let your sense of reason or any potential excuses interfere and tell you that you "can't do something." Remember, this is your dreams list. If you can't dream something big for yourself, no one else will. What you write on your list will likely inspire you, motivate you and excite you. These dreams may make you realize things about yourself that you never allowed yourself to think about. But most importantly, this list will define desires and dreams that may have been buried or abandoned by the complexities of everyday life.

In those audio cassettes that my dad made us listen to, I remember hearing a saying that has had a profound impact on my life. The saying was, "whatever the mind can conceive, and believe, it can achieve." At the time, I'm quite sure that I didn't grasp it fully. Over the years, it has become clearer. You see, there are multiple parts to it. The first component is that you must *conceive* of what it is that you want. You must identify your life's dreams, take the action necessary to list them out, and then use your mind to make them seem totally real to you. You need to accept them as something that will happen in your future. This is the first step in making your dreams become realities.

STRATEGY 4: Eliminate any negative thoughts, feelings, or influences when creating your "dreams list" and believe that anything is possible.

For many, however, their internal governors, or self-limiting beliefs, will not allow them to conceive anything more than mediocrity for themselves. If they were to think about something that they felt was too unattainable, their minds would shut down to the concept. Unfortunately, the reality is that they could far surpass these goals if they would simply come up with a greater vision for themselves.

The second component of that incredible statement is that you must *believe* that you can accomplish the task that you set for yourself. Many people come up with brilliant plans only to abandon these plans due to their self-limiting beliefs. Unfortunately, I see this in people all the time

I remember a seminar I held in Las Vegas several years ago. A lady in the seminar was really down on herself. I sat and visited with her for over two hours telling her that she could do anything that she set her mind to accomplishing. I told her repeatedly that I could tell by simply talking with her that she was an intelligent, articulate, capable person who had a lot to offer. She continued to disagree with me and tell me that I was wrong. No matter what I told her, she refused to allow herself to think positive thoughts about herself. It was one of the saddest things that I have ever seen. The saddest part is that it is something that I have grown accustomed to seeing.

I've come to the harsh realization that there are an overwhelming number of people whose experiences growing up were far different than mine. When I was growing up, I never had the slightest doubt that I could have the life that I set for myself. I always knew that I could have whatever it was that I went after. Unfortunately, this is not the same type of upbringing that everyone experienced.

I've worked with people over the years who have shared stories with me about how their parents always told them how worthless they were. I've talked with people who shared stories with me of how their parents, family, or loved ones shot down nearly every dream that they ever set for themselves. While some of these parents and others may have been well-intentioned, the problems that they've caused in the minds of their children are deeply rooted. If you are one of these people who have had this type of experience, I'm sorry. I promise you, however, that I am going to do whatever I can to help you to overcome these challenges so that you can reclaim these dreams and go after them with a renewed vigor that will make them a reality. I've done it with many people and I can do it with you too.

The reality is that *you can have just about anything that you want in this life*. The key is that you must conceive it, and believe it, if you are to achieve it. You must envision yourself having the life you want. If you think about it, there are very few things that you have ever truly wanted that you were not able to attain. The difficulty with most people is that they only go after the smaller things in life and never work towards their greater goals or work towards achieving those things that truly mean the most to them. By not working towards the things they really value, they are not only limiting their financial success, but also their personal satisfaction with their lives.

What I've learned from working with some truly wealthy and successful people is that the process of achievement is the same whether you're going after something small or shooting for something much bigger. Understanding and implementing the process, makes those big goals seem much less daunting and far more doable. As you continue to achieve bigger and better things for yourself, things that previously seemed unattainable will seem easily achievable. This is one of the major differences between the big-time achievers and others. The most amazing part of this is that you can apply the same process and get the same type of results in your own life.

By far, the biggest obstacle to your achieving bigger goals is your ability to set them for yourself. *You can do great things*. All you have to do is learn how to accomplish them. When you set bigger

40

goals, your mind will go to work on plans for accomplishing them. While your conscious mind may only be working when you do, your subconscious mind is plugging away, working on solutions to your challenges twenty-four hours a day, seven days a week. Put it to work.

STRATEGY 5: Create a "Values List" for your life.

An extremely valuable and important exercise that an ultra-successful mentor of mine once shared with me is to create what he referred to as a "values list." For many people, this may sound somewhat vague and ambiguous. What is a "values list?" Well, your values are simply the ideas and beliefs that you have about the relative importance of the things in your life. By understanding these values, you will be more likely to go after the goals and dreams that are best-suited for you and your individual situation. I don't mean to say that your goals will be lower than someone else's, they'll just be different. You need to make sure that your "life ambition ladder" is leaning up against the right wall so that you will have the motivation necessary to keep climbing it. Your values are a big part of this.

For instance, if you value security highly, choosing to leave your job and start your own business might cause a great deal of stress for you. On the other hand, if you value wealth above security, staying in a safe, secure job at an average wage would be a frustrating experience. If you value security and wealth equally, you will experience what is known as the "frustration of values conflict"- worrying that any decision you make might be the wrong one. Let me assure you of something: *If you simply make no choice, you've still made one.*

It's important to realize that the emotions involved in deciding what the right ambitions are for you are all mental and have nothing to do with what is the right or wrong decision. This is why it's so important to identify your values before your specific goals are set. Acting consistently with your values brings you a feeling of emotional balance, security and pleasure. Acting against your values brings fear, guilt, frustration and emotional imbalance. These are negative feelings that can derail you off of your track to success. The good news is that you can eliminate those negative feelings.

You have two choices: you can either change your actions to support your values, or you can change your values to support your actions. Don't compromise on those things that you hold most important. In order to determine if your actions and your values are working together or in conflict, make out a written list of your values. List those things in your life that are the most important to you such as your faith, your family, your friendships, charity, health, travel, career, home, free time, peace of mind, even respect, or wealth and fame.

Making a list of your values can help you focus on accomplishing what's most important. This is an incredibly important step on your path to prosperity. Many people are tempted to skip it. Don't.

STRATEGY 6: Recognize a universal truth: you become what you think about.

Another saying from those audio cassettes along with a number of classic personal development books that my wealthy mentors have had me study over the years is that the strangest secret in life is that *you will become what you think about.* Understanding the unmistakable reality of this statement is the first step in making your escape from the "Artificial Wealth Trap". It is the first step in regaining control of your life. It is an introduction to your own personal power source for overcoming all obstacles in your life.

STRATEGY 7: Learn that you can make things happen or you can make excuses but you can't make both.

Truly believing in yourself, and what you can do, means overcoming obstacles, doubts, doubters and objections. You can do it if you will follow a plan, step-by-step, patiently and with true determination. To merely "try," thought at least an attempt, is just not going to be enough.

42

You must make a commitment to your success. You must give it your all. As with anything in life, this may involve temporary set-backs, but the end result is that you will simply step back and redirect your efforts to achieve your goals.

It's important to recognize that you didn't fail, you just made a wrong turn on your journey. You've probably heard about Thomas Edison, who finally figured out the key to the light bulb after more than 1,000 unsuccessful attempts. When asked how he managed to deal with so much "failure," his response was that he had never failed. He said that he'd simply discovered over 1,000 methods that didn't work. Now is not the time to give up, it's time to figure out your next course of action in working towards your goals, and then take it.

Unwavering faith in yourself, your abilities, in your hopes and dreams, and in your absolute determination to achieve them will put you on the path to success. These strengths will allow you to overcome the obstacles and the "doubting Thomases" in your path. Remember, *if you are willing to do what it takes to live like others won't, you can live a life that others don't.*

STRATEGY 8: Enlist the support of your "team members" to increase your collective strength.

In escaping the "Artificial Wealth Trap," just like quitting smoking or any other major life change, having the support and understanding of those who are important in your life will make your journey that much easier. If the important people in your life are working toward the same goals as you, your task becomes half as difficult, and your escape from the "Artificial Wealth Trap" twice as fast. When someone dreams *with* you and believes *in* you, no obstacles are insurmountable. Even better, when you recruit others into this process of changing their thoughts, you will see that they too will begin to change their lives as you begin to change yours.

Once this happens, you will find that the excitement and enthusiasm of those around you will help you to maintain your own. You will then find yourself surrounded by like-minded people whose primary objectives are success for themselves and others. This mentality, just like a negative mentality, is contagious. By surrounding yourself with positive reinforcement, you will greatly expedite your attainment of the life you want most.

STRATEGY 9: Create a "vision board" to keep you focused on the life and dreams that you want to achieve.

One of the easiest ways to keep your dreams fresh in your mind is to use what I refer to as a "vision board" as a daily reminder. The exercise of creating a vision board is basically just like it sounds. I want you to put together a collage of pictures that portray the way that you want your life to look. Whether you go to the store to find magazines, search for images on the internet, or use some of the pictures that you may have taken of your own life, put together a visual image of the life that you want for yourself and see what it looks like. Create the image on your "vision board" and make that image burn itself into your mind.

For many people, this may seem rather simplistic, like more "fluff," but again, it is based on results. We humans, as a species, are visual creatures. We have gone to great lengths to develop art, visual media, literature, fashion, etc. that pleases the eye. These things aren't necessary for survival, but they have been cultivated and highly prized since early man drew his world on rock walls. The reason for this is that it's a fact that what we see, we remember.

By creating a vision board, you will put a sharp, fresh image in your mind every time you look at it. By keeping your mental image crisp and new, you will consciously and subconsciously gravitate toward those actions that will get you closer to making that image real, because to you, it is already a reality. When you are facing set-backs or difficulties, and you will, go back to that vision board and refresh that image in your mind. You will find that you also refresh your determination and energy to reach that ultimate vision.

The next step in your "Artificial Wealth Trap" E.S.C.A.P.E. Plan is to define your goals-those specific objectives on which you've decided to invest your time, effort, energy, and money. Whereas dreams and values are your mental attitudes, goals are the physical objectives that will help you achieve those dreams. To get the most benefit and satisfaction, your goals should reflect the most important values in your life.

There are specific parameters that make up a goal. To be effective, a goal must:

- **Be specific and measurable**- You must be able to define your goal in dollars, numbers, or specific terms, like the size and style of house, or the exact job that you want.
- **Have starting and finishing dates**- You need both starting and ending dates for accomplishing each goal. These target dates will help you determine where your time and energy would be best spent.
- **Be put in writing**- Not writing down your goals is a huge mistake. When your goals are written down, you can better plan, organize and control the paths that will lead you to accomplishing them.
- **Be written in terms of results and not processes**- By result, I mean that it defines the way your life will be after you have accomplished your goal. The process involves the steps, time and resources it takes to get there. That will come later.

Focusing on the result, not the process, creates a road map from where you are to where you want to go. The process will take shape after you have your goals defined.

STRATEGY 11: Write out a "pledge statement," sign it, and carry it with you.

Having your goals list is a wonderful motivator and a powerful way to help keep you focused on the results you want for your future. But the "Artificial Wealth Trap" has its own ways of sucking you back into its depths. Temptation is everywhere and corporations, the media, and even our own conditioning make it easier to give in to the temptation than to resist. We are basically made to feel guilty if we deny ourselves or our family a luxury item, as if somehow we are being "deprived" of something necessary. In order to ease your escape and overcome temptation, you need to make a promise to yourself that you will stay the course.

I don't just mean to look in the mirror once a day and say, "I'll do it." That works for some people, but most of us need more help. Make it a pledge, an affirmation with yourself, to take steps, daily, weekly, annually, etc., to move toward fulfilling your goals.

This type of a pledge can really work if you commit to it. The fact is that once you commit yourself in writing, especially if others witness that you have done it, you are more likely to keep on track to avoid potential shame or failure. So make your statement pledge for escaping the "Artificial Wealth Trap" and keep it with you for times of temptation.

Here's how I want you to do it:

Start out by writing your goal as a statement.

"I WILL accomplish...."

Next, tell yourself HOW this will help you.

"By accomplishing this, I will..."

Last, tell yourself WHY this will help you in your life.

"This is important because it will enable me to..."

To better illustrate this for you, let's take a look at an example. Let's say that you've always wanted to be a millionaire. Your statement pledge could start with the overall goal.

"I WILL become a millionaire.

The next part would be to give a time frame for making it happen.

"I WILL become a millionaire by the time I am 50 years old."

Then tell yourself how this will help you.

"By accomplishing this, I will become financially independent."

Then decide why this will help you in your life and why it's important to you.

"This is important because I will be able to provide a stable financial life for my family so that I can spend more time with them and it will give me the money necessary to achieve my dreams."

Finally, I want you to sign your written statement. My telling you to sign it may sound odd, but when you sign this contract with yourself, you are promising that you will work towards these goals. You may even want to have someone you respect or who you want to hold you accountable witness it for you. Remember to always keep your statement with you. Whenever you get a chance, pull it out and read it to yourself again. Continue to reinforce your goals by reminding yourself of exactly how you will better your life by ignoring the temptation of instant gratification and working towards the end result of true, long-term satisfaction.

STRATEGY 12: *Identify and eliminate destructive values from your life.*

Let's delve a little deeper into some key concepts that can make a major difference to you in your life and in your journey of success. Too often, we start down a positive path to achieving a life-long or necessary goal, like escaping debt or discontinuing detrimental behavior, only to veer off that path by our own hand. What I mean by this is that our own bad habits and our own destructive values serve to sabotage us. Why on earth would we do this to ourselves?

I have come to the conclusion that some people are just afraid of success simply because it is something different. In a strange way, a negative situation, like financial hardship or an unhealthy lifestyle, is oddly comfortable to many people because it's familiar. They say they want to change, but they actually fear change, or they fear the failure that comes when they can't stick with the strategies that made them successful. To rationalize or justify their position, they fall into a trap of being consumed by destructive values.

Most of our values are positive, but destructive values always lead to personal failure and must be changed in order to achieve, and maintain, a successful, fulfilling life. Some destructive values include:

1. The desire for something for nothing. Symptoms of this negative value include gambling, cheating, or stealing.

2. The desire to feel superior to others. Symptoms of this negative value include gossip, prejudice, bigotry, aloofness, criticism, and blame.

3. The desire for continuous, instant pleasure. Symptoms of this negative value include overspending and overindulgence in food, alcohol, or drugs.

The quickest and easiest way to defeat the temptation to engage in these negative activities is to be honest. Being honest with yourself and identifying destructive values is the most important step in their elimination. Destructive values are parasitic and drain energy and resources that could be spent on the things that you value most. Giving in to these emotions will serve to rapidly undo any successful steps that you have taken. Destructive values are roadblocks in the way of your escape from the "Artificial Wealth Trap."

You must establish the elimination of any destructive values as one of your primary goals. You've got to be careful as you go through this strategy however. Don't use your list to become self-critical. Remember, this list is intended to help you improve your current situation, not for you to use to beat yourself up. The whole point of this exercise is not the list itself, but what you do with this list. You need to create a plan to eliminate these destructive values from your life. If reaching your goals is more important to you than these destructive values, then do what it takes to not just create it, stick to it.

STRATEGY 13: *Make a conscious effort to recognize negativity and do what it takes to move yourself away from it.*

Negative behavior, negative thoughts, and even negative emotions can do irrevocable damage to your success, *if you let them.* Sociologists and psychologists have known about these threats for years, but have thought of them mainly as threats to mental or social health. Applying them to financial success and happiness is a relatively new concept. When you can conquer social negativity, internal negativity, and negative emotions, you can repel the attacks and threats to your success. Most people find that eliminating the negativity has a side benefit of exponentially increasing their personal satisfaction, both with themselves and their lives in general. After all, the point of success, however you define it, is to be "happy."

Negative emotions will also hinder our successful escape from the "Artificial Wealth Trap." This negativity can rear its ugly head in a number of ways, whether we are the ones feeling the emotions or they come from external sources. Anger, rage, jealousy, hatred and fear can unravel all the positive strategies that you have in place. You can't do much about controlling the negativity of those around you but you can avoid those people that exhibit this negative energy. Sometimes this can be difficult to do, but being around a negative person can drag down even the happiest of souls.

Do whatever you can to distance yourself from these people. If they ask you why you seem to be acting strange or stand-offish, talk to them about the importance of a positive mental attitude and how their negativity is acting as a hindrance to your success. If they can't understand this, you may have to create even greater distance in the relationship. Chances are, however, that you may even serve as a positive influence on them after they've had a chance to think about it. This may even lead them to change their negative behavior. If not, so be it. Just don't allow yourself to be negatively impacted by the attitudes of others. If you find yourself encountering this type of situation, do what it takes to move yourself away from it.

STRATEGY 14: Spend the majority of your time on those goals and objectives that are the most important to you.

One of the greatest discoveries of philosophers over the centuries is that our lives reflect the thoughts that occupy our minds. At this point, we've already created our Values List and our Dreams List. We mentioned that we truly are happiest when we're spending our time and resources on the things and people that we value the most. Knowing which dreams and values are the most important to you will help you to make certain that you focus your energy on achieving the goals and objectives that will give you the most satisfaction.

Since we become what we think about, make a conscious effort to spend the majority of your time thinking about those things that are the most important to you.

STRATEGY 15: Begin each morning and end each evening with a visualization of your goals.

Always remember that the strangest secret to achieving extraordinary levels of success is that *we become what we think about.* The greatest part of this is that since we can control what we think about, we can control what we become. The important thing is that you must put thoughts in your mind that will produce the type of results that you want to come to fruition in your life.

What most people don't, or simply forget to, realize is that we really have two minds: our conscious and our subconscious. While our conscious mind is only working while we are aware of it, the subconscious mind is working 24 hours a day 7 days a week. It will continue to work on that which we program it to focus. For this reason, I want you to set aside a moment of time, even if it's just 5 or 10 minutes each morning when you wake up *and* 5 or 10 minutes each evening before you go to bed, to focus on what your life will look like once you accomplish the goals that you've set for yourself.

When you look back on your life in the coming years, I want you to say with absolute certainty: "I always knew that I could do it." In fact, I want you to say that today. Start practicing saying that phrase now. Relish the feeling of accomplishment that you'll have and use that as your daily inspiration along with the great examples and advice you've learned in this chapter.

That said, let's get down to business with the STRATEGIZE portion of the "Artificial Wealth Trap" E.S.C.A.P.E. Plan.

Part II:

STRATEGIZE

CHAPTER 4

PLANNING YOUR WORK, AND THEN WORKING YOUR PLAN FOR PROSPERITY

Think of yourself as on the threshold of unparalleled success.
A whole clear, glorious life lies before you. Achieve! Achieve!

Andrew Carnegie

Having a dream to chase after is extraordinarily important as the starting point for anything. It's especially important in following a plan for creating a life of Real Wealth. However, even the most optimistic dreamers must take the time to set out a plan for how they intend to accomplish their dreams and the process of building wealth is no different. Building a life of financial freedom requires setting out a plan and then following that plan to make the dream become a reality.

In this Part of the book, our focus is on the STRATEGIZE portion of the "Artificial Wealth Trap" E.S.C.A.P.E. Plan. This is the phase of the process that requires us to take an inventory of ourselves and our finances to determine exactly what it is that we will need to do to reach our Real Wealth destination. By mapping out our course, we can begin to truly see the virtual inevitability of accomplishing our objectives. There are always certain steps involved in any worthwhile endeavor and such is the case with wealth building.

Do what it takes to go through this chapter and complete all of the exercises and assignments contained in these strategies. This is not something that is optional. It is mandatory for anyone who truly wants to escape or even avoid the "Artificial Wealth Trap" altogether. By going through the steps that will make up your journey, you will see that the accomplishment of your dreams is easily within your reach. *You can have the life that you want if you will do what it takes to set out and follow a plan for how to get it.* It all begins with a starting point.

STRATEGY 16: *Determine your current fiscal condition.*

One of the biggest obstacles that most people face in putting together a financial blueprint is that they don't know where they currently stand financially. Whenever I meet with a client for the first time, I always ask them to tell me what it is that they would like for me to help them to accomplish. Early on in my career, the response nearly always had to do with items of a tax or legal concern. More and more, however, people began asking me a considerable number of financial planning questions. This made sense to me since I've also worked with people on their finances for a number of years. What didn't make sense to me was how little that people knew about their current financial situation.

In order to work with someone on anything, it's imperative that you first begin with an understanding of their starting point. Whether it's a physical fitness training program, a legal plan, or anything else, we've got to start somewhere. To gauge the treatment necessary, you first have to identify the existing condition. This is definitely true when it comes to getting a firm grasp on your finances.

Knowing where you are starting from will be the first step in determining how you get to where you want to be. To do this, you've got to assemble a grouping of items that can help you to determine your current fiscal condition. Some of the things that you will need to identify include the following:

1. Your income and income sources;

2. Your expenses and debt; and

3. Your overall financial condition.

Oddly enough, many people simply have no idea where they stand with regard to these three areas. Most people probably have some sort of a ballpark figure of how much they make each year but they don't necessarily have a good understanding of how the cash flows into and out of their lives. We'll be taking a closer look at each of these items as we focus on this portion of our E.S.C.A.P.E. Plan.

Through this process, you will be evaluating, and probably changing, the manner in which you keep your financial records, how you spend your money, and even how you structure your expense plans. This is an invaluable process if you are unhappy, or even just discontent, with your current financial situation. *If you want to get different financial results, you will have to do things differently.* Let's start with the most important player on your team, yourself.

STRATEGY 17: Evaluate your understanding of where you currently stand financially.

I want you to take some time right now and think to yourself about how you felt when you read that initial strategy. If you're like most people, you probably thought to yourself, "Do I know enough about my current financial situation?" I want you to be completely honest when you answer that question. Think about it. Do you have a decent grasp on your financial affairs? Do you know where you stand?

It's highly likely that your answer to these questions was "no." If you answered "yes," good for you. You are already in a rare group of people who have taken the time to actually assess their financial plans and are situated to do something about them. If you answered "no," don't worry, you're not alone. The good news is that the information in this chapter is designed to assist you in making sure that you do get a better handle on your current financial condition so that you can begin to make it better immediately.

To do that, you've got to have a good understanding of the measurements that reflect your current financial affairs. As mentioned above, you need to be familiar with your income and your expenses. I don't mean that you are simply aware of how much comes in and how much goes out; I want you to have a good understanding of *how* it comes in and *how* it goes out as well. To measure this, you've got to have a system.

STRATEGY 18: *Create a records management system.*

In order to get a handle on your current financial position, you've got to have immediate access to your important records. This means that you will need to establish a "records management system." Establishing this type of system will make things much easier for you in accurately assessing the state of your economic condition. As beneficial as this can be, most people never take the time to do it.

The challenge is that people don't get excited thinking about going through the organization process. I can just about hear most of you moaning at the prospect of creating your records management system. Believe me, I've heard all kinds of reasons why this is supposedly so difficult to complete. The good news however, is that I can give you hundreds, or perhaps even thousands, of dollars' worth of reasons why it is worth it for you to take the time to do this. It's quite possible that not having a good records management system in place is costing you thousands of dollars per year that could be going into your plan for prosperity. I want to help you change that.

First, I can tell you that getting a records management system in place can save you a great deal of money. Even better, it can save you more of your valuable time than you can imagine. A few hours spent setting up a filing system and creating a place that is just for keeping records will save you hours of time in the long run. Not only that, having your receipts and records kept up-to-date can also prevent you from losing money on missed tax deductions. It can help you to eliminate the loss of important warranty or guarantee information, late fees for missed bills, inaccurate creditors' or bank records, even proof of loss for insurance. This may not seem exciting at first but I can assure you that once you see the potential of more money for yourself it will begin to get your blood pumping.

But what exactly do I mean when I tell you to create a records management system? If you step back and look at things, records management is simply being somewhat organized. It means knowing what records you need and where to find them. It means setting aside an hour or two each month to stay up to date. It means saving time and money when it comes to looking for important information for dealing with financial matters. Just as important, it can keep you on track, and show your progress, in your financial improvement goals.

The key to creating an effective records management system is not necessarily to follow a specific plan for record keeping but to institute a plan that you will actually follow and understand for yourself. To do that, first go to the store and get yourself a filing box for your documents. Buy yourself some file folders for your box and then put together a system that makes sense to you. Following any type of plan will help you to get started. The key is to actually begin.

STRATEGY 19: Formulate the categories for your filing system.

Sometimes people tell me that they aren't exactly sure how to properly establish their records management system because they don't know how to put the process in motion. Basically, following a records management system refers to the *process* of grouping your records into individual categories of expenses. There's no absolute plan for the "correct" way of doing this. As I mentioned in the previous strategy, the most important part is to devise a system that works for you. The key is to then *use the system*. It's been my experience that if the system is too difficult to follow, you'll never execute the strategy. It's important that you do.

To follow this strategy, there are certain steps that you need to take. Set aside a specific time to focus on putting your system into effect. Dig out all of your receipts and records as an initial step. Once you've gotten your receipts and records together, begin going through them, separate them and place them in chronological order by month. After that, make sure that you have set up an area or filing cabinet just for your records. Begin utilizing some sort of record keeping file, chart, or software program. Don't get overwhelmed at the thought of doing this. Whether it's as simple as a piece of paper to remind you where things are or a complex software program, the key is that you have something. Remember, Microsoft Money comes with most personal computers and is very easy to operate. If you don't like that particular program, find one that you do like and begin using it.

Now comes the time to actually begin sorting and filing your records. By this I mean that you need to create and label a file folder for each of your separated piles. For example, let's say that one stack or pile that you have separated is for a credit card. Put the bills and receipts for this credit card in the folder. Create a folder for each of your other stacks as well. Each bank account, investment account, insurance policy, medical receipt, warranty, etc., should have its own labeled file.

You may be tempted to lump like items together. That's fine as long as the files will be manageable. Warranties or major purchases with guarantees, for example, may be able to be combined into one file, but if you have more than one credit card, it may be difficult to sort through several monthly statements and sets of receipts. Remember, don't make this too complicated. It will take time to do this but it will be worth it. A minute now to create separate files could save you hours in the long run.

STRATEGY 20: Give yourself a complete fiscal fitness examination.

Ask any medical expert and they will tell you that you should have a yearly physical examination to make sure that you are staying on top of your physical fitness level. As a financial planning strategist, I encourage people to go through what I refer to as a "fiscal" examination. The reason for both the physical, as well as the "fiscal" examination, is to help you to identify your current condition and identify the areas that need further attention. Personally, before I enter into any vigorous activity, I always go to the doctor to make sure that I am ready for it. Similarly, you need to assess yourself before you enter into a major financial program. This assessment is exactly what

I mean when I recommend that you give yourself a complete fiscal fitness examination.

A "fiscal" examination is nothing more than taking the time to review the information that you've accumulated through the previous strategies along with the information that you will compile through the next few strategies. Once you've done this, the next part of your examination is to consider everything in relation to where it is that you want to go, and then to figure out what needs to be done in order to get there. Just like a physical examination, there will be certain tests that need to be administered and calculations that need to be performed.

In addition to the financial snapshots that you've taken regarding your current situation, you need to factor in some of the things that you may be faced with in the future. The strategies contained in this Part of the book will help you with that. By taking the time to do this at the beginning, you can avoid some of the costly mistakes that others have made by getting into activities that they were not "fiscally" ready to take on. Not only will these help you to increase your likelihood of success with these activities but you can also prevent potential dangers as well.

STRATEGY 21: Prepare a family financial statement.

Now that you've completed the various strategies that make up your fiscal evaluation and have come up with your "diagnosis," it's now time to take the findings of your check-up and assess the extent to which you need to improve your finances. A *family financial statement* is the first step in that plan. A family financial statement is essentially a snapshot of your current net worth and can help you immensely in taking control of your current and future financial situation and spending.

When I meet with people and talk with them about putting this statement together, I often get looks of bewilderment. There is a sense of confusion on many of the faces that I see since they've never really thought about their family as a group that would need a financial statement. Some of them tell me that it seems too much like a business rather than being personal. My response is, "good, now you're getting the picture." I believe that one of the keys to your success is to indeed treat your family like a business. As such, you will need a family financial statement.

The good news is that putting this statement together is a lot easier than it may sound. First, go through the information that you should have compiled when going through the steps earlier in the chapter and make a list of all of your assets. Your assets essentially comprise everything of value that you currently own, along with their current, estimated values. Think about it as taking an inventory of your assets and making a list of what these assets are worth. That doesn't mean the cost to replace these assets but more of a measure of what you might reasonably expect to receive if you were to sell them.

Be realistic when you do this. When it comes to your personal items, don't fall into the trap of thinking that your stuff is worth more than it really is. Put on your banker's hat and think to yourself what a banker would tell you that your assets are worth. To be safe, come up with your number and then let the "banker" in you deduct a good 10% from your number. This will give you a more reasonable representation of the value of your assets.

In putting your list together, don't leave out frequently overlooked assets like stocks and bonds, any retirement accounts, or even the cash value of any life insurance that you may have. Once you've identified all of your assets, simply add up their total value.

The next step in the process is to make a list of your liabilities. Liabilities are basically the debts that you currently owe. This will be things such as your mortgage, your student loans, any home equity loans, car loans, or credit card debt. Once you've listed those out, add up the total amount of all of your liabilities.

To complete your family financial statement, all you have to do is to subtract your liabilities from your assets and this gives you your family's total net worth. Now that you've identified your current condition, you can now move on to the strategies that can help you to greatly improve things.

STRATEGY 22: *Identify and evaluate your expenditures.*

The first rule of financial management is to keep track of your money. One part of this is to figure out exactly what it is that you are spending your money on. Only when you identify the *flow* of your money can you make the necessary decisions and apply the appropriate strategies. Most people simply never take the time to do this. In fact, most people really have no idea how they spend all of their money. Until you can figure this out, it will be enormously difficult to gain control over your finances.

To do this, you'll need to go through the paper work that you put together in your records management system. An easy thing to do first is to take a look at your check register and review your checks. Answer the following questions to better identify the outflow of your money:

- Who did you pay?

- How much did you pay them?

- What did you pay them for providing?

- Is this a regular expense or a one-time only expense?

Go back at least 3 months (6 months is even better) to determine the expenses that use up your money.

For those who don't write checks for most of your items, go through your receipts. Whether these receipts are for items that you paid for with cash or with credit cards, you can get a pretty good idea as to where your money has gone when you review them. If you don't have any receipts, take a look at your past several credit card statements. Go as far back as necessary to identify your expenses. Some of these expenses may have occurred quite a while ago but you may still be paying them off. This should tell you something. Whatever you've got to do, review your records to find out what you've been spending your money on. If you can't spot the leaks, it will be rather difficult to fix them.

Once you've taken a quick look at the expenses that have taken up your money, take the next step which is to make a list of the places where you spent your money. Put them together in a list so that you can evaluate these expenses in light of their size and how often they occur. Many people who feel that they haven't really spent that much money find out that it is a lot of little expenses that have added up to a big whole. Even worse, you may discover that those little expenses have added up to a "black hole" for your money.

STRATEGY 23: *Prioritize your expenses and rank them by necessity.*

One of the most important tasks for getting a handle on your finances is to determine which expenses are truly necessary and which are not. While this may sound rather simplistic, let me assure you that it's more challenging than you might realize. This is the way that people fall into the "Artificial Wealth Trap" to begin with. If you ever hope to get out of the trap, or stay out of it, you've got to learn to prioritize the importance of your expenses.

In working with families, I often encounter expenses that one of the family members deems essential that another family member finds frivolous. For instance, I worked with a family one time who just couldn't understand how they continued to find themselves "behind the eight ball" as they referred to it. After taking a look at their spending habits, it didn't take me long to understand how they got into the situation. The husband said that the only thing that he ever spent money on outside of essential family expenses was golf. Well, this "only expense" was a pretty major one. As it turned out, he was spending more than $500 per month on average (over $6,000 per year) on these golfing expenditures. When I pointed this out, he seemed shocked. The difficulty was that he had never taken the time to add everything up. He forgot to include a lot of the "incidentals" that came along with golf.

When he saw how much he was spending, he realized that he might need to manage his habits a little better. I simply pointed out to him that he needed to take the time to think through how important golf was to him to see if it was worth all of the expense involved. In no way did I tell him that he needed to give up golf. Getting to play golf was something that he greatly enjoyed and I encouraged him to keep it up. To be able to afford it however, he had to find the money to pay for it while at the same time saving enough for his financial future. One way to do this was to stick with the same clubs for more than a year. By falling into the trap of continually buying the latest, greatest new driver or putter to come out, he was wasting huge sums of money.

Until you take the time to sit down and prioritize the expenses that use up your money, you will never be able to find the money necessary to build up your nest egg. That's why it's so important to not only identify your expenditures but to prioritize them as well.

Using the list of identified expenditures that we came up with in the previous strategy, the next step in our process is to rank each expense in order of its importance. Start out with the absolute necessities of food, clothing, and shelter. Be careful about that clothing one however. A new pair of shoes every month doesn't qualify as a necessity just because it falls under the category of clothing. Similarly, food and shelter need to be managed. Two of the biggest snares that pull people into the "Artificial Wealth Trap" involve paying more than they can afford for their food and their housing.

Spending money on housing is something that I am actually in favor of when it comes to the *purchasing* of housing (rather than renting) considering the fact that a home is an appreciating asset. I typically encourage people to purchase as much of a home as they can reasonably afford since this is the biggest investment that most people will ever make. Remember, I said the most that they could reasonably afford, not the most that they could qualify for in terms of obtaining a mortgage. Sometimes it's even a good idea to stretch a little bit when it comes to affording a home. Just keep in mind that it's important to do plenty of research before you purchase any piece of real estate to ensure that you pick the right property.

The next of the so-called "necessities" is a different matter altogether. Food is an area where people quickly lose track of their expenses. I've worked with so many people over the years who have had no idea how much money that they were spending on food until they went through this exercise. Once they found out how much they were spending on food and drinks, they were just about sick. Now, don't get me wrong, I like to eat a good meal as well as anyone and I want you to know that I'm not one of those people who will tell you that you've got to give up lattes. The key is to make sure that you've allocated your expenses properly so that you can *enjoy* the food and your lattes. Remember, we've all got to have food to survive but there's a fine line between meeting our needs and breaking the bank.

When going through this exercise, be realistic in making your rankings. Ask yourself whether you could make it if you were to cut back on this expense each month. Even better, ask yourself what would happen if you didn't incur this expense at all this month. Remember, one of the things that separates my most successful clients from others is that they realize that *if you will live like no one else, you can live like no one else.*

STRATEGY 24: Determine which expenses can be reduced (or eliminated) immediately.

Once you go through the process of ranking your expenses in order of importance, it's likely that you'll find some areas where you were surprised to find that you were spending so much money. In fact, there may be some items that you will decide to eliminate from your expense plan altogether once you see how much of your money they've taken. Until you take the time to realize how much money you're spending and exactly what you're spending it on, you won't be able to make these reductions.

Once again, don't interpret this strategy as my telling you to eliminate *everything* in your life that is not essential. This is something that I hear a lot of financial advisors telling their clients to do and I disagree with them completely. We've been given a tremendous opportunity to live a wonderful life. If you go about things in a way that deprives you of all enjoyment, you will have missed out on many of the great things that this life has to offer. While I certainly believe that it's important to accumulate wealth for the future, don't forget to enjoy the present. The key is to identify ways to do both. Eliminating expenses that don't help you financially and that don't give you enjoyment is a great place to start.

In the next Part of the book, we will be focusing our attention on strategies for "Creating" wealth. There are three key ways to do this. First, you can increase your income. Second, you can decrease your expenses in order to free up more of your money. The third way is the best which is to combine the first two approaches. When you begin to follow a plan for increasing your income while at the same time decreasing your expenses, you will experience the type of exponential growth in your wealth that can lead to financial freedom. The most important part, however, is to have a plan and to begin following the plan.

STRATEGY 25: Identify negative money mindset obstacles.

I'm often struck by how much that people underestimate the importance of mindset when it comes to the accumulation of wealth. What I mean by this specifically is that most people mistakenly believe that the only way to gain control over their finances is to go into an "expense freeze mode." In this type of situation, people look to put a halt to all of their expenditures to a point where they begin to feel pain. While the feeling of pain can often serve as a great motivator, this type of pain is just the opposite.

I've worked with countless individuals and families over the years helping them to steady their financial ships. Perhaps the biggest mistake that I see people make is that they go to extremes in their attempts to gain control over their financial affairs. I firmly believe that it's important to adhere to sound strategies and principles with extreme diligence, but I also believe that there is a balancing act in following these strategies. For many people, they get out of balance and they end up way off track. Essentially, they will pick a direction to go in, and then they follow it too closely. This is a mistake.

It may sound strange for me to state that someone could adversely affect themselves by following a strategy too closely. Let's take a look at why I've come to believe that this is true. Think to yourself about a time when you set a goal for yourself that you found especially difficult to achieve. One that most people can relate to is a diet. Think about how you felt when you were on that diet. If you're like most people, all you thought about was how awful it felt to have to stick to it and deprive yourself of food. You felt like you were missing out on things when you stuck to your diet and you felt like you were cheating if you didn't stick to the diet. Whether you were successful or unsuccessful, either way you felt bad.

This is the reason that most diets don't work. It's the same way with budgets. The fact is that the overwhelming majority of people trying to adhere to an impossibly strict diet or an overly strict budget end up failing. The reason for this is that they can't handle the pressure. They implemented an extreme plan that completely deprived them of any enjoyment. Without some sort of motivation, these people are doomed to failure. This is not just a lesson for others, it's a lesson for you as well.

What you've got to realize is that when you set impossibly difficult behavior requests for yourself, you've established a great deal of pressure that leads to a negative mindset. Remember, you created this pressure for yourself. You've created something where you end up feeling awful no matter which way that you go with things. By going to extremes, you've created a negative situation that leads to failure. You must identify any negative money mindsets and work to eliminate them from your life.

STRATEGY 26: Set goals for eliminating any negative spending habits.

What I've found is that those who are the most successful tend to think a bit differently when it comes to taking control over their finances. Sure, it's important to formulate a plan and then to follow that plan to completion, but most people miss a key step in the process. That step is the establishment of both short-term and long-term goals.

Setting goals for accomplishment, and then following those goals, is perhaps the single greatest thing that you could possibly do for yourself. This is one of the things that I've observed in every single one of my most successful clients and something that I've seen in my own life as well. The most successful people in the world got that way by setting goals for themselves and then following them through to completion. Earlier in the book in the Part on "Envisioning," we talked about the importance of setting worthy goals. The process is the same when it comes to *formulating* and *strategizing* our plans.

The first step in doing that is to get more specific with your goals. As I mentioned in the previous strategy, one of the biggest obstacles that people face is the difficulty to stick to their plans. This is a negative money mindset issue because it causes us to think too much about negative issues. What we need to be focusing on is our goal and how good it will feel when we accomplish it. Rather than setting enormous, all-encompassing singular goals, it's important to set forth intermediary steps on the footpath to financial freedom.

These footsteps will take the shape of both short-term and long-term goals. There is a saying that has always had a major impact on me and it is one that I've often found myself discussing with people quite often in assessing their successes. The saying is:

Life is hard by the yard, but it's a cinch by the inch.

If you think about it, you've probably experienced this in your own life as well. Like many others, you've probably found yourself overwhelmed at times when you consider the incredible tasks ahead of you. If you focus on the enormity of the task in its entirety, you will experience nothing but discouragement and frustration. However, if you can break things down into smaller, "bite-size chunks," you will discover that you can do just about anything that you set your mind to accomplishing. For this reason, it's imperative that you set specific goals when it comes to eliminating any negative money mindsets or spending habits. Don't try to go "cold turkey" and eliminate these all at once as it will only set you up for probable failure. Instead, break it down into doable tasks and achievable goals.

STRATEGY 27: Establish wealth accomplishment objectives for yourself.

Perhaps more than any other measurement, the family financial statement that you completed in an earlier strategy gives you the clearest representation of where you stand financially. Over the years, I've had a number of clients tell me that taking a look at their family financial statement was rather eye-opening. I've had my fair share of clients who have told me that looking at this number was eye-opening in a positive way and I've also had plenty who have said that it impacted them in a negative way. The key is that you've got to put it together to see where you are currently situated.

Once you've done this, it's a great time to sit down and formulate a plan of accomplishment that is consistent with the items that you came up with in drafting your "dreams list" from the previous Part of the book. If, for example, you wrote down that one of your dreams was to have a one million dollar net worth, now you know how far or how close you are to realizing your dream. If you said that you wanted to be completely debt-free, you now have an exact measurement of what it will take to reach that milestone. These new measurements are what I refer to as your "wealth accomplishment objectives."

If you haven't taken the time to formally establish your wealth accomplishment objectives, now is as good a time as any. Set aside some time when you can sit down and really think about exactly what it is that you would like to achieve from a wealth accomplishment standpoint. Write these objectives out in clear statements and keep a copy of them where you can easily access them and then assess your progress. These will become your core financial objectives. By focusing on them regularly, you will gain much needed motivation for staying on target.

STRATEGY 28: *Create a cost estimate for accomplishing your dreams and objectives.*

For most people, the choices that they make in life are often dictated by the *cost* rather than the *importance* of the activity. The best illustration that I think I've ever heard on this came from a married couple that I worked with as clients. Talking with the clients one day about how well they had done financially, I asked them what it was that first got them thinking about the life that they wanted to live for themselves. Their answer was one that I've never forgotten.

When I spoke with them, they told me that one night they were going out to dinner for their anniversary. To celebrate, they went to a fine restaurant and had a nice dinner, but neither one of them particularly enjoyed the experience. In talking with each other afterwards, they realized that they really hadn't enjoyed the dinner as much as they could have because they both ordered from the right side of the menu rather than the left side. When I looked at them with a questioning look on my face, they pointed out to me that the right side of the menu is where the prices are listed.

They explained that neither one of them really ordered what they would have preferred to eat for dinner but what they felt was more "economically edible." Rather than having what they really wanted, they settled for what they felt was more financially appropriate. They each told me that this gave them a feeling of emptiness that they pledged to eliminate. The bottom line was that they said that they were tired of ordering their meals and living their lives based on price. They wanted to have the ability to order based on what they wanted without letting price be the determining factor of what they could experience.

That illustration was something that drove them to set goals for themselves that they *wanted* to achieve rather than what they felt like they *ought* to achieve. They began to set goals for themselves that would enable them to live the types of lives that they most wanted to live. They began employing strategies that would provide them with the type of financial freedom to experience life to the fullest and they have certainly done so.

One of the saddest things that I encounter is seeing how people will often forego something that could have made a tremendous impact on their lives because they mistakenly believed that they couldn't afford it. The truth, however, is that they probably could have afforded these things if they had simply reallocated their resources and focused on those things that were the most important.

When you created your "dreams list," we told you to take money out of the equation. The reason for this is to enable you to identify what it is that gets you excited. Sometimes, the only way for people to list out what they really want is to take away their self-limiting beliefs so that they can be as honest as possible. In completing your list, cost was something that was eliminated from consideration. Now, however, it's time to see what it's going to take financially for you to accomplish those dreams.

In this strategy, you need to determine how much it will cost for you to achieve your goals and dreams. For some of these things, it will be easy. For others, it may be difficult to come up with a dollar value. Regardless of the expense, keep in mind that just because your dreams may be expensive doesn't mean that you should abandon them. It just may mean that you have to determine the order in which you go after them. Remember, your job was to tell us your dreams. It's our job to show you how to develop a plan for going after them. Through the strategies in this book, you will develop just such a plan.

STRATEGY 29: *Measure the distance for the trip to your Real Wealth destination.*

Once you've taken the time to compile a family financial statement and a cost estimate for accomplishing your objectives, you can now determine just how far you will be traveling on your trip. Don't focus too much on the distance or you may end up feeling overwhelmed or you may end up letting negative and self-limiting thoughts derail you. I've worked with people who completed this assessment and felt like the journey was too long to ever embark on. I've also worked with people who felt like this was nothing more than a quick road trip.

Either way, it's important to take the time to evaluate just how far, or how close, you are from reaching your desired destination.

In order to establish the type of goals necessary for reaching your destination, you have to know the distance that must be covered. For instance, let's say that you want to be worth a million dollars by age 60. If you are currently 40 years old, you know that you have 20 years to get there. If you also know that your current net worth is $200,000, you know that you need another $800,000 to reach your goal. By measuring the distance, you know exactly how much wealth you must accumulate and in what time frame. Now that you know this, you can begin to run the necessary calculations of how much wealth you will need to build each year and what type of return you need to be generating on your money to build this amount. This will give you a specific measuring device that will help to motivate you in reaching your goals. Never underestimate the importance of measuring the distance that must be covered.

STRATEGY 30: Set a reasonable timetable for arriving at your destination.

One of the biggest frustrations that I see people encounter comes from setting unrealistic timetables for accomplishing their objectives. They set out to accomplish something that virtually guarantees failure and then they get depressed that they were not able to achieve these goals during the short time period that they set. This is a major cause of people abandoning their plans for success. For this reason, it is imperative that you set a reasonable time frame for reaching your destination. The hardest part of this deals with the balancing act of not being too ambitious or too conservative.

It's important to realize that different people have different goals. This is as it should be. Since we all have different personalities, feelings, and interests, it's only natural that we would all have different aspirations. These different aspirations necessitate different time frames. For instance, if one of your goals is to climb Mount Everest, you need to take into account that there are only certain times of the year when the weather conditions allow for your ascent. Additionally, you've got to factor in an appropriate level of training prior to making your summit attempt. Depending on your starting point, you will need to establish your own personalized time frame.

Be reasonable but *be ambitious*. This is where our practical side interacts with the dreamer in us. Don't let the mental barriers get in the way of going after what you want most in life. Accomplishing your dreams gives you a sense of accomplishment that can bring immense happiness. I'm sure you've heard the saying, "it's not those things that we did in life that we regret, it's those things that we didn't do." You can either be a person who achieves their dreams or one who just dreams of achieving. The best part about it is that the choice is yours. Set your mind to making your dreams a reality.

STRATEGY 31: Spend at least one hour per day brainstorming your voyage to Real Wealth.

As you learned in the first Part of this book, the strangest secret for achieving success in life is that we become what we think about. With that thought in mind, it seems pretty obvious that we must focus on our journey. However, life has a way of side-tracking us down paths that lead us away from, rather than toward, our destinations. The most successful people recognize that these distractions exist and they make sure that they concentrate on doing whatever they can do to make sure that they focus their energy on formulating ways to overcome these distractions.

Because there can be so many distractions out there waiting to take us off of the pathway to prosperity, it is imperative that we set aside specific time to focus on our trip. The recommendation that I give people is to set aside at least one hour each day doing nothing but meditating on your plan. During this time, think about ways to accomplish your objectives. Develop new thoughts and ideas about what you must do to get to where you are going. This time may be difficult to schedule early on as it may seem unimportant. However, once you begin to see the benefits, it will become something that you cherish and can't bear the thought of missing.

Be sure to have a pen and a pad of paper handy during these times so that you can write down your ideas. Rest assured, not all of your ideas will be good ones. However, some of your ideas will be great. Go through the process of writing them down and reviewing them on a regular basis. Keep a record of all of your ideas in a file folder or folders. Some of those ideas that weren't so good may lead you to an idea that can make all the difference. By taking the time to focus on your objectives, you will find that your mind goes to work on ways to make them happen. Since you become what you think about, you will become a person who focuses on formulating solutions. Once that happens, you will become unstoppable.

STRATEGY 32: Plan your work, and then work your plan.

One of the best pieces of advice that I've ever received was to plan my work, then work my plan. If you break this down, it's really quite simple. By now, you should understand the importance of going through a detailed process of deciding exactly what it is that you most want to achieve with this gift of life that we've all been given. While it's certainly important to spend the time necessary in planning out what we want, you must then put the plan into action.

Over the remainder of this book, we will be providing you with strategies for achieving whatever it is that you've set for yourself, no matter the size. Once you design a specific plan for how you will make it to each milestone on your journey, the key now is to *work your plan*.

By sticking to the working of our plan, we will know that we are on pace to achieving those things that are the most important to us. When times of discouragement occur, which they naturally will, we will know that as long as we stick to our plan and work the strategies, we can and will reach our destination. You've planned your work, now it's time to work your plan. That's what the remainder of this book is all about.

Part III:

CREATE

CHAPTER 5

WINNING THE CREDIT GAME
AND DEALING WITH DEBT

A credit card is a money tool, not a supplement to money.
The failure to make this distinction has supplemented
many a poor soul right into bankruptcy.

Paula Nelson

To become financially free, you've got to get a handle on a number of different areas. Perhaps the most important area to begin with is your debt and credit history. No doubt about it, your debt and credit history can be your greatest asset and ally, or it can be your biggest financial enemy. In short, your credit rating can work in your favor or, it can work against you. By effectively managing and controlling your debt and credit, you can more easily attain the necessary financing for a number of assets and activities that can help you to escape from the "Artificial Wealth Trap."

Whether you're purchasing a home, a car or even an appliance, your credit score in conjunction with the amount of consumer debt you presently owe, will dictate how much you have to pay in finance charges. Does this mean you must have a good credit score and low debt to become financially successful? Absolutely not! Anyone can achieve financial success. The information in this chapter will provide you with the strategies that you need to follow in making that happen. Having your finances under control and a strong credit file will give you access to a number of financial tools that will help you to succeed with your personal and business finances.

As we get started in dealing with the issues of credit and debt mastery, we've got to review the strategies that you and your family need to follow to win in the credit game and defeat devastating debt.

For starters, we have to be more active in managing our debt rather than being passive about it. Most Americans make the common mistake of following the "What's my monthly payment?" mantra when making buying decisions. By following this approach, they end up in a never-ending, vicious debt cycle. One wrong move and the late payment penalties and charges start to snowball until this debt inevitably becomes a financial avalanche!

Just remember that the rules of managing your debt have changed dramatically over the years. Not only that, the number of financing options that have emerged in recent years are also far too many to mention. You've got to watch out for credit card companies that are forcing quicker paybacks on money charged. Another red flag is that these credit card companies also require you to pay more finance charges than ever before. Because of this, your first line of defense is to reduce your debt through every possible means.

The next thing that you need to do is to control your credit and your credit rating. In this book you will learn how to get a free copy of your credit report, how to go over it, what to look for and how to correct it. You will also learn how your credit score is computed based on the information contained in your credit report. On top of that, I will show you the specific strategies to significantly improve your credit rating.

Most lenders use your credit rating (also known as your FICO score) as a basis for approving your loan application so it is vitally important for you to know the following information:

1. The contents of your credit report;

2. Your credit score; and

3. How to manage your credit.

This chapter will also provide practical tips and advice on your spending habits. We'll cover this in more detail later in the book but it's something that can't be addressed too much. You've got to realize that most of the money that you'll be making in your lifetime will go into mortgages, auto loans, and other bank financing products so it only makes sense for you to know how the banking system works.

Like it or not, life is about making choices. The strategies contained in this book are designed so that you can make the right ones. No matter how prepared you are, things happen unexpectedly in your life that can throw your life out of whack. Believe it or not, your financial success doesn't depend on how smooth your sailing was, it actually depends more on how well you navigate the rough waters. The strategies contained in this chapter will help you to navigate the choppy credit and debt waters as effectively as possible.

STRATEGY 33: *When you're in a fix, it pays to keep your positive attitude more than your credit.*

When everything seems to go wrong and nothing seems right, don't stay down in the dumps. Make every effort to maintain a positive attitude and to stay focused. The harsh reality is that life will oftentimes throw a wrench into even the most well-oiled machinery with events such as:

- Bankruptcy caused by overspending on non-essential items or products
- Downsizing, layoffs or company shutdowns
- Losses in business and /or investments
- High costs of hospital bills and medicines
- Marital problems such as divorce or separation
- Problems with children (financial or otherwise)

All of us at some point in our lives will experience one or more of these ordeals. In these times, you must exert every effort possible to maintain a positive attitude. Rather than settle on the issue and its repercussions on your life, stay focused and face your future with greater resolve.

Trust me when I tell you that it'll take you much, much longer to recover if you engage in self pity. During times of great stress, your mental attitude is the only thing you have absolute control over. Your mind will work for you or against you. Don't allow yourself to be sidetracked by your misfortune. Never dwell on the negative. Look on the bright side, pick yourself up, and start all over again if necessary.

Keep in mind that I'm not telling you that everything will be ok simply because you've got a positive attitude. What I'm telling you is that you have in your possession a collection of strategies that can make your life better. That, in and of itself, should put you in a better frame of mind.

STRATEGY 34: Calculate your debt-to-income ratio to determine the depth of your hole.

To effectively manage your debt problem, you may want to consider taking a closer look at your overall financial standing as far as debt and credit are concerned. The key indicator to your actual financial status is the debt-to-income ratio. This is determined by estimating the percentage of after-tax income that you and your family have to spend on non-mortgage debts each month. Having this information readily available makes your job much easier.

You first need to list all of your short-term indebtedness. This could include any of the following:

- Auto financing loans
- Bank loans
- Student loans
- Department store credit cards
- Gas cards
- Other credit cards
- Any other pending loans

Your debt-to-income ratio (which does not include any first mortgages, utilities, and phone bills) should be below 15% for it to be considered a relatively acceptable level of indebtedness. If your debt level goes beyond 15%, you may have to consider taking some drastic measures before things get out of hand.

For your convenience, I have included a chart that can more or less give you an idea of your estimated debt-to-income ratio.*Debt-to-Income Ratio Chart*

Debts	Minimum Monthly Payment
Credit Card/s	$
Car Loan/s	$
Student Loan/s	$
Bank Loan/s (excluding mortgages)	$
Other Loan/s	$
1. Total Monthly Payments* *not including mortgage, utilities, and phone bills	$
2. Monthly Take-Home Pay (after-tax income)	$
3. Debt-to-Income Ratio Divide subtotal #1 by #2. This is the percentage of after-tax pay that's used to pay off your non-mortgage debts	
4 Debt-to-Income Percentage Multiply subtotal #3 by 100	%

Ratio	Percentage	Rating
0.0 – 0.05	0% - 5%	Excellent
0.0 – 0.10	6% - 10%	Good
0.11 – 0.15	11% - 15%	Not So Good
0.16 – 0.19	16% - 19%	Trouble Ahead
0.20+	Above 20%	Drastic Action Needed

Now would be a good time to take stock of your overall financial standing, even if at the moment you're not experiencing any financial problems.

Ask anyone who's been through tough times and they'll tell you that financial problems can take a turn for the worse within a relatively short span of time. An unexpected personal or family emergency, loss of job or any crisis can radically turn your comfortable life upside down almost overnight. If you're in financial trouble or you want to get out of debt, it is important that you regularly review your overall financial standing. You should calculate your debt-to-income ratio every quarter until all your debt has been settled or your debt ratio is at a comfortable level.

Once you've taken this step, I strongly recommend that you continue monitoring your debt-to-income ratio on a semi-annual or annual basis just to make sure that you're on the right track. A great strategy when it comes to paying off your debt is the following:

1. List all of your pending obligations, from the highest to the lowest interest rate.

2. Budget at least 25% of your net monthly income toward paying off these debts.

3. Pay off the minimum monthly amount due on each debt (usually 2% of the outstanding debt) and then apply the balance of your budget to paying off your highest interest rate debt, which is normally a credit card.

4. Continue this process until all of your debts have been paid off.

STRATEGY 35: When the bills loom larger than available cash, use offensive, not defensive strategies.

When most folks are neck deep in debt and there's not much money to go around, most of them just want to hide and let the bills and overdue notices go unopened. Oftentimes, they just let the phone ring unanswered or ignore any knocks on the door for fear that it's from a creditor or bill collector. Denying or avoiding your financial problems isn't going to help you. In fact, it's just going to make it worse. The key is to nip your money issue in the bud before it spirals out of control.

To keep this from happening, the best time to act is now. Instead of avoiding or hiding from your financial problems, work with your creditors in updating your overdue accounts with them. Find out from their calls and notices the best way to settle your obligations. Believe it or not, creditors will advise you of their every move for the purpose of motivating you to update your accounts so there's no need to hide anymore.

Take the offensive. If you know you're going to be late in paying your bills, do the following without delay:

1. Call each of your creditors and tell them why you won't be able to pay on time. Be truthful, sincere, and direct with them, but don't give excuses.

2. Ask for their help. Find out how you can work out the payments with them without damaging your credit rating. Some creditors may be willing to work out a compromise with you. Credit card companies are a different story. They may not be as open-minded as your other creditors. Try reminding them that once a year (usually at Christmas) some credit card companies offer the "skip next month's payment" promo and ask if you can take advantage of that type of offer now. If the customer service representative seems uncooperative, ask for the supervisor who's in a better position to decide on such arrangements.

3. Don't ever make promises you can't keep. Any goodwill you've established with your creditors will vanish in an instant if you make this mistake. Make sure you can deliver on your commitments.

STRATEGY 36: Avoid payment-lengthening debt consolidation loans.

One tempting option when plagued by seemingly insurmountable debt is to consider debt consolidation loans with a bank, credit union, or even through a finance company. At first glance, it may seem like a reasonable choice. By consolidating your debts into a single monthly payment, your total monthly payments will come down and provide some cash flow relief. If considered in the long term, however, this kind of loan often leads to financial ruin since the short-term payment relief comes at the cost of an even greater debt burden spread over a longer amortization period.

At first, it seems like a brilliant idea until you start computing for the total payment to be made on the debt consolidation loan. The trade off is that lower monthly amortization payments come at the expense of paying off the balance over a longer payment period. When the same amount of money is borrowed over a longer period, at even the same interest rate, there is more interest to pay. This means that you are actually putting yourself deeper into debt. Most people never take the time to run the calculations. They're so focused on the immediate relief from the lower payments that they fail to see the net result. This is how creditors pull you down into the depths of the "Artificial Wealth Trap."

STRATEGY 37: When considering a loan, find out what your total payments will be.

When Americans apply for financing, they commonly ask the following questions:

1. How much is the down payment?
2. How much is the monthly payment?

The question they should be asking is: How much are the total payments? Truth be told, it is the total payments and not the amount of a single payment that will wipe out your savings and adversely alter your long-term wealth-building efforts. This is the primary problem with debt consolidation loans.

Another drawback of a debt consolidation plan is the possibility of a higher interest rate. A debt consolidation loan places the lender at a greater risk. More risk means a higher interest rate. The objective of any lender is to lend out money at reasonable rates to prospective borrowers who can provide proof that they can repay it. However, if your debts are already spiraling out of control or you have a record of late payments, you will most certainly be turned down for the debt consolidation unless you can provide collateral (such as home equity) to underwrite the loan.

In effect, the lender agrees to lend you money based on your house, which is a better credit risk. In the event that you fail to make your loan payments, the lending institution can then sell your home for the money that you owe. This is another reason for the high rate of foreclosures that we are experiencing in this country. It's not just "sub-prime" or "alt-A" mortgages that are hurting us, it's also a result of debt consolidation loans not being serviced.

Even if your record at the credit bureau qualifies you for debt consolidation, don't be surprised if the interest rate is outrageous. Debt consolidation loan rates from finance companies range from 15% to 28% per annum. At these rates, the borrower will only be getting deeper into debt. Curiously enough, despite the high interest rate, with an extended payment period, the amortization payments for a debt consolidation are still substantially lower. Most borrowers don't realize that they're at the losing end of the bargain. Once again, this is the "minimum payment mentality" that got people in trouble in the first place.

STRATEGY 38: *Apply extra principal payments first to accounts with the highest rates.*

There are several strategies you can adopt to free up some money for debt reduction. We'll be covering a number of ways to do this when we focus on money-saving strategies for freeing up cash flow in a later chapter. However, we need to take a look at these options as often as possible so that they can begin to sink in to our minds so that we can increase the likelihood of our actually implementing them. Some of these strategies include:

- Life insurance cost cutting strategies
- Tax deductions from a small business
- Increasing allowances on a W-4 form
- Car insurance cost cutting strategies

From these strategies, you could easily free up $100 in savings each week or $400 in extra cash per month or much more. You can then use this extra money to reduce your pending loan obligations. With some extra money to use for debt reduction, it would be easy to be tempted to pay off the accounts with either the fewest payments or the ones with the smallest balances. Even though this may seem logical, it is ill-advised as a debt reducing or wealth-building strategy.

Your goal should be to use your money where it will do you the most good. Don't forget that the higher the interest rate, the higher the percentage of your money that goes into paying off the interest rather than your remaining balance. This is definitely a no-win situation for you. Your best bet would be to pay off the accounts that charge the highest interest rates. For instance, credit cards and department stores typically charge at least 18% per annum. It would make perfect sense to pay off these high-interest accounts using the extra money. Another strategy for this would be to pay more than the minimum monthly payment especially for credit card accounts.

STRATEGY 39: Compute your interest savings to determine if a low-interest credit card is worth the yearly fee.

Some credit cards like MasterCard and Visa have either an annual fee (typically ranging from $20 to $55 or more) or an exceedingly high interest rate. Some cards often have both. You need to consider this before you sign up for one of these cards.

Before you decide on a card, it's a good idea to plan how you intend to use your credit cards. This will help you to determine which card is best for you. If you intend to religiously pay off your balance in full each month, a no annual fee card is the best choice for you since the interest rate is not a consideration. If you do keep a balance, a lower interest rate would be to your advantage. The higher your debt, the less the annual fee becomes a percentage of the total cost.

There is a point where the annual fee becomes a factor in determining which credit card to use, especially if you keep maintaining smaller balances. The formula is simple enough. You only have to estimate your average monthly balance for the year to convert your annual fee to the equivalent interest. The annual fee divided by your average monthly balance is the amount of interest to add to the interest rate charged so that you can figure out the actual interest expense. The rule of thumb is: the less your average balance, the less the add-on interest.

For instance, let's figure the actual interest charged on a credit card with 18% annual interest, $5,000 average balance, and a $30 annual fee. The formula to make this determination is: annual fee ÷ average monthly balance = add-on interest + annual interest = actual interest rate. Considering the facts listed above, the formula would look like this:

$$\$30 \div \$5,000 = 0.6\% + 18\% = 18.6\%$$

By running this calculation, you can figure out the impact of the annual fee and compare the true cost of the card against other options. When the actual interest rate of a low-interest rate card exceeds the actual interest rate of a no- or low-fee credit card, you are better off carrying the low-fee card and cancelling your other cards with higher actual charges.

STRATEGY 40: Learn and understand the three uses of credit to be more effective in using it.

One of the strategies that I've learned in my career as a lawyer is to think things through in a logical manner so that they make more sense. What I've learned from working with extraordinarily successful and wealthy clients is that they follow this same strategy when it comes to money. Specifically, they taught me that there are really only three uses for credit. To be successful in your wealth-building strategies, you definitely should know these three uses. Basically, you can use credit to purchase any one of the following:

1. Perishables or consumables – these include groceries, dinner dates, airline tickets, fuel, heating and phone bills, etc. When purchased on credit, you're still paying for these bills even after the goods and services are long gone.

2. Depreciables – these usually refer to goods and services bought on installment and whose value depreciates or declines over time such as cars and SUVs, flat screen TVs, MP3 players, cell phones, appliances, furniture, designer wardrobe items, etc.

3. Appreciables – these are purchases that provide higher returns than the interest charged for the use of the credit. In essence, it is a form of investment that provides a decent return for your money.

Among the three uses, buying appreciable items is obviously the best use of credit. In effect, you're simply borrowing money at a low rate and investing it at a higher rate of return. Examples of appreciables include:

- A home with a mortgage;
- Rental real estate;
- Education expenses; and
- Leveraged business expenditures.

The term "leveraging" means using borrowed money to make more money. This is often referred to as OPM (other people's money). This concept can enable you to control a much greater amount of assets than you would otherwise be able to control which can thereby enable you to build more wealth at a much quicker pace.

STRATEGY 41: *To eliminate high-interest credit card debt, make extra principal payments each month of $25 to $100, PLUS the minimum payment, PLUS the amount of the purchases.*

Your high-interest credit card should be the focus of this strategy. By paying more than the minimum monthly payment, you can rest assured that you will be paying off your obligations in half the time.

To cite an example, let's assume that your credit card balance is $2,200, your minimum monthly payment is $120, and you purchased $220 in new expenses this month. By applying the "extra principal payment" strategy, you should send a check for $440 itemized as follows:

Purchases this month	$220
Min. monthly payment	$120
Extra principal payment	<u>$100</u>
Total Payment	$440

This approach will help you to accomplish multiple goals all at the same time. First, you will be paying for your purchases as you incur them, which is always a good strategy. Second, you'll be taking care of the minimum payment. And third, you'll be applying additional principal payments which will enable you to reduce your overall debt much more rapidly. This will not completely eliminate your debt challenges overnight, but it will help you to make some major progress.

STRATEGY 42: *Total and pay all perishable purchases that appear on your credit card statement.*

Using your credit card to pay for your perishable or consumable purchases is the worst possible way to use your available credit line. To keep from digging yourself into a hole, add up all of your perishable purchases such as groceries, medicines, gas, electricity, water, phone etc., and include that amount in your monthly payments. Then keep track of your perishable/consumable purchases on a quarterly basis so you can gauge your accomplishments in managing your credit. This is a little strategy that can make a big difference.

STRATEGY 43: *Use debt shifting to pay off your credit cards in half the time with the same monthly payment.*

Keep tab of your credit card expenses by listing the accounts and credit balances along with the interest rate for each.

Name of Establishment	Current Balance	Interest Rate Per Year
1.	$	
2.	$	
3.	$	
4.	$	
5.	$	
6.	$	
7.	$	
8.	$	
9.	$	
10.	$	
11.	$	
Total Balance	$	

To fast track the reduction of your credit card debt:

- You should apply for a low-interest credit card with the highest possible credit limit for which you qualify. Look into credit cards offered through banks located in the State of Arkansas for the lowest rates. The state's constitution contains a usury law which forces banks to keep their rates low.

- You should also use transfer checks that you would be receiving with your credit card to transfer balances from higher interest rate accounts and pay off all of these balances if possible. Then continue to make the same payment as your previous credit card with the lower rate card and eventually you will pay off your debt within a shorter period of time.

- As mentioned in the previous section, categorize your credit cards from the highest interest rate to the lowest rate and pay extra to the highest charging card.

STRATEGY 44: *To get out of the late payment cycle, do whatever it takes to increase short-term cash flow.*

The most direct manner to secure debt relief and manage your credit more effectively is to increase your cash flow. We'll be covering a number of ways to do this in a later chapter. For now, however, there are eight strategies you can implement to quickly free up some cash to pay off your pending obligations. These are not meant as lasting solutions but merely to provide short-term answers to your cash flow problems. Just remember that in the long run, your discipline and financial planning is still needed.

1. Check your home equity. Some financial advisors advise against this strategy. My opinion is to explore all of the options that are available and make your own decision based on the facts of your individual situation. An equity loan could consolidate several of your pending loan obligations into a single payment at a much lower interest rate with the benefit of a tax deduction on the loan interest.

2. Review your life insurance policies for any possible cash values. You may want to dispose of them for more affordable term insurance policies.

3. Try to borrow short-term funds from your relatives, friends, coworkers, and other available sources to prevent you from being penalized with late payment and bad check charges. Be careful with this one. If you can't pay them back quickly, avoid using this strategy since it has the potential to cause more difficulties for you.

4. Set up a small business where there's minimal investment but where you can avail yourself of some additional income and tax incentives. We'll take a much closer look at this option in later chapters.

5. Increase your allowances on your W-4 to augment your take home pay. Once again, this is a strategy that will be covered elsewhere in more detail.

6. Put in overtime whenever possible, provided that you get paid for it.

7. Consider getting a second job until you're free and clear.

8. As a last resort, borrow from your 401(k) or any similar retirement plan until your creditors stop bugging you. Be sure to weigh the potential ramifications of this and seek professional assistance before taking any action. Remember, this is an absolute last resort.

Another strategy for getting out of the late payment cycle is to not wait for your creditors to call you. Be proactive and call them periodically to update them on your repayment strategies.

STRATEGY 45: Get control of all of your credit bureau reports.

Like it or not, the credit bureau would be the first place your prospective creditors and employers would go to verify the information that you provided in your loan or job applications. For this reason, it's important that you have control of your credit bureau reports and the information that they contain.

A credit bureau is a private credit data gathering and reporting agency. The three largest credit bureaus in the U.S. are Trans Union, Experian, and Equifax. These credit bureaus have their own computer systems with nationwide coverage and are financed by member establishments that include companies, retail outlets, banks, finance and mortgage companies, as well as other lending institutions. These members pay an annual membership fee and pay another fee for each inquiry. Only members of credit bureaus have access to your credit file but any registered business can become a member.

Just remember that it is your responsibility to maintain an accurate and up-to-date credit file and not the responsibility of the credit bureau. You can accomplish this through the following strategies outlined in this section.

A credit bureau simply gathers all the relevant information provided by its members about their customers, their accounts and payment patterns, and then records it in its files. If a member happens to provide incorrect information about one of its customers, that information is nonetheless included in the credit bureaus' files. It is not the responsibility of the credit bureau to evaluate your credit rating or to recommend approval or disapproval of your loan application. It primarily provides a copy of your file to members who request it and they make their individual decisions based on the information they receive.

Before the enactment of the Fair Credit Reporting Act of 1970 (FCRA), no one had the right to know what was contained in his or her credit file. If there were any inaccuracies in the report, no one could do anything about it. With the FCRA, you have been given considerable power to control your credit file, provided you know how to use it. Needless to say, having a negative or erroneous credit file could have a serious drawback to your wealth-building efforts.

STRATEGY 46: Pull your credit file now and once per year.

In December of 2004, the three major credit bureaus launched a web site, toll-free number, and address where all customers with a credit file may be able to receive a free report each year from each credit bureau. The issuance of free annual credit reports by the three major credit bureaus was mandated through the Fair and Accurate Credit Transactions Act that was signed into law by President Bush in December of 2003.

Through this law, you can now access your credit report over the Internet, by phone or by mail and it allows you to order one free copy from each credit bureau every 12 months. To access your free credit reports, you need to provide the following personal information:

- Your name
- Your home address
- Social Security number
- Date of birth
- Previous home address (if you moved in the last two years)

Furthermore, each credit bureau may have to ask you some other personal information that only you would know, such as your monthly amortization payments. This is done to maintain the security of your credit file.

You can order your free credit report through the following:

Web site: www.annualcreditreport.com

Phone: 1-877-322-8228

Mail: Annual Credit Report Request Service
P. O. Box 105281
Atlanta, GA 30348-5281

Accessing your credit file via the Internet is the recommended option since you would be able to receive your report almost immediately. If you order your report by phone or mail, you should receive your free copy within two weeks.

I cannot emphasize enough how important it is to access your credit report at least once a year and to correct any erroneous entries on it. Your credit file may be used in different aspects of your wealth-building efforts. Some of the reasons for having a credit-worthy credit file are:

- To obtain loans
- To buy insurance
- To apply for a job

Without a doubt, a credit-worthy report can be one of your biggest allies in your efforts to get out of debt and on the path to financial prosperity.

STRATEGY 47: Obtain all "information reports" on yourself and your family.

Aside from credit bureaus, there are other nationwide agencies that gather information about you and your family that are also worth checking for accuracy such as:

Medical Information Bureau Report

This bureau gathers information on your health and medical conditions that you may have reported in the past. Health and life insurance companies are most interested in this kind of information as part of a medical background check whenever an insurance company is deciding whether to insure you.

> Medical Insurance Bureau (MIB)
> P. O. Box 105
> Essex Station
> Boston MA 02112
> 1-866-692-6901
> www.mib.com

Comprehensive Loss Underwriting Exchange (CLUE)

A subsidiary of Equifax, CLUE is a data-gathering agency that is the main resource for auto insurance companies in determining whether to underwrite a particular auto insurance policy. CLUE maintains a record of all the claims made on your vehicles in the past five years. CLUE does not maintain a record of your traffic violations (you can obtain this information at the Department of Motor Vehicles) or claims that you may have made on another person's insurance when it was their fault.

Comprehensive Loss Underwriting Exchange (CLUE)
National Consumer Service Center
P. O. Box 105108
Atlanta GA 30348-5108
1-800-456-6004 (Choice Point)

Records from CLUE and MIB can be obtained for free if you have been denied insurance coverage for any reason. Otherwise, the report costs about $8 in most states.

Social Security Personal Earnings and Benefit Estimate Statement

This report contains the estimated amount of Social Security benefits that you and your family may be entitled to at present or upon your retirement. It also reports your total earnings whether you're self-employed or an employee.

It is vitally important that you check on the Social Security Administration's (SSA) record of your earnings at least on an annual basis. The money that you will be receiving from the SSA upon your retirement will be based on the figures reported each year. The SSA automatically sends an earnings and benefits statement to all American citizens age 25 and over, who are not yet receiving benefits.

For more information, you can contact:

Social Security Administration
1-800-772-1213
www.ssa.gov

Each of the agencies mentioned and their reports can positively or adversely affect your financial future. Negative or erroneous information on any of your reports could sabotage your financial security. A poor credit rating could mean a higher interest rate on your loans or if you are ever even granted a loan. In a similar manner, a negative insurance report could mean higher auto, health, and life insurance premiums. An incorrect earnings statement with the SSA may mean smaller pay-outs of retirement benefits. Considering their impact, it pays to keep all of your records up-to-date.

STRATEGY 48: Exercise your credit file "Bill of Rights".

It is said that ignorance of the law is no excuse. This also applies to knowing your rights and privileges mandated under the Fair Credit Reporting Act and other relevant statutes. Use this knowledge to gain control over your credit file.

You should be aware that the Fair Credit Reporting Act and other pertinent acts give you the right to:

1. Get a copy of your report from a credit bureau based on your credit file.

2. Be aware as to who has asked about your credit file over a certain period. This may include employers, stores, suppliers, and banks, among others. These are known as inquiries. Every time you apply for a loan or even for a job, companies may look into your credit file. Credit bureaus make a record of each inquiry at the bottom of your credit file. Be forewarned that too many inquiries could set off a potential red flag or warning to your prospective creditor or employer that you could be overextended in your loan obligations. By law, inquiries should only remain on your credit file for up to two years.

3. Ask the credit bureau to re-verify and reevaluate any information in your credit file that is incorrect.

4. Get missing but positive information added to your credit file. If you know that the omitted information could boost your credit rating, you should exert every effort to have it added to your file by the credit bureau.

5. Have any disparaging credit information removed from your file after seven years and any bankruptcy information purged from your credit file after ten years.

6. Tell your side of the story in your credit file. By law, you are allowed to add a personal statement of 100 words or less to your file.

7. Maintain the privacy of your credit file from anyone other than bona fide members of the credit bureau.

8. Transfer your credit file from one state to another every time you move to another area.

9. Avail yourself of the small claims court to resolve any disputes with the credit bureau regarding erroneous information recorded in your file. This works to your advantage in terms of shorter time periods for hearings and lower legal expenses.

10. Find out exactly why you were denied credit. Remember, you are only allowed 10 days to ask the institution that turned you down. This privilege gives you the precise information you need to determine why you were refused credit in the first place and the identity of the institution that provided such information.

11. Remain silent about any negative credit information that has not been recorded in your credit file.

The information above is a listing of your rights and privileges under the Fair Credit Reporting Act. Don't hesitate to use these rights to protect your credit file and boost your rating. But don't forget that it is your sole responsibility to maintain an up-to-date and credit-worthy file. It's not the responsibility of the credit bureau.

It's your job to see to it that your credit record truly reflects your actual financial situation. If you need a free copy of the Fair Credit Reporting Act for your personal reference, you can get in touch with the Consumer Response Center of the Federal Trade Commission (FTC) at 1-877-FTC-HELP or visit their web site at www.ftc.gov.

STRATEGY 49: Do not switch your credit cards each time a bank offers you a lower interest rate card.

Choose to stay with one credit card instead of jumping from one card to the next every time the bank sends you a lower interest rate card in the mail. By opting to remain with a single credit card, your credit-worthiness will considerably improve. Lending institutions prefer to see a long-term relationship with fewer creditors. Moving from one credit card to another creates an impression of instability.

STRATEGY 50: *Avoid signing a mortgage agreement that contains a prepayment penalty.*

A prepayment penalty is a fee that may be charged to a borrower who pays off a loan before it is due. This is a common provision included in many mortgage contracts. In an effort to maximize their earnings, most banks and lending institutions incorporate a prepayment penalty clause as a way of discouraging a borrower from paying off the loan before its maturity date. Unfortunately, most borrowers are not well-versed with the legalese of mortgage contracts and end up signing the document without fully understanding the repercussions and ramifications of their actions. One option would be to seek legal assistance before entering into such a binding agreement. The best option is to not enter into any mortgage contract with a prepayment penalty clause at all. Avoid such an arrangement at all cost. It is usually a lopsided agreement in favor of the lender.

The bottom line with all of this information is that you need to be an active player in your personal financial situation. You are in the position that you are currently in as a result of your actions up to this point. If you are less than pleased with these results, you've got to do things differently. The way to do this is to learn the strategies and actions that will produce different results. The information in this chapter is a great start, but there's much, much more. Keep reading!

CHAPTER 6

CREATING "IMMEDIATE INCOME"

Capital is to the progress of society what gas is to a car.

James Truslow Adams

I t's been said that there are two types of people in this world, those who sit around and wait for things to happen and those who go out and make things happen. I once heard someone add a third group to this list referring to those who look around and wonder to themselves, "what in the world just happened?" Whichever group that you may consider yourself to be a part of, the greatest aspect of it all is that we each have the ability to move into another group. The key is that *we must learn how to do it.*

Now, why would I begin this chapter on "Creating Immediate Income" with this information? The primary reason is that it ties directly into the topic that most people find to be the most important when it comes to their finances. That topic is wealth *creation*, or more specifically, making money. The whole concept of "making" money indicates the necessity of doing something, of *making something happen*. When we talk about the American Dream, it's important to note that America was the first country to ever coin the term "making money." The term demonstrates the fact that money is out there to be made for those people who put forth the time, effort, and energy to "make" it.

Throughout this book we've been taking a look at a plan for making an "E.S.C.A.P.E." from what I refer to as the "Artificial Wealth Trap." In reviewing this plan, there are six core components which each reflect one of the letters in the "E.S.C.A.P.E." acronym. The first two Parts of the book covered the first two action components which were to *Envision* and *Strategize* wealth. In this Part, we talk about the "C" in the acronym, *Create*. I know that there will be some who will skip straight to this Part without reading the first two which is a big mistake. The first two Parts form the foundation upon which our wealth is built. It's vitally important to work through each of those steps in the wealth process.

Now that the foundation has been established, this Part of the book deals primarily with learning strategies for bringing more money into our lives. If you want to become wealthy, you must learn to produce the fuel that powers the engine. This means that *you must learn to create more money in your life*. To do this, you must become the type of person who makes things happen. There are a number of strategies that can help us to accomplish that objective.

STRATEGY 51: Understand the difference between making money and building wealth and then focus on doing both.

While the process of creating income is viewed by most people as the most important, many people take it a bit too far and view it as the only component on which they should focus their efforts. In fact, many people don't recognize the difference between "creating" income and "accumulating" wealth, which we will cover in the next Part. For these people, it's all about making money and nothing else. They are so focused on making as much money as possible that they never take the time to learn how to take things to the next level which is to *keep* some of the income that they generate. Ironically, these people often find themselves similarly situated to those who don't make much money in that they're also living paycheck to paycheck just with larger paychecks. This is an especially devious and devastating part of the "Artificial Wealth Trap" in that it catches up with people who feel like they're doing well only to find themselves inadequately prepared when the time comes to retire or when things take a downturn. In those times, we must have enough money to take care of ourselves.

In this Part of the book, we will be taking a look at ways to put more money in your pocket so that you can not only survive but thrive in any sort of market condition. The caveat that I would give you is to make sure that you don't stop here. Be sure to move through each Part of the book and the E.S.C.A.P.E. program as a whole in order to achieve maximum results and reclaim the American Dream of financial independence for yourself and your family. In order to do that, you've got to apply some fundamental wealth creation strategies. Let's begin with one of the most important.

STRATEGY 52: View cash as the fuel that powers your financial engine. Without it, you won't get anywhere.

In referring to the concept of wealth creation, we are focusing primarily on means of creating income. Plain and simple, this means bringing more of that valuable green stuff, that cold, hard cash, into our lives. As the saying goes, "cash is king." That saying needs to become somewhat of a mantra for your life. When it comes to operating our lives, it is virtually impossible to do so unless we have the requisite amount of cash necessary. I equate this to an engine. Unless you provide it with fuel, the engine will not run. It is the same thing with our financial lives. It takes a great deal of cash to keep things running.

In my life, I've been beaten up a time or two by people for seeming to care too much about making money. I've had people tell me that I shouldn't worry so much about ways to make money either for myself or for my clients and students. These people have told me that I need to realize that the Bible says that, "money is the root of all evil," and that it's not important. Let me take the time right now to let you know my feelings on the matter. These people are ridiculous. Nowhere does it say that money is the root of all evil. The Bible says that, "the *love* of money is the root of all evil," not money, in and of itself. There's a big difference. And for those who say that money is not important, they're dead wrong (and probably dead broke as well). Money is vitally important. It's crucial. It is a form of energy without which we would cease to exist. It is essential.

Perhaps the biggest difficulty that many people have, however, is in understanding the proper role of creating income in the overall wealth process. Many people take the activity of making money too far by focusing on this aspect exclusively. I think I've made it clear that I'm all for making as much money as morally, ethically, and legally possible. In fact, I've never met anyone who has specifically told me that they don't want to make any more money. Actually, it seems that just the opposite is true. Nearly everyone I talk with says that the most immediate and primary thing that they need in their lives is more money. If only they had more money, they believe, everything would be great and they could live the lives that they've always dreamed of. What they fail to realize is that more money, in and of itself, will not make them wealthy. Even further, it will not provide them with the financial independence that comes with building real wealth.

STRATEGY 53: *To produce additional cash (or fuel) for your financial engine, you must master the proper use of the "and then some" strategy.*

In dealing with methods for increasing the amount of income that we are able to generate, there are additional steps that must be taken. These are the steps that I've observed my most successful clients taking and the ones that I've taken myself. It is these steps that separate the successful from the rest of the pack. One of these steps is to ensure that you are making enough income to pay for your necessary expenditures "*and then some.*" The difficulty with most people is that they build up their expenditures to take up all of their current income "*and then some.*" The proper method for implementing this part of an overall wealth plan is to gain better control and mastery over our concept of the "and then some." This is where most people fall into the "Artificial Wealth Trap."

These people end up finding themselves stuck on what has been referred to as the "hedonic treadmill" where they spend everything they make in an effort to somehow buy happiness. They continue to buy things that they believe will make them happy only to find that their "happiness" quickly dissipates, or even disappears, soon after they make that purchase. Each time they make more money, they end up spending even more on those things that they think will bring them the elusive feeling of happiness. They go through life as if they were on a treadmill, running like crazy but never really getting anywhere. If you can gain a better understanding of the role of making money in the overall wealth process and correctly apply the concept of "and then some," your decisions will be easier to make and you'll find yourself much happier, and much better off financially.

STRATEGY 54: Balance the two essential ingredients to cash flow: increasing income and decreasing unnecessary expenditures.

To become the type of person who makes things happen, *you must have cash flow.* The two sources of this flow are *increasing income* and *decreasing expenses.* It's actually quite simple if you break it down into these core components. It is basically a formula that looks like this:

Cash Flow=Increasing Income + Decreasing Expenses

The point of this really hit home with me when I read a quote by someone who I view as one of the wisest people who has ever lived, Benjamin Franklin. The quote read as follows:

> *"There are two ways of being happy: We must either diminish our wants or augment our means - either may do - the result is the same and it is for each man to decide for himself and to do that which happens to be easier."*

The quote may have been pertaining to the concept of happiness but it really struck me as to how applicable it is to the pursuit of real wealth. I couldn't help but think that these were also the two concepts that must be mastered if one were to attain any appreciable amount of wealth. Indeed, these two strategies were necessary ingredients to achieving financial success as well as happiness. After thinking on the matter, I tried to determine which one was more important. I soon realized that they were each extraordinarily important in their own right but the mastery of both simultaneously is what expedites the process and enables wealth to change from a mere dream into a reality. By utilizing these methods, I realized, I could have whatever it is that I wanted. This is something that has helped me in my own career and something that I've witnessed employed in the lives of my most successful clients as well.

These are the only methods of providing more capital. It is in the balance of these two things that fortunes are made. Both of these methods are necessary. Unfortunately, most people come across potential ways to make more money and they blindly chase these strategies. While there's nothing wrong with this, it's important to remember that *there is no amount of money that you can make that you can't outspend.* Making money, along with decreasing unnecessary expenses to create cash flow, is essential if you ever plan on escaping the "Artificial Wealth Trap." Remember, this is merely one step in the overall process but it's a crucial step for building the momentum necessary to build real wealth. To complete that step, the following strategies must be followed in order to create some immediate income.

STRATEGY 55: *Identify your current cash needs and your current sources of income.*

Since, creating wealth involves increasing cash flow, the first step in doing that is to identify your current cash needs and your current sources of income. You've got to identify your starting point so that you know what type of road that you have ahead of you. This can be as simple as sitting down and using some of the information that you gathered in the previous section on strategizing and using it to identify where your money comes from and, more importantly, where it goes.

When you take a look at your current sources of income, then look at your current expenses, you can better identify where any potential difficulties might lie. You can also identify which of your current expenses are truly "cash needs" and which are just "cash wants?" In working with clients over the years, I've come to the realization that most people have a great deal of difficulty distinguishing between the two. "Cash needs" are those things that you simply can't live without, whereas "cash wants" are things that we'd prefer to have but could certainly get by without. Those "cash wants" may be keeping you from pulling yourself out of debt and moving toward wealth.

Once you've identified all of your current sources of income and the cash needs that are truly necessary, you will be positioned to establish what I refer to as your "cash flow equilibrium level." Getting a handle on your current position is crucial to your ability to stay on track and to escape the "Artificial Wealth Trap." Just like reading any other map, your road map out of the trap and onto the road to prosperity requires you to first identify your starting point.

STRATEGY 56: Establish your "Cash Flow Equilibrium Level."

No matter how much I talk with people about their finances, I never cease to be amazed at how many people just don't have any real idea as to where they stand financially. Most people think that if they're paying all their bills and paying them on time, they're ok, right? Unfortunately, this may not be the case. In fact, they may actually be sinking deeper and deeper into the "Artificial Wealth Trap." Just keeping up is not enough. Financial independence comes from generating enough income to pay all of these bills "and then some." This "and then some" is then put to work building our wealth for us rather than requiring us to have to do all of the work ourselves. By truly studying and understanding what I refer to as your "cash flow equilibrium level," you can better see just how far into the trap you may have fallen. Better yet, you can see how far you need to go to escape your current trap and begin building the real wealth that you and I both know that you are capable of amassing.

Identifying your "cash flow equilibrium level" will help you determine exactly what's happening to the money that's coming into and then moving out of your life. Once you are aware of this measurement, you'll be better positioned to address which component of the cash flow criterion that most needs your focus. You may be amazed at the money that you are letting slip through your fingers in pursuit of instant gratification instead of building future wealth. Knowing the cash flow that you need to satisfy your current necessities is essential to good financial health and critical in building the type of wealth that will enable you to become truly financially independent.

Not having this knowledge just embeds you deeper and deeper into the trap and prevents you from creating the wealth you deserve. Remember, if you want different results, you must do things differently. Knowing your "cash flow equilibrium level" can be a real eye opener and can help you prioritize your spending habits. That alone is a big step towards making your E.S.C.A.P.E.

STRATEGY 57: Develop a focused plan for mastering your "Velocity of Money."

The next strategy is to develop a focused plan for your "velocity of money." When I refer to the "velocity of money" I mean the speed at which money comes into and flows out of your life. This is different from the "cash flow equilibrium level" as it is not a measurement of the *amount* of cash coming and going from your life but a measurement of the *speed* with which it moves. For some of you who may be caught in the "Artificial Wealth Trap," that velocity of money may seem like it travels away from you at the speed of light. Many people I talk with say that their paycheck or other income seems to be spent before it even gets to their account. And unfortunately, they're not just joking, they really mean it. They've already allocated that income, albeit improperly, to those trappings of the "Artificial Wealth" lifestyle.

People who really want to make good on their escape from the "Artificial Wealth Trap" need to get a better handle on their cash flow. Not only that, they need to master it to an extent where they have a thorough understanding of how their money comes in and how it goes out.

At this point, it's time to really sit down and decide on a plan to help you gain control over your velocity of money, by creating more cash "flow." Specifically, I mean that you need to increase the flow both by creating more income streams, and also by making good choices on where and how you spend your money. Once you decide on your plan, follow it stringently, except to make positive changes that will help you reach your financial goals and help in your escape. Positive changes are those that increase the "inflow" and decrease the "outflow." One of the dangers in applying this formula is the danger of falling into what I refer to as the "Poor Man's Temptation." The next strategy will help you to avoid and overcome this temptation.

STRATEGY 58: *Avoid falling into the "poor man's temptation" when cash flow gets tight.*

In financial situations, and in most areas of life, you want to be proactive rather than reactive. But when there is more debt than money, most people want to hide, to shut down, and to cut back on everything. This is a defensive strategy. It is what I refer to as the "Poor Man's Temptation" because it is the default position that most people fall back on and the one that keeps them from ever rising out of their current situations. This is exactly the opposite of what you need to do when you are faced with this situation. You need to be proactive. You need to go on the offensive in this type of situation.

You may have heard the saying that "it takes money to make money." That saying is at least partially true. In many instances, you do have to spend money in order to make money. My caveat here is that you need to spend money in such a way that will bring some sort of positive return. If that spending is not a necessity to your lifestyle, and it won't directly benefit you financially, you need to reexamine that spending habit. Offensive strategies involve healthy spending that really amounts to investing in yourself and in your future wealth. By spending your money wisely, you are being offensive. When you employ the proper spending habits, you are increasing your velocity of money. By doing so properly, you can turn what once was a disadvantage into an advantage.

Think about it from a business' perspective. If a business were to fall for the "Poor Man's Temptation," it would probably go out of business. In fact, this is one of the reasons why so many businesses fail. They aren't thinking like productive businesses, they're thinking like individuals and thereby make the mistakes that individuals make, such as falling for this temptation. For instance, what do you think would happen to a business that decided to stop spending money when things got a little tight. Necessary expenses like advertising might be cut which would thereby virtually guarantee a decrease in new customers and new business. If they cut back on something like customer service, it's likely that they would then lose much of their existing business as well.

Successful businesses understand the proper usage of offensive rather than defensive strategies. This is another invaluable lesson that I've learned from working with clients who've taught me the importance of these amazing strategies. I've applied this thinking in my own life and have gotten the same type of tremendous results. The best part about it is that it can work equally well for you in your life. The key is to make the first move and to take control, instead of being controlled.

STRATEGY 59: Reduce your unnecessary expenses to increase your necessary resources.

In order to reduce your debt and work your way out of the "Artificial Wealth Trap," you need the cash with which to pay it off. To get the cash, you need to increase your cash flow and your velocity of money. Earlier, you looked at your income sources. One of those income "sources" was to moderate your spending habits to increase your "cash flow equilibrium level." There are dozens of strategies that you can use to instantly increase your cash flow by freeing up wrongly allocated expenditures. If applied properly, you could easily free up at least $100 per week. That $100 per week is more than $400 per month in extra cash. Even more amazing, that is $5,200 in extra cash over the course of a year. This money could be used for a variety of things that can help you to escape from the "Artificial Wealth Trap" and enable you to begin building real wealth. As the effects of your new strategies kick in, you will be able to easily see how there is free money to be found in having this knowledge. Even better, that knowledge can prove quite valuable as it builds up and begins growing exponentially through the power of compounding which we'll spend quite a bit of time looking at later in the ACCUMULATE Part of the book.

All of this is a result of simply freeing up an extra $100 per week. Realize that the most powerful point in this strategy is that this $100 a week increase in cash flow comes from found money, not from your paycheck. You are not working harder or taking on another job, you are working smarter with your current income. I often hear people say that this sounds like magic. Well, you will soon learn that proper planning works like magic, especially when you utilize the miracle of compounding growth.

STRATEGY 60: Stop making "interest-free loans" to the Government by making appropriate W-4 adjustments.

Another very important wealth creation strategy is to stop making interest free loans. Now you may say, "Wait just a minute, has he lost his mind? I don't make loans period, much less interest-free loans! Is he crazy?" You may honestly believe that this is the case, but your actions may tell me otherwise. You see, having too much withheld from your paycheck for income tax is exactly that, an interest-free loan to the government. This is another example of a key distinction between those who understand wealth strategies and those who don't. Those who don't understand the rules of the wealth game actually look at tax time as a wonderful time of the year. The reason for this is that they look at their tax refund as some sort of "bonus" that they can now spend on more consumer goods that end up keeping them further in the clutches of the "Artificial Wealth Trap."

The truth of the matter is that they are really just being repaid the balance on the "loan" of their money to the government. The difficulty is that the loan was made on an "interest-free" basis. Let me assure you, if there was a bank out there willing to operate this way, by making interest-free loans, they would go out of business in short order. It works the same way for you. You may not "go out of business," but you've certainly improved your chances of falling deep into the "Artificial Wealth Trap" and staying in your current financial position. That puts a whole new perspective on your withholdings, doesn't it?

There is a simple solution to reduce or eliminate this interest free loan. You need to add an additional allowance, or allowances, to your W-4 tax form. What's even better is, as you work to create new tax deductions, or qualify for additional tax credits, you don't have to wait until next year to receive the accompanying refund. That's right, get your refund now instead of waiting until you file your tax return next year. Simply by adding one extra allowance to your W-4 form for every $3,400 you have in current or new deductions will literally allow you to receive your "extra refund" now instead of later. Even better, you will stop making an interest-free loan to the government, and start putting that money to work for you.

STRATEGY 61: Use the leverage potential of the internet to provide added fuel for your financial engine.

Wealth creation strategies focus on freeing up non-working cash and non-income producing assets so that they can begin providing for additional cash flow. Selling an item, or items, that you find that you no longer need is a relatively quick and easy way to produce quick income and increase your cash flow. This strategy is one that I've seen many people employ to provide an initial amount of cash to get started with in making their E.S.C.A.P.E. from the "Artificial Wealth Trap." The question for most people when getting started with this strategy is, "how do you turn this dead weight into cash?"

In the age before the internet, selling unnecessary personal items could have involved setting up a booth at a trade fair or flea market, having a garage sale or even visiting a pawn shop or local auction house. The problem with those options is that you can only reach a relatively small target market. Because of that, you typically received a less than stellar price for the item(s). The bottom line is that the more potential customers you have the ability to reach, the higher your potential sales numbers and very often, the higher the price. This can easily be accomplished with the advent of the internet

The internet has become a powerful sales and marketing tool. Online selling, be it through classifieds or auction sites such as eBay, gives a huge prospective marketing base to the seller. Best of all, it does so with relatively little expense.

The best way to get started is to look around at your "stuff." What do you have that is just collecting dust or taking up space? Old technology, collectibles, retro items, even clothes can be turned into quick cash by taking advantage of online auctions. If you don't have a lot of "stuff" to sell but have the necessary skills to effectively utilize the internet sales portals, you might even consider creating a business that can offer the service of online selling for others who may not have the time, or the computer savvy to do so. With all the options out there, there is no excuse for not taking advantage of one of the online tools to put quick cash in your pocket. We cover the potential of cashing in on the internet in much greater detail later in this Part of the book by devoting specific attention to the topic and the multitude of strategies available. The idea of considering this type of activity as a potential business ties in perfectly to our next few strategies.

STRATEGY 62: Reduce your tax expenses by "taking care of business" and not taking it personally.

One thing I always tell people is to treat their finances like a business. This will help you to be more objective in your decision-making. It will help you to increase your cash flow, while learning to adjust your spending by focusing more on the things that will help make you more money. I refer to this adjusted spending plan as making *calculated expenses*.

Businesses do this every day. A successful business is one that watches its base line, its cash flow equilibrium, and calculates how to use its available cash in ways that will help it continue to succeed. The best part about this strategy is that you can do the same thing by really "taking care of business."

By "taking care of business," I mean that you need to start some sort of home-based business. Doing this can enable you to take advantage of many, many cash flow advantages. The question then becomes: *What kind of business?* Well, that's up to you. The point is to find something that fits your interests, fits your financial budget, fits your available time, and fits the amount of risk that you are willing to take. Think about this process as the business of you becoming wealthy. For some of you reading this right now, you may already be doing this. Others of you may be at a point where you are seriously thinking about one type of business in particular. Still others of you are just getting started and the whole idea seems rather overwhelming. Don't worry. This is something that you can ease into and should be done at a pace that suits you and your individual situation. I'll give you some guidance a little later in the chapter on how to determine if you're ready to take this step or to make the leap, depending on your circumstances. With our help, you can make this jump quicker and more effectively and safely than if you were on your own. This is what we do.

Starting your own home-based business can be one of the most rewarding activities that you ever undertake. Not only for the excitement, but also for the many financial advantages it can bring. Properly implementing this strategy can give you a pay raise by literally saving you thousands of tax dollars each and every year. What most people don't realize is that the U.S. Government has established hundreds of pages of tax code that give tax advantages to businesses.

Businesses are given preferential treatment under the tax code. The challenge is that many of the people who actually do realize this mistakenly believe that this preferential treatment is reserved only for those largest of companies with enormous payrolls. This misconception can cost you thousands of dollars and can keep you stuck in the "Artificial Wealth Trap." It's important to know that while personal tax deductions and credits are being reduced or eliminated, Congress is continually adding bigger and better tax breaks for businesses to stimulate the economy. Businesses' bottom lines, their cash flow equilibrium levels, are raised significantly by these breaks. Individuals, meaning you, can't take advantage of these savings. So to reap the tax dollar benefits provided by the government, you must become a business. Our point here is to provide for more capital though a reduced tax obligation. This is explained in much greater detail in the PRESERVE portion of the E.S.C.A.P.E. plan where we've included an entire section on methods for legally paying less in taxes.

There are hundreds, if not thousands, of business tax savings strategies that your home-business can implement. The key is that you've got to have a business to gain access to them. Before you make the decision to take that step, there are some things that must be taken into consideration. These next few strategies take a look at that process.

STRATEGY 63: *Identify sources of income and insure that they are adequate to meet your expenses before leaving a position which provides steady income and cash flow.*

It seems like every time I speak with any sort of group of any appreciable size that there is always at least one person who comes up to me and asks if I think that they should leave their job to devote themselves full-time to a new business endeavor. My answer is essentially the same as it is with virtually every tax, legal and/or financial question I'm ever asked: *it depends.* The answer depends on whether the person has additional sources of income that can sustain them while they are waiting for their new business dealings to pay off. This is one of the most common mistakes that I see people make. The mistake is that they cut off an income stream before they've ensured that an alternate source is fully established.

One of the biggest groups of aspiring business operatives that I encounter are those interested in getting involved with real estate. In the real estate world, it has been my experience that the people who have the most long-lasting and enduring success are those that have their activities segmented into two separate and distinct areas. The first area is to ensure that they have income streams that provide the necessary fuel to power their engines. The second area is a longer term type of outlook that enables them to build wealth for the long run. Without the proper balance, the end result is rarely achieved.

STRATEGY 64: Develop a dual system of efforts for creating income and building wealth simultaneously.

I remember when I was growing up, my Dad was actively involved in investing and developing real estate. In addition to these activities, he taught real estate seminars. People would often ask him the question, "if you're making so much money in real estate, why are you teaching real estate seminars?" He always answered them honestly by telling them that he taught seminars as a means of generating income while he was building up his fortune with long-term real estate strategies. Since he was successful in the real estate arena, people were interested in paying him for his knowledge, experience, and expertise. He developed a dual system for creating income (making immediate money) and building long-term wealth simultaneously.

He operated his real estate business differently than most people because of this dual system approach. He was not dependent on his real estate activities to pay the bills. Real estate was done to pay for retirement, not every day expenses. His primary strategy was not to "flip" houses for the immediate cash flow that he might generate. He was in it for the long run. Because of this strategy, he was able to build up a great deal of wealth. Even better, now that the properties are paid off, he and my mother receive monthly income in amounts that would not be available in many other investment arenas. He applied the wealth principles that he was teaching other people and was able to accomplish a great deal in doing so both in his position as an educator as well as in his capacity as an investor. However, in order to operate the long-term strategy, he had to have immediate cash flow. He didn't leave his "day job" that provided him with the income to meet his living expenses. He adopted the dual system for dual success in both wealth creation as well as wealth accumulation rather than putting all of his eggs into one basket.

In working with people in the field of small business, I work with them on applying this dual system to make the transition out of their jobs and into a new endeavor. I'm often asked if I think that they've reached the point where they should leave their jobs and devote themselves completely to their preferred business activity. I remind them that a lot of this can be made easier by revisiting the information compiled when going through the Dreams List and Values List exercises that we outlined earlier in the book. However, most of these people are asking me from a purely financial perspective.

The advice that I typically give people is to make sure that they have streams of income that can sustain them before they make that decision. This is the first determination that someone considering leaving their job to start a new endeavor needs to make. After that, the person needs to consider the type of activity or business venture that they will be involved in before they make the major decision of leaving their employment. A great number of people have contacted me as an attorney to let me know about real estate deals or investments or business opportunities that they chased after that failed to generate the amount of money that they had anticipated. As you can imagine, their stories don't paint a pretty picture. If they had only followed a system, they would have fared much better.

STRATEGY 65: Learn to protect yourself against the contagious diseases known as the "paralysis of analysis" and the "desire to acquire."

One of the biggest challenges that people face is that they get so excited about the prospect of making more money that they fail to sit down and think through the consequences of giving up their current income. In speaking with some of these people, they have told me that they wanted to be the type of people to go out there and make things happen rather than continuing to work a job that they don't like, making less money than they feel they are worth. I tell them that while this is all well and good, they need to formulate a plan for the transition.

In putting this sort of plan together, it's important to take a look at a couple of maladies with which people often find themselves afflicted. The first is what is referred to as the "paralysis of analysis." Chances are, you've heard quite a bit about this one. This condition occurs when people decide to spend so much time analyzing things that they become paralyzed, they do nothing. On the other hand, people often suffer from what is known as the "desire to acquire." This happens when people work so hard to overcome the paralysis of analysis that they end up going after the first thing that comes their way without spending the necessary time thinking things through. To become wealthy, you've got to master these maladies.

No matter what you decide to do, remember, I'm always in favor of people following their dreams. Go out there and make things happen. Just be sure that the things that you make happen are part of a well thought out, long-term plan for wealth. Over the next few chapters, you'll be given access to a number of powerful strategies that can help you to put a great deal of money to work for you in building real wealth for yourself. Before we take a look at those, there is one final strategy that we need to be aware of as we study the art of wealth creation and the strategies involved in it.

STRATEGY 66: Recognize the role of cash flow and continue to build multiple sources of income to provide fuel for your financial engine.

There are certain wealth creation strategies that must be done on an ongoing basis regardless of where you might find yourself in the real wealth cycle. Once you've taken the time to understand the importance of a properly flowing cash flow machine, it's time to analyze your existing situation and look for ways to expand. One way to do this is to conduct a monthly assessment of your cash flow, your equilibrium level, and your personal velocity of money measurements. Hopefully, you've been keeping some sort of chart or notes to measure this. If not, you need to start.

When you take the time to assess these creation strategies, you will gain a greater recognition of their importance. Additionally, you'll find yourself much more motivated to look for newer, bigger, and better ways to increase your cash flow. This can take the form of increasing your existing sources of capital or in identifying potential new sources. It's been my experience that once you really get the hang of it, you'll end up doing both.

The most important part of the Wealth Creation process is to begin focusing on the process itself. By doing this, your mind will become a greater asset to you than you could ever imagine.

CHAPTER 7

INCREASING CASH FLOW
WITH MONEY-SAVING STRATEGIES

There are but two ways of paying debt - increase of industry
in raising income, increase of thrift in laying it out.

Thomas Carlyle

S howing or telling people how and where to spend the money they earn can be tricky because most people like to spend their own money the way they want. They resent being told what to do by anybody. Let me assure you that I'm not going to try to tell you where you have to cut spending. I am, however, going to give you some strategies that you can use that have worked quite successfully for me, my most successful clients, and many other people in helping them to escape from, or completely avoid, the "Artificial Wealth Trap." The final decision about what cuts to make rests with you. Only you can decide what's most important to you and what you are willing to cut back on or eliminate. The goal of this chapter is to give you some guidance on how to best make these decisions so that you can increase your cash flow.

One of the things that these concepts assume about you is that you value your time. Part of the reason you spend your money the way you do is because you try to save yourself some of that valuable time. Because of this, these recommendations focus on areas that won't take a lot of time, but will result in substantial savings and a way out of what I refer to as the "debting disorder."

For most people, spending money is a lot easier, and more fun, than earning it. I certainly realize that this is the case so you can rest assured that I am not going to tell you to stop having fun and turn into some sort of penny-pinching, stay-at-home miser. In fact, I strongly disagree with those financial advisors and those books that push people in that direction. Like most diets, those strategies don't work since most people aren't interested in following them. As far as I'm concerned, you can still spend money and can still have fun, but there's a difference between spending money carelessly and spending it wisely. Spending too much and not spending efficiently puts pressure on even the largest incomes. The result is that savings dwindle, or cease to exist altogether. When that happens, you can't achieve your financial goals and you'll more than likely end up caught in the "Artificial Wealth Trap." This chapter will help you to keep that from happening by showing you some ways to free up a lot of the cash that you may have improperly allocated.

As we begin our journey toward mastering money-saving strategies, let's start with the basics. Sometimes, when you dive into the details too quickly, you miss the big picture. So, before I jump into the specific areas where you can trim your budget, I want to share some overall keys to successful spending that I've learned in my years of working with wealthy clients that have helped me immensely. These principles are woven in and out of the recommendations I will make about your spending.

STRATEGY 67: Live within your means.

The best piece of advice that I could ever give you is to live within your means. This may sound like an extraordinarily basic strategy but it's one that few people ever truly master. The reason for this lack of success is that people spend too much time comparing themselves to others. This doesn't work in determining whether you are living within your means because spending too much money is a relative problem. Two people can each spend $50,000 per year, but the result for each can be drastically different. If one of these people earns $60,000 annually, and the other one earns $45,000 per year, you can immediately see a big problem. One of them is saving $10,000 a year while the other one is going into debt by $5,000. So you must first learn to live within your means. That's certainly easier said than done so we've got to determine how we go about accomplishing this objective.

STRATEGY 68: Stop letting other people dictate your spending habits.

The first step is to stop letting others dictate your spending limits. You probably have friends who are big spenders. We all have friends like this. Society collectively refers to these people as "the Joneses." When you go out with them, you know you may spend too much just to keep pace. Don't get me wrong; I'm not telling you to abandon your friends, just find another activity to share with them that's not so costly. Don't allow them to dictate your spending. You may even have to take drastic steps to keep this from happening. If necessary, take only a little cash and no credit cards when you go out with them. That way you can't overspend. This may sound extreme but the temptation to overspend can result in extreme financial distress if it's not overcome.

How much you can safely spend while still working toward your financial goals depends on the goal you set for yourself and determining where you are now. We will assist you elsewhere in this material with a method of determining the amount you should save in order to accomplish your financial goals.

STRATEGY 69: Look for the best value.

A spending habit that distinguishes my wealthy clients from those who are not as financially prosperous is that they always look for the best value. As most of you know, it's often possible to find high quality and low cost in the same product. Conversely, paying a high price is no guarantee that you have bought a quality product. Cars are a good example. Whether you're buying a subcompact, a sports car, or a four-door luxury sedan, some cars are more fuel-efficient, last longer, retain their value, and cost less to maintain than others that have the same sticker price.

When you evaluate the cost of a product or service, you need to think in terms of total, long-term costs. Suppose you're comparing two used cars. There is a reliable minivan that costs $22,000 and there is a nice crossover sedan for $25,000. On the surface, the van appears to be cheaper. But the price of the car is just the starting point in the expense of owning it. If the van is more costly to operate, maintain, and insure over the years, it will cost you much more than the $3,000 you save on the initial purchase price.

The point is, paying more for a higher quality product can actually save you more in the long run. But be sure to do your homework before you buy high ticket items of any kind, no matter the market. Make certain that you're aware of the cost of ongoing service, repairs, maintenance, and other fees you may incur in the years ahead. Include the prospect of resale value in your calculations as well.

STRATEGY 70: Set your priorities for spending before making wholesale spending reduction decisions.

If you decide you want to cut your spending by ten percent, one way of doing this is that you could simply reduce your overall spending by that amount. Or, another way that you can reach the same goal is by cutting some spending categories more than you do others. You need to set your priorities and then make your choices about where and how to cut your spending to accomplish the ten percent savings.

Whenever people take the time to truly assess their spending decisions, they find out that much of their spending is by habit rather than by conscious decision. You may find that you shop at certain stores because they are the most convenient rather than because they are the best stores for value. To master your spending habits, you need to really look at what you spend and where you spend it when you are deciding where to make your cuts.

Keep in mind as you read these strategies that they are general concepts and may not apply to your particular needs. Some will make sense for you to try and others won't. Start your spending reduction plan with the areas that come most easily, then work your way through them. Keep a list of the options that you might want to try later as you get more accustomed to spotting good areas to reduce your spending. These are things that might take a bit of a sacrifice, but will help you to achieve your spending and savings goals faster. That so-called "sacrifice" may not seem like much of one when you consider it more as a trade for something more valuable.

No matter which of the ideas you choose for yourself, rest assured that keeping your expenditures lean and mean pays enormous benefits. After you implement a spending reduction strategy, you'll reap the benefits not only for the present but also for years to come. Eliminating fat doesn't always mean you have to do without something, either. You might have to learn to buy differently, or think about your purchases more, but that's easy once you get accustomed to it.

I'm often struck by the advice given by some of the "financial gurus" out there who advise their "disciples" to completely give up almost all of the things that they enjoy most in life. I don't buy into this line of thought. You will find that a few of these savings concepts are more practical for some of you than for others. While reading through these, you might come up with ideas that are more suited to your personal needs. Write them down and develop your own strategies that can be combined with the ones you find here. The bottom line here is that it's your life. We just want to help you to enjoy it more by taking money off your list of items to stress over.

STRATEGY 71: Recognize that job number one is distinguishing your "needs" from your "wants."

Do you actually need or just want to buy a particular product or service? First of all, learn to differentiate between your "needs" and "wants". Learning to distinguish between your "needs" and "wants" can actually save you more money in the long run.

"Needs" are things that sustain you such as food, clothing, shelter, and transportation. In contrast, "wants" are items that enhance and probably improve the quality of your family's life. For example, you need clothes to keep you warm and to protect you from the elements but buying designer wardrobe items to look stylish is a want. One of the biggest areas of temptation and justification for spending more than one can afford deals with the area of these so-called "necessities" of food, clothing, and shelter. This is where many people fall into the "Artificial Wealth Trap" without realizing it.

Unfortunately, millions of Americans have problems distinguishing between their actual "needs" and those things that are more accurately categorized as "wants." These people have an uncontrollable urge to buy non-essential goods to the point of putting their personal finances in jeopardy. Donald Black, a psychiatrist at the University of Iowa College of Medicine, and Susan McElroy, psychiatrist at the University of Cincinnati, have both conducted pilot studies with subjects that are deemed "compulsive shoppers." These are people who simply cannot stop shopping, even though they know that their behavior is causing serious problems to themselves and their families. Such people routinely spend the bulk of their paychecks on personal items, and spend hours each day planning their next trip to the shops. They are often in debt for thousands of dollars, frequently write checks that bounce, and exceed credit limits on multiple credit cards. They may even be forced into bankruptcy. The worst part of it all is that they keep on spending.

Compulsive shopping is probably closest in nature to a series of psychiatric complaints known as impulse control disorders. But it also resembles obsessive compulsive disorder (OCD), a strange complaint that causes sufferers endlessly to repeat pointless tasks like washing their hands, or to hoard obsessively. This is an honest-to-goodness behavioral disorder. It is exactly what we're referring to when we mention the concept of the "Artificial Wealth Trap."

The good news is that if you're fortunate enough not to be afflicted with this disorder then you don't have an excuse for not getting your finances in order. All you need is a dash of conviction, some planning, and a measure of discipline. You may be caught in the trap right now, but there is a way out.

STRATEGY 72: *Don't establish a budget; follow an "expense plan" instead.*

Most financial "experts" tell people that the key to setting their financial affairs in order is by developing and following a budget. I tend to steer clear of using the word "budget" since it has a negative connotation with most people. Budgets, like diets, often fail because of their inflexibility. I prefer to utilize what I call an "expense plan." An expense plan is really nothing more than a financial blueprint for how you plan on spending your money. It simply tells you what amounts you can afford to spend on certain allotted items and how much you need to save out of your next paycheck. An example of a recommended plan for your paycheck is as follows:

60% - You should reserve 60% of your monthly paycheck to be directed toward paying off all household-related expenses such as groceries, rent, utilities, transportation, clothing, etc.

10% - Then allocate 10% for your retirement savings. You'll need this money when you're unable to work anymore.

10% - You also need to set aside 10% for long-term savings in case of an emergency where you need to get your hands on some cash fast.

10% - Another 10% of your paycheck should be set aside for short-term savings. You may need this money for some unexpected expenses such as credit card bills.

10% - The remaining 10% is yours to do with as you please; it's referred to as your, "do whatever feels good" money. Use this as an incentive to give your family and yourself a treat for a job well done. After all, who ever said that saving money shouldn't be fun? For many people this is the money they use to contribute to their favorite charity.

The key to this expense plan is to understand that it is not meant to be made up of hard and fast rules. The best plans enable their practitioners to exercise some flexibility and creativity to make their expense plans their own. To do this, you'll have to find out which plan works best for your family. It would be pointless to set an unrealistic or undesirable target for yourself and your family and you would set yourself up for failure as it's highly likely that your family would only have a hard time achieving it. That's not to say that it should be all fun and games but we've got to be realistic. I recommend that you get your spouse and kids involved in the planning and implementation. This is not only important for getting the best results, it will also teach them to be responsible and make them feel like they are playing a part in the family's welfare and well-being.

One of the things that makes this suggested plan different from others is the, "do whatever feels good" money. Many advisors will tell you to deprive yourself of all unessential items completely. I disagree with this philosophy because it usually only works for those die hard fanatics. Don't leave this incentive out of your family's monthly expense plan. This is designed as a way to give yourself some motivation and to reward yourself for sticking to your plan. The important thing to remember is to reward your family and yourself every time each month's planning target is attained. Be sure to remain consistent with your plan. If you fail to hit your target, you don't get to spend that money. This motivates everyone to stay on target and to meet the next month's goal. This strategy teaches essential lessons that will get you out, and keep you out, of the "Artificial Wealth Trap."

STRATEGY 73: *Don't buy "wants" on credit.*

A good rule to follow when it comes to buying consumable goods on credit is: if you have to borrow to buy something then in all likelihood you can't afford it. Just keep in mind that a credit card is actually a debt card. I think that attitudes would be different if the issuing bank called it a debt card rather than a credit card. I've seen credit card companies entice people with slogans such as, "give yourself some credit." Imagine their results if the slogan more accurately reflected the reality of the situation by saying, "get yourself in debt." This definitely provides a more accurate portrayal of what is actually happening since every time your card gets swiped at the store counter, you're only putting yourself deeper and deeper into debt.

This "kind" portrayal of the process by the credit card companies is what draws people so deeply into the "Artificial Wealth Trap." Living on credit has become an indispensable part of our lives today. Unfortunately, so many people are neck deep in debt that it makes having a decent life impossible for them. The worst part is that they got stuck in the trap by trying to get a piece of that elusive "decent life." Did you know that credit card debt in the U. S. is over $750 Billion? If you consider yourself an "average" American, then you probably have at least 8 credit cards.

Now, don't get me wrong. Credit cards themselves are not inherently evil. The evil comes into play in how the credit cards get used. According to the most recent study by the Federal Reserve, 43% of American families spend more than they earn every year. It's no surprise that personal bankruptcies have doubled in the past decade, topping 1.6 million last year, according to the U. S. Bankruptcy Courts. All of this has to do with the behavior that people have been trained to demonstrate when it comes to credit cards.

To escape the trap, we've got to learn how to use credit cards properly. Buying items on credit that depreciate in value, such as cars, clothes, and vacations is hazardous to your long-term financial health. When it comes to certain expenditures, you should buy today only what you can afford today. If you must carry a debt for consumer purchases for several months or years, then chances are that you really can't afford the items. Consumer debt is extraordinarily expensive and reinforces the bad habit of spending more than you can afford. The more you engage in this behavior, the deeper entrenched you become in the "Artificial Wealth Trap."

STRATEGY 74: *Eliminate all credit card debt with double-digit interest rates.*

The best investment that most borrowers can make is to pay off your credit card debt with double-digit interest rates. Most people simply don't realize the trap that is associated with these enormous interest rates. Perhaps an example will help to illustrate the destruction. Let's say for instance, that you have a $3,000 credit card balance financed at 19.8%. If you're paying the required minimum payment of 2% of the balance or $15 (whichever is greater), it will take you 39 years to pay off the loan. On top of that incredible length of time, you will also be paying more than $10,000 in interest charges!

The credit card companies are making billions of dollars by encouraging people to run up these charges. They focus cardholders' attention on adhering to a "minimum payment mentality" to take their minds off of the total cost. These companies are very good at what they do. They've spent millions of dollars getting you to fall into the "Artificial Wealth Trap" and it is in their best interest to make sure that you don't get out. It's no wonder that so many people fall into the trap. By following the strategies, you can get yourself out and stay out.

But what should you do if you're already caught in the debt trap? To pull yourself out, all you have to do is to simply pay more than the required minimum of 2% of the loan balance. You need to do whatever you can to pay 10% to 15% (or even more if you can afford it) of the loan balance to shorten the payment period and reduce the interest charges. Always give first priority to paying off your high interest debt.

STRATEGY 75: *Formulate an expense plan for keeping food from eating your savings.*

When it comes to assessing our expenses, the amount that we spend on food is one area that can make an enormous difference in our pocket books. Unfortunately, there is no good way to eliminate this category.

You must buy food, but the reality is that most of us can buy what we truly need for a lot less than we are currently buying it. The quickest example is that people tend to shop for convenience rather than value. Buying in bulk is a good example of a way to get around this and to save money on food.

Some stores specialize in selling larger quantities or packages of a product for a lower price because they save money on the packaging and handling. Basically, you save money on the individual servings of the product. While I'm certainly not an expert on the matter by any means, I've done some informal price comparisons between these kinds of stores and regular grocery stores, and I've often found that they charge between thirty and forty percent less for the same items. All of this is without the hassle of coupons or driving all over town to see which stores have the best prices this week. That type of mindset is what keeps people in a lower economic condition than they might otherwise find themselves. Many people spend hours cutting coupons when they could have spent that time learning to make more money. My point in talking about savings here is not to engage in defensive mentalities but to form habits that can result in getting maximum results with minimum efforts. That's the most important economics lesson that you could ever learn.

Another warning about wholesale or super stores is that you'll be tempted to buy things that you don't need or really want. These stores sell everything from toothpaste to tires and computers. Make sure that you have a full list of what you need and then stick to the list. Deviating from the task at hand can be costly. As we say with other areas, plan your work and then work your plan. Stay on target while at the store so that you can reach your destination when it comes to your financial goals.

STRATEGY 76: Stop taking your savings out to dinner.

When talking about the expense of food, few things add up like the expense of eating out. Eating meals out or getting takeout can be a real time-saver, but it can also take a big chunk out of your finances. If it's done too often and too lavishly, it can lead you back to Square #1.

Keep in mind that you are paying someone to shop, cook, and clean up for you. There are always those who really hate to cook, or can't cook. If you are one of these people, choose restaurants carefully and order selectively. This is one of the biggest areas where I see people spending money that could be much better utilized.

There are also specific areas where you can avoid spending too much. For example, avoid beverages, especially alcohol. Most restaurants make big profits on beverages. The healthier option, and perhaps the wealthier option, is to drink water instead. Another tactic that I've heard espoused is that you can order vegetarian oriented meals. These dishes, including pasta and rice dishes, generally cost less than meat dishes. This may be a strategy that works for you. Then again, if you're a carnivore like me, it may not be worth the effort.

You've got to understand that I'm not suggesting that you live on bread and water. That violates the key point that I emphasize when dealing with clients and students which is the ability to exercise your own personal freedom. Our objective is not to tell you what you have to do but to give you options. The secret to life in general is to have as many options as possible. You can have dessert, and wine too, if you want. But do you need to have them every time you eat out? If your answer to that question is yes, then figure out how to make sure that you can afford it. If you're open to alternatives, try having appetizers and dessert at home, where they are much less expensive. Another benefit of this is that it can give you an opportunity to visit with friends without all of the distractions that you typically encounter at a restaurant.

STRATEGY 77: Shelter your finances.

Housing and all of the costs associated with it typically take out the largest chunk of your monthly expense plan. It's important to realize that housing is not just the house or apartment in which you live. You have to take into account the expense of your utilities, furniture, appliances, maintenance, and repairs. People often overlook areas where they can save money in this category. By identifying areas where you may be losing money, you can better afford the expenses associated with your largest investment.

When it comes to housing, we're talking about both home ownership as well as renting. First, we'll look at those who rent. Rent can take up a sizable portion of your overall expense plan. Considering the size of this expense, you've got to apply strategies to reduce it as much as possible. Many people consider rent to be a fixed and inflexible expense. That's not necessarily true. There are a number of things that you can do to cut it down in size. For instance, you can move to a lower-cost rental unit, even though it may not be as nice. It may be smaller, lack a private parking space, or be in a less popular locale. Remember, however, that you are not building up any equity when you are renting. If you can live with these trade-offs, you could save quite a bit of money each and every month on your rent. The less you spend on rent, the more you can save toward buying your own home or building up money for other purposes.

Another strategy that clients and students of mine have mentioned as a great way to save is to share a rental, if possible. This is certainly not for everyone as there are some people who couldn't bear the thought of living with someone else. Living alone has its benefits, but financially speaking, it can be a luxury. One option for reducing your rental expense is to rent a larger place with roommates. The benefit of this is that your rental cost should go down considerably, and you'll get more home for your rental dollar. I had some clients who moved into a large luxury home that each of them individually couldn't have dreamed of affording. Together, however, they were living in luxury. Bear in mind that there are some drawbacks to this situation, too. You have to be able to share your space and you'll need to give a little in some areas. Think things through and determine if this is something worth exploring.

Regardless of where you live, learn to negotiate with your landlord. Every year, it's likely that your landlord will raise the rent by a certain percentage. If the local rental market is soft, or your living quarters are deteriorating, stand up for yourself. You may have more leverage and power than you realize. If you always pay your rent on time and are a good tenant, a smart landlord won't want to lose you. It takes time and money to fill a vacancy. You should be able to reason with any landlord and show them that a comparable rental costs less elsewhere. Even if you can't beat the rent increase, you might at least be able to negotiate some improvements to the place. A smart landlord knows the wisdom in the statement, "a bird in hand is worth two in the bush."

STRATEGY 78: *If possible, buy housing rather than renting.*

One of the strategies that I am a huge proponent of is the approach that, if possible, you should always buy rather than rent. In the long run, this is probably the best idea. The reason for this is that you are building equity which is an asset. If you can get a 30-year fixed-rate mortgage, your payment on the principal remains constant. Only your insurance, maintenance, and taxes are subject to increases due to inflation. Of course, there are other expenses associated with home ownership that are often overlooked. Be sure to factor all of the expenses in before making the decision to buy a home.

Once you do have your own home, try to save on homeowner expenses. As every homeowner knows and will tell you, houses drain your cash flow, even if they are in good shape. You should be careful to watch this area of your expense plan. Be realistic in what you can really afford. The most common mistake is to overstretch when buying and then there is too little left over for other areas of your life. If this is the case and you have nothing left for other things, like vacations, eating out now and then, hobbies, or saving for retirement, your dream home can become a financial prison.

STRATEGY 79: *Avoid adopting the "arrogance of poverty mindset."*

The challenge that I see people facing more than perhaps any other becomes overcoming the desire to live in a nicer home than they can afford. I've dealt with a number of people over the years who suffer from what I refer to as the "arrogance of poverty mindset." Forgive me if this comes across as offensive but I believe that this mentality is what keeps people from ever reaching the next level. The challenge here is that people feel like they're too good to live in a certain part of town because it doesn't provide the proper level of prestige. The only way that they can afford to live in the "appropriate area" is by renting.

These people end up paying more to rent an apartment in an exclusive neighborhood than they would pay to own their own home in a less exclusive area. They feel like they're successful since they're living in the neighborhood that provides them with status. This "status minded" move is what keeps people stuck in the "Artificial Wealth Trap." It is an arrogance that ensures poverty. The difference between these people and my most successful clients is that the wealthy people realize that building equity is more valuable and more lasting than building fleeting status.

To make sure that you don't get in too deep, calculate how much you can afford to spend monthly on a home by figuring your other needs first. Although real estate can be a good investment, it can also eat up a great deal of your discretionary money. You must remember to allow for any remodeling and renovation that might have to be done. This is a never ending process, so you need to allot a certain portion of your money each month for it.

Some people also feel the need to move up to a bigger, more expensive home every few years. This is one of the classic symptoms associated with being caught in the "Artificial Wealth Trap." The remodeling and renovation process starts all over again. Be happy with what you have, at least for a while. The world will always have people with bigger, nicer houses for you to buy. I know this because I have seen it happen to so many people over the years and I saw it happen to me personally.

Years ago, I built my own home in a nice subdivision. I was very proud of the home and couldn't have been happier. Unfortunately, I had some friends who began to build their own new homes that were bigger and nicer than mine. Well, I couldn't have this happen. I immediately went to work building a bigger, better home so that I could prove that I was on top. The result was that I ended up with more home than I could reasonably afford and I was forced to downsize.

The lesson that I learned in that instance was that you will guarantee your unhappiness if you are continually trying to find happiness by outdoing others. This is the "Artificial Wealth Trap" at work. Do what it takes to stay out of it.

STRATEGY 80: *Identify expenses associated with your housing and look for ways to reduce them.*

Another great strategy for building equity is by refinancing your mortgage. This step may seem like common sense, but many people don't keep up with current mortgage rates. If interest rates are quite a bit lower than when you purchased your home, it might save you some serious money to look into refinancing. One quick word of advice is to find out what you will save before you sign anything. A point or two saved on your financing may not be balanced by the fees you pay up front for doing the refinance. Run the calculation before you run to the closing table.

One strategy that you might also want to think about is an appeal of your property tax assessments. In some areas of the country, housing prices have actually gone down in the last few years. If you're still paying property taxes based on a higher valuation, you may be able to save money by appealing your assessment. Call your local tax office to find out what you need to do. You'll probably need to prove that the property is worth less today than at the time of the assessment. You can do this by using the sale prices of similar properties in your area. If you have refinanced your mortgage recently, you may have a recent evaluation of the worth of the property in the appraisal.

In working with clients over the years, I have also learned that one thing you can do with your house is reduce those utility costs. There are times when you have to spend some money to save money. A great way to do this is to insulate an attic to save on heating and cooling costs. You could also install water flow regulators in the shower heads and toilets; it never hurts to save water. If you live in an area where garbage rates depend on the amount you throw away, recycle. Recycling means less garbage, which means lower trash bills. Besides that, it's a great way to help the environment. Those old appliances can waste electricity, too. You should look into upgrading when you can afford to do so without going into debt.

STRATEGY 81: *Stop driving yourself to the poor house by getting a handle on car expenses.*

It's no secret that this country is car crazy. In most of the world, cars are a luxury. If we adopted that mindset and thought of cars as more of a luxury than a necessity, Americans might have far fewer financial problems. There are a number of difficulties associated with our obsession with cars. They not only pollute the air and clog the highways, they also cost you a bundle and contribute a great deal to the debting disorders that run rampant among consumers. Buying the best car you can and using it wisely can save you money.

The problem is that cars are not built to last. Car makers don't want you to keep your car for years and years. They want you to buy a new one. New models are constantly being introduced and advertised. You are bombarded with slick advertisers pushing you to buy the newest and the best. Buying a new car every few years is an expensive luxury, even when interest rates are very low. This part of the "Artificial Wealth Trap" can be costly as people try to project the image of driving the latest, greatest car to prove how successful they are to everyone.

To stay out of the trap, don't try to keep up with others when they show off their new cars every year or two. They may be running themselves into financial ruin just trying to impress everyone. The better option is to let others admire you for your financial wisdom. One rule that financial advisors advocate that you follow in buying a car is the "eight year rule." The rule states that you should buy a brand new car and keep it for 8 years or buy a four-year car and hold it for 4 years. This provides the best cost per miles driven. I disagree with this a bit in that I am typically against buying a brand new car. As we all know, the value of a car drops significantly as soon as it is driven off of the car lot. I prefer to let someone else take the initial impact of that financial hit.

My preference is to purchase a late model vehicle with low miles so that someone else has to pay for the experience of having a brand new car. I have found that this strategy can save literally thousands of dollars and still enables you to have a nice, virtually new car. This is not only my preference but one that I've employed personally and seen employed by some of my wealthiest clients. In the end, however, the choice is yours. If you will follow the strategies in this book, you can purchase whatever type of car that you prefer. The key is in attaining the proper balance for your life as a whole.

Another quick caveat with regard to cars is to avoid using them as a status symbol. I've got quite a few clients who are professionals who like to use their cars to project a successful image. They tell me that picking up a prospective client in a new car can make a favorable impression. However, I caution them that it might also make these prospective clients wonder about the fees that they are charging as well as questioning their money management skills. When you buy a car, remember that the cost doesn't end with the sticker price. You are responsible for gas, insurance, registration fees, maintenance, and repairs. Don't just look at the front end costs. Think about the total long-term costs of ownership.

STRATEGY 82: *Avoid borrowing money for expensive consumption purchases.*

The main reason people spend more than they can afford on cars and other consumable goods purchases is that they can get the financing on them very easily. This is one of the primary offenses that cause people to fall into the "Artificial Wealth Trap." The rule of thumb that I tell people is to avoid borrowing money for expensive consumption purchases. This is especially true for items that depreciate in value like cars do. A car is most definitely not an investment and you should factor that in when purchasing one.

Here are a few practical and dollar-saving tips when buying a new car:

1. Wait to make your actual purchase until the last day of the month. Dealers have quotas, and they are more lenient on a good deal when their quota is looming; and

2. If you are making car payments, make extra payments and pay your car off as soon as possible. Keep making the car payments into a savings account to be used to purchase your next car. Drive your car at least six to eight years. Save enough money so that when you purchase your next car, you can purchase it by paying cash combined with your trade-in. This gets you out of the car payment cycle and will save you a great deal of money over your lifetime.

STRATEGY 83: Don't consider leasing as a way to save money on a vehicle.

Some people look to leasing as a way to save on luxury items. In most situations, leasing is even more expensive than borrowing money to buy a car. Leasing is like a long-term car rental. We all know how rented cars are treated. The same is often true for leased ones. This is one reason that leasing is so expensive. The practice of leasing cars or buying them on very long-term credit is becoming the norm in our society. This is caused by misinformation spread by car makers, dealers, and the media. It's another example of how we've been taught to do things the wrong way. By doing things the wrong way, people end up further and further behind in their efforts to achieve financial freedom.

Operating a car that one cannot afford is one of the chief obstacles to becoming financially free. Maybe you've realized that your car is too expensive to operate. It could be that the maintenance costs and insurance are just too high. Or, maybe you have bought too much car. This often happens when people finance their auto purchases. They are talked into paying much more than they can realistically afford. The good news is that you don't have to keep driving that mistake. While it may be a blow to your pride, sell or trade your expensive car and get something more financially manageable. The sooner you switch, the more money you'll save. Getting rid of a leased car can be a challenge, but even that can be accomplished, if you're motivated.

I can assure you that the embarrassment of downgrading your vehicle will pale in comparison to the embarrassment of going broke.

STRATEGY 84: *Avoid the temptation to "dress to excess."*

Anyone who knows me very well knows that I like clothes. Some might even say that I'm obsessed with clothes. My response is that I simply believe in the adage that one should "dress for success." The key is to make sure that you don't fall into the trap of dressing to excess.

I'm sure that my collection of clothing would likely exceed the average but I'd also bet that the amount that I spend on clothing is competitive with anyone. The way that I stay competitive is by sticking to timeless traditions. A rule that I learned early on was to not chase the latest fashions. Fashion designers and retailers constantly try to tempt you to buy more. Don't do it. A strategy that has served me well is to throw out the magazines and find your own style and stick with it. In most cases, you simply do not need an entire new wardrobe every year. If you buy classic designs, you can make them last several years. By purchasing accent pieces, such as a tie, shirt, scarf, or blouse, you can give your wardrobe a fresh look for a fraction of the price.

Additionally, if you want the effect of a new look every year, rotate your wardrobe. Store last year's purchases away next year and then bring them out the following year. The best advice that I could give you is to buy basic, classic styles. Don't let others dictate to you what you will wear. I'm all in favor of dressing for success but I can promise you that you don't want to be the best-dressed person with a debting disorder.

I know that I mentioned accessories earlier but be sure to minimize those accessories and stick with the basics. Shoes, jewelry, handbags, and other extras can cost large amounts of money. Be realistic in determining how many of these accessories you really need. Do you need one style of shoe in every color with a handbag to match each pair? Make your choices carefully. Buy those things that will last and still remain nice looking for years to come.

STRATEGY 85: Stop financing vacations that you can't afford.

For many people, vacations are a luxury. For others, regular vacations are an essential part of their routine. Vacations have become somewhat of a status symbol and a measuring device of how well we're keeping up with the Joneses. This is another path that leads directly into the "Artificial Wealth Trap." While I am a strong advocate of taking time to travel and experience other locales, you must keep in mind that vacations are not long-term investments. The strategy here is simple: Do not use your credit cards to finance your travels. You may be living it up in the lap of luxury and relaxation while on vacation but ask yourself how relaxed you will feel when the bills come in.

A better approach is to try to economize while still enjoying your time off. Try taking shorter trips and explore the area around your hometown. Check with your local tourist bureau, or state tourist bureau, to find interesting sites that you never realized were in your own backyard. Often they will send you a packet of information that includes coupons that you can use to receive discounts.

If you do decide to take a trip to a popular destination, try to travel during the off-season. You'll find that the rates are quite a bit less on both airfares and hotels. Also check in the paper for ads selling tickets that were bought but couldn't be used. When you're shopping around for the best fares, check the internet. Tour packages can also save you money if you find one that suits your needs. As mentioned before, look for the best value. There are deals out there if you are willing to look for them.

STRATEGY 86: Tie in vacations with business trips.

A great way of reducing your total travel costs is by tying in a vacation with a potential business trip. This provides an opportunity to multi-task by maximizing your time away and offsetting a great deal of the expenses. If you work for an employer who sends you away on a business trip to a desirable location, consider taking the family along with you if possible. In many instances, your employer will allow you to do this and will allow your family to stay in your accommodations with you thereby lowering your cost. The best part about this is that many of these business trips may be scheduled in locations that you would not be able to afford to stay in if you had to pay the costs yourself.

I also have a number of clients who have their own businesses who work this strategy to their advantage quite well. They look for business-related events held in places where they would like to travel and they attend these events on a tax deductible basis. If their family members are actively involved in their business, they are able to take them along with them and fully deduct the cost. This ends up saving them huge amounts of money and allows them to take vacations that might seem extravagant were it not for the business purposes. Later in the book, we will be taking a look at how you can start your own business and take advantage of this and many other tremendous tax benefits.

STRATEGY 87: *Don't let the health club keep you from joining the wealth club.*

Expenditures on exercise are almost always money well spent, but you don't have to join a trendy club to get the same benefits. If you belong to a gym or club for the social side, either dating or business purposes, you will need to decide if it's worth the added expense.

An alternative might be a low-cost exercise facility. These are common in most places today. In some areas, you might find the local school gym is open to the public to use. Colleges and universities often have tennis courts, tracks, pools, basketball and racquetball courts, and weight rooms that are available to the public. Makes some calls and find out. You will have the best opportunities in larger cities, but even in smaller areas you can find these facilities.

Lots of healthy exercise can be done indoors or out, free of charge. As an active runner, I enjoy the opportunity to get outside and experience the outdoors whether at home or on the road. Even better, it doesn't cost anything to do it. If you're dedicated to building your body, you may want to buy some basic gym equipment to use at home. Be careful about this though and give it plenty of thought before you buy. Lots of rowing machines and free weights end up in a closet after the first week. A good way to get a good deal on this type of equipment is to find some of these well-intentioned people who are looking to unload their equipment at a bargain.

STRATEGY 88: Understand that good health care provides good wealth care.

Health care is a big issue now and the cost for this service is going up fast. If you have health insurance, it probably covers most of your health care needs. However, many plans require you to pay for certain expenses out of your own pocket. Be sure that you are familiar with your policy so that you can make allowances for any extra medical expenses in your budget.

Keep in mind that medical care and supplies are like everything else in that prices and quality vary. Medicine in the United States is a big business. A conflict of interest can arise when the person recommending the treatment benefits from providing that treatment. There are many cases of unnecessary surgery and other medical procedures. For any major diagnosis that might require drastic treatment, be sure to get a second opinion. Most insurance companies will allow this.

If you don't have health insurance, you may end up paying a larger amount out of your own pocket. It's wise to investigate buying some coverage, even if it is minimal. Shop around and find the right policy for you at the right price. This area is so important that we've included an entire chapter to it in the PRESERVE Part of the book.

Alternative medicines (holistic, chiropractic, acupuncture and others) are gaining attention in the media today because of their focus on the treatment of the whole person, not just a symptom or two. While this may not be the best idea to pursue if you have an emergency, it may be worth investigating if it interests you. Eventually, this may lead to inexpensive health care. One word of caution that I must give you is that most insurance companies do not cover the cost of this type of treatment so be sure to check that out.

If you must take certain prescriptions on an ongoing basis and pay for them yourself, you might try ordering by mail. This can often bring down your cost and is convenient for refilling prescriptions, if you think ahead. Your health plan may be able to provide more information about this.

STRATEGY 89: *Insure your wealth by learning about insurance.*

The area of insurance can be a minefield for the unsuspecting customer. You really need to study the different types of coverage to evaluate what types that you might need. You also need to learn what types of coverage to avoid. We've included an entire chapter for helping you with this later on in the book. For now, here are some of the most common ways in which people waste money on insurance.

Low Deductibles

The deductible is the amount that you pay before your insurance kicks in. On an auto policy, for example, if your collision deductible is $500, you will pay this amount for damage and your insurance company will pay the rest. Low deductibles are great if you have an accident, but they are costly to maintain. The lower the deductible, the higher the premium you will pay. You will probably still save money if you pay the lower premium for the higher deductible in the long run. Just remember if you have a low amount in savings not to get too carried away with a really high deductible because this could cause you a hardship if you do have a claim.

Knowing What to Insure

You need to determine what you should insure. If you have something that you couldn't replace without creating a financial hardship, then you should insure it. You must decide what types of coverage are worth the cost. For most people, dental and home warranty plans are not needed. If no one is dependent on your income, life insurance doesn't make much financial sense either. By identifying unnecessary insurance expenses, you can free up a great deal of money that could be better utilized in your overall financial plan.

STRATEGY 90: *Review various strategies for reducing debt and freeing up cash and apply as many of the strategies as possible.*

As you have seen, debt reduction and curing the debting disorder involves adopting a simple strategy for successful saving. In particular, it's a strategy that has to be applied to credit card debt. If you learn nothing else from this material, learn that strategy. Like any successful strategy, you have to be willing to put a plan into action. The best plan available to reduce your debts is simply to avoid them in the first place. You can avoid them by eliminating easy access to credit or credit cards.

If you use credit cards, only charge what you can afford to pay off that month. Never borrow for anything except long-term investments. If you pay your balance in full each month, you don't need to keep credit cards that charge you an annual fee. If you have a credit card that charges an annual fee, call the company and tell them you want to cancel that card to get a competitor's card that charges no fee. And just remember to keep only one card for emergencies.

When you are able to apply these simple concepts to your daily life, you will see a difference in things. It may take a while, but you can do it. The most important aspect of debt is to recognize its effect on your long-term financial picture and then do something about it.

CHAPTER 8

SAVING MONEY BY MANAGING INSURANCE

If you cannot make money on one dollar-
if you do not coax one dollar to work hard for you,
you won't know how to make money out of
one hundred thousand dollars.

E.S. Kinnear

A major part of creating wealth involves identifying ways of increasing the available cash in our lives so that it can be used to establish or supplement our investment accounts. One way to do this is by increasing the amount of income that comes into our lives. For many people, this is much easier said than done. You may find that you're already doing as much as you can do to bring in the money but you still find yourself with cash needs. This requires taking advantage of the other way to increase cash flow, which is to reduce expenses. One of the quickest and easiest ways to effectively reduce expenses is to gain control over insurance.

The concept and practice of insurance has been around probably as long as people have owned assets. The first form of insurance appeared in the form of community togetherness. When an individual or family encountered a hardship, such as a fire or the death of a provider, the community would band together and chip in to rebuild or provide assistance to the deceased provider's family. Not long after, the concept of insurance as a business developed, and it has remained the same ever since.

In simple terms, insurance is the spreading of risk and consequences of a peril over a large number of people so that the costs remain more manageable than if the individual encountered the hardship alone. In essence, by buying insurance you are accepting a small, predictable loss (the premium) in exchange for a potentially larger, unpredictable loss (the peril).

As simple as this concept sounds, managing insurance costs can be an expensive and daunting task for any individual or family. The insurance industry is one of the richest industries in the world and it becomes obvious that your insurance premiums are paying for more than just the claims of other policyholders. Since insurance costs take up a large percentage of many families' household income, it is imperative that everyone understand how insurance works and what types of coverage may be best for themselves, their family, and their personal and business assets. Failing to come to an understanding about insurance can lead to one becoming "insurance rich and cash poor." Of course, what is worse is when one truly has an emergency and finds himself or herself unable to survive because they did not have enough insurance.

In this chapter, we're going to be discussing many specific strategies for insurance. Some of these strategies will demonstrate when insurance should be a part of your plan. Yet as you will see, we will also discuss some strategies for when insurance may not be necessary. This can provide you with a great way to free up some additional resources without compromising your safety or security.

STRATEGY 91: Do not buy life insurance if you are single with no dependents.

Life insurance should be used only to prevent a financial hardship that would be created if the insured dies. Primarily, it is meant to replace income, which may be required to support dependents. In spite of this, a large portion of all life insurance policies owned in this country is designated to protect the lives of single people with no dependents. This is a glaring example of how well salespeople are trained and how little we've learned about money and insurance. So, this first strategy is simple: If you are single, invest your money elsewhere.

STRATEGY 92: *Do not buy life insurance on children.*

As we just stated, life insurance should be purchased to protect assets and care for dependents left behind. Although children may be an emotional asset, they are usually not financial assets nor do they have minors of their own. Parents buy life insurance on children because they are told by a salesperson that it is the loving, responsible thing to do. The truth, however, is that insurance coverage belongs on the income-providing parent(s) or providers, not on the children.

Often whole and universal life insurance is sold as a method of building enough cash value to pay for a college education for the child who is insured. A $50,000 life insurance policy on a one-year-old child could cost $250 per year and have cash surrender value of $5,000 when the child reaches college age. If $250 per year is invested correctly in a mutual fund, a college fund of over $20,000 can be accumulated in the same amount of time. This is a much better use of your money.

There could be a rare exception to this strategy if your child was to become a television or movie star and you became disabled, making the child the family's primary breadwinner. In this circumstance, life insurance on the child might be prudent. Yet in just about any other instance, follow this strategy and avoid buying life insurance to cover your children.

STRATEGY 93: *Purchase life insurance only to replace the lost income or services of a provider.*

There may be instances where you need less income than the provider's salary to maintain your standard of living, but you should always ensure that your cash flow needs coincide with your income replacement calculations and, if necessary, adjust accordingly. In that

151

figure, be sure to consider including the value of any indispensable services that are provided for the dependents by the spouse or partner. Some examples of essential services are daycare, a full time nurse, handy-worker, chauffeur, teacher, cook and house cleaner. These are services often provided by a non-working or part-time spouse/partner that will need to be replaced.

The formula to figure the necessary amount of insurance you need to purchase is:

Annual Income Needed x 10 = Amount of Insurance Needed

For example, if it was determined that you would need to replace $50,000 a year of income/services, you would need a policy with a face value of at least $500,000 and the proceeds invested with an average annual rate of return of 10%.

STRATEGY 94: Buy only term life insurance and devote the rest of your financial plan to prosperous living.

Term insurance is pure insurance protection with no bells, whistles, fancy packaging or investments to buy. Therefore, the premiums per $1,000 of insurance are the lowest of any form of life insurance. If the insured dies within a given period of time, the company pays the agreed upon sum of money to the beneficiary. Once a term policy is purchased, future stability is guaranteed up to age 70, 90 or even 100, depending on the company that issues the policy. As each of the terms for the insurance comes to an end, the insured will discover that the cost of the insurance for the next term will increase. Why? Since the risk of death is greater as a person becomes older, the cost of the insurance is greater.

Term is the least expensive type of life insurance, often up to 80% less than the insurance-plus-investment policies like whole life and universal life. Term insurance pays salespeople far less in commissions and, therefore, is not always offered by agents, if you don't insist. Although most people falsely believe that term insurance cannot be purchased as you get older, the truth is that both annually renewable term and level premium term guarantee your insurability to age 90, and with some companies, to age 100.

STRATEGY 95: *Never buy universal life insurance as an investment vehicle.*

Universal life insurance was created after people started to catch on to what a poor investment it was to purchase whole life insurance. To redirect the exodus of policyholders from whole life into non-insurance investments that bring a much greater return to insurance companies, the insurance industry created a life insurance policy that is a term insurance policy attached to a separate investment account. With universal life insurance, a portion of the inflated insurance premium is directed into a separate investment account that usually pays a variable interest rate. The portion of the premium that is invested consists of whatever is left over after the insurance company deducts its monthly insurance fees, management fees and commissions.

For example, let's say you purchased a universal life policy with a $100,000 death benefit and yearly premiums of $2,000. You are promised an 8% rate of return on the investment portion of your account. A full 30%—or $600—of the first year's premiums is deducted for insurance, commissions and fees. That leaves only $1,400 to be applied to the investment account. Would you go to a bank with the intention of investing $2,000 in a Certificate of Deposit and paying a $600 charge for this opportunity? I certainly hope not. You wouldn't let a bank charge you those fees and you shouldn't let an insurance company, either.

Furthermore, there are other items to consider (if you read the fine print) that most salespeople will not tell you:

- The "guaranteed" interest rate is usually guaranteed for the first year only.

- The portion of the premium which goes toward insurance increases each year, thereby reducing the investment contribution even further.

- High surrender charges are applied to your "savings," if you decide to cancel your policy.

If necessary, the death benefit portion of a universal life policy can be adjusted, but the investment account would be similarly affected.

STRATEGY 96: *Never buy variable life insurance as an investment vehicle.*

Of all the investment life insurance policies, variable life insurance is by far the best of the three choices, but is still not as good as buying term insurance and investing the difference. The variable life insurance most often sold today is actually "variable universal" life. Many of the arguments for variable life are the same as those given by sales agents for whole and universal life insurance. Variable/universal life insurance is similar to plain old universal life. The major difference is that universal life provides you with a low fixed/variable rate that is determined by the insurance company. Variable life allows you to invest in equities, typically through mutual funds, and allows you to pick the investments and move your money among the investments when you so choose. Your cash value is dependent on the growth of the equities within the stock market.

When the life insurance agent tries to sell you a variable life policy, he or she will show you tables of the projected growth of variable life versus a regular taxable mutual fund highlighting the benefits of tax-deferred growth and tax-free borrowing. Of course, at face value, you would be a fool not to invest in variable life, if you believe the sales illustration. In the information that follows, we will set the record straight on key selling points.

"Investment return" assumption

The rate of return assumption is just that, an assumption—not a guarantee. Your investment can actually lose money in the first few years, according to stock market conditions. But, this is the case for either the variable life policy or the standard mutual fund investment.

"Cost of term insurance" assumption

In the agent's sales chart, you are shown the same investment contribution amounts for both the variable plan and the regular mutual fund investment. That is not true. If you buy level premium term and invest the difference, your insurance costs are usually one-third of what variable life will charge you for commissions and fees. In reality, because term is such a bargain, more net cash will be available for investments.

The "you'll pay tax on your mutual fund investment earnings annually" assumption

You are led to believe that you will pay taxes every year on the growth of your mutual fund account. The reality is that the majority of your earnings will grow tax-deferred automatically in your mutual fund, because most of the growth is from unrealized capital gains. You will not owe taxes on capital gains until you sell those particular fund shares. You will, however, be taxed on any dividends you receive from the mutual fund.

The "you'll pay the same tax rate for variable life or plain mutual funds" assumption

What the salespeople won't tell you is that you will forfeit the more favorable capital gains tax rates for the much higher income tax rates, if you invest within a variable life policy. For the time being, the top capital gains tax rates for long-term gains are much less than the top rates on ordinary income.

The "you pay any taxes owed out of your mutual fund account" assumption

It is rare (and not recommended) that anyone would pay a tax liability on an investment from that same particular investment. Besides, you won't have much (if any) tax liability to pay anyway, unless you sell shares of that mutual fund.

STRATEGY 97: *Never buy credit life and credit disability insurance when getting a loan.*

Wherever and whenever you borrow money, many loan officers and financial institutions will attempt to attach credit life and credit disability insurance to your loan. All loans are targets for this overpriced insurance, including auto, boat, personal and business loans. Usually, you will need to sign for acceptance of this insurance, so read your contract carefully, and do not affix your signature to this section unless a signature is required in order to decline credit life/ disability insurance. The purpose of credit life insurance is that it pays off the balance of your loan should you die. Credit disability makes your loan payments for you should you become disabled or unable to earn income. Both are usually included as a package and financed as part of your loan.

At first glance, this sounds like a good thing so it begs the question: "What's wrong with the concept?" The challenge is that credit life and disability are overpriced by as much as 800%! You will never get wealthy overpaying for anything by that much. Lenders are always very aggressive in pushing credit life and disability, and finance managers usually receive big bonuses or commissions when you are coerced into buying the insurance. Many lenders will even indicate that if you don't take the coverage, you won't get the loan. In truth, it is against federal law for anyone to require that you take their credit life or credit disability unless the cost is already included in the finance charges and interest rates, which in many states would violate usury laws.

Credit life insurance is actually a form of decreasing term insurance, which means that the insurance pays off only the balance of your loan, even if you are down to your last one or two payments. For instance, if you financed $18,000 for the cost of an automobile and were to die the first month, the insurance would pay off the full $18,000. However, at the end of the term of the loan, often 48 to 60 months later, the amount paid off would be as little as one month's payment.

Credit life actually protects the financial institution and not your heirs. Your heirs get nothing from the policy. It only guarantees that the

156

financial institution will collect its money if something happens to you. Credit life and disability insurance is usually financed into the loan, which means that you end up paying compounded interest on insurance you never needed in the first place.

These two insurance gimmicks, with interest, can add as much as 10% to the cost of anything you purchase and finance. If you feel strongly about having your loans paid off in the event something should happen to you, don't buy credit life and disability insurance. Instead, substitute inexpensive level term insurance for expensive credit life insurance, and your premiums can decrease by as much as 90%, saving you hundreds of dollars a year for the rest of your life. This is the type of savings that you are looking for if you hope to create wealth.

STRATEGY 98: Replace expensive mortgage life insurance with inexpensive term insurance.

Another gimmick in the lucrative insurance business is mortgage life insurance. The sales pitch is logical and emotional. If you die, wouldn't you like your home mortgage paid off so the payments wouldn't be a burden on your dependents? Of course you would, but mortgage insurance is certainly not your best alternative. Mortgage life is nothing more than a decreasing term insurance policy (explained earlier) where the beneficiary is your mortgage company—and not your dependents.

STRATEGY 99: Carry a minimum of $50,000 property damage liability coverage on an auto policy.

The next several insurance strategies we will discuss involve auto insurance. Of course, pursuant to the law in every state, everyone who owns and drives a vehicle must carry some sort of automobile insurance. At the very least, in most states everyone must have a property damage liability policy. Property damage liability coverage protects you against damage to other people's property. Many insurance companies offer liability policies with coverage in the hundreds of thousands of dollars. While it is always speculative whether that amount of coverage would ever be necessary, everyone should carry at least $50,000 in liability coverage.

STRATEGY 100: *Consider eliminating collision and comprehensive coverages if the value of your vehicle drops below $2,000.*

Collision and comprehensive insurance are optional coverages (if there is not a debt against the car) but are appropriate for most policyholders. Collision insurance pays for repairing or replacing your vehicle if it collides with another vehicle or object. Comprehensive insurance policies pay for losses from incidents other than collision, such as fire, theft, glass breakage, vandalism, windstorm, and falling objects. Both collision and comprehensive coverages are subject to deductibles. For example, a $250 deductible means you are responsible for paying for the first $250 of repairs (minus depreciation). The insurance company will then pay the balance.

Do not pay a premium that is greater than 10% of the amount that your insurance company will pay. Remember, the insurance company will only pay you for the current market value of your vehicle minus the deductible - not what it will cost to replace it.

STRATEGY 101: *Check to see if your personal injury protection (PIP) and medical payments provide duplicate coverage, and if so, eliminate the overlap.*

There is one absolute truth when it comes to the topic of insurance, and that is that claims will not be paid twice. Check to see if your personal injury protection and medical payment coverages are duplicated. PIP coverage is available in certain states and, because it allows injured parties to collect without litigation, is designed to lower the cost of automobile insurance. The common components usually include reimbursement for medical expenses, lost income, property damage and compensation for death. PIP limits or minimum coverages are determined by each state. Check with your Insurance Commissioner's office for details.

Medical coverage policies pay for medical expenses caused by a car accident to a family member(s) or other person(s) riding in your automobile. Coverage applies even if you are in another person's car or walking. Coverage is similar to what a medical insurance policy would cover. Remember, you cannot collect twice for the same medical expenses if you already have your own hospitalization policy.

With these two types of policies, there is often an overlap because passengers already are covered by your bodily injury coverage or their own medical insurance. Check with your insurance company to examine these areas of your insurance policies and eliminate such overlap.

STRATEGY 102: Get rid of hidden insurance that is costing you extra money every year.

When it comes to policies offered by insurance companies, gimmicks fall mainly into two categories: insurance attached to purchases and insurance attached to loans. Insurance, when attached to purchases, includes extended warranties and service contracts that are supposed to cover repair costs for stereos, appliances, automobiles or other major purchases. Insurance attached to loans is actually life or disability insurance with fancy names like credit life, credit disability and mortgage life. These are intended to pay off your loans if you lose your ability to work or lose your life.

Many times these insurance contracts and clauses are slipped into purchases and loans without the complete awareness of the buyer or borrower. Your first objective is to search your purchase and loan papers to find and cancel unnecessary coverages. Second, mentally gear yourself to refuse ever again to buy these high-priced gimmicks, no matter what the sales pitch.

159

STRATEGY 103: *Never buy or finance extended warranties on appliances and electronics.*

An extended warranty will pay the cost of repairing an item you buy after the manufacturer's warranty runs out. The real purpose of an extended warranty is to add to the dealer's profit at your expense. The odds are only about 15 out of 100 that you will have a claim. You pay for the warranty in advance, even though you get no benefit until the manufacturer's warranty runs out.

If you finance the amount of the extended warranty, you will be paying interest on the cost of a contract that won't be in effect for as much as one to three years. The warranty is a limited guarantee and does not cover normal wear and tear or rough handling, or in the case of a video recorder or camera, dropping the equipment. The cost of the warranty is astronomical compared to the amount of money the dealer actually pays for the real repairs. Salespeople are normally paid big commissions for intimidating you into saying "yes" to extended warranties. With the advancements in technology, the cost of replacing these items is close to the cost of repairing them which makes warranties even less attractive.

STRATEGY 104: *Never buy or finance extended warranties on an automobile.*

Extended warranties are supposed to cover major repairs or maintenance not covered by the manufacturer's warranty, either during or after the original warranty term. There are so many loopholes, conditions and limited chances of collecting that an extended warranty turns out to be one of the biggest potential rip-offs in your financial plan. Since most extended warranties on new cars do not start until the original warranty runs out, you have paid in advance for something you won't need for three to seven years. Service contracts are also prepaid, so that the dealer gets your money long before you might need the service. If you add the cost of the warranty to your loan, you end up paying as much as 40% extra.

STRATEGY 105: Cancel your extended warranties and get a refund.

Normally, you can have an extended warranty or automobile service contract canceled and recover the unused portion of the cost. Put your cancellation request in writing and include the loan number and the date purchased. Ask for a refund of the unused portion of the insurance. Alternatively, have one or more payments knocked off of the end of your loan, to equal the amount of the unused portion. Many financing institutions require the dealer to reimburse them for any warranties that are canceled. A few of the new extended warranty contracts, however, like other forms of insurance, have a high cancellation penalty, which simply allows the dealer to keep the unused portion of your extended warranty money, even if you cancel. The important thing here is to read your contract and act now.

STRATEGY 106: Do not waste your money on flight insurance, free accident insurance, student accident policies or hospital indemnity insurance.

Our last strategy for insurance looks at several types of policies which are simply a waste of money. One such type is flight insurance. This insurance pays if you die in a plane crash. As a general rule, over-priced specialty insurances are a waste of money. Most charge cards automatically insure you for free, if you charge your plane ticket on them. Regardless, if you need life insurance, buy term, since it will pay regardless of how you die and dollar for dollar is a much better value.

Another insurance policy which is generally worthless is so-called "free accident insurance." This accidental death and dismemberment insurance usually will pay $1,000 or so if you die or are maimed in an

161

accident. It may sound like you have nothing to lose, but by taking this coverage, you are subjecting yourself to endless sales pitches, telemarketing and direct mail to try to sell you increased limits of this worthless coverage.

Next, let's look at "student accident policies." This insurance is offered through your child's elementary or secondary school and usually runs $30 a year for school hours coverage and around $150 for coverage around the clock. This may sound like a minimal amount but you've got to remember that specialty coverages like this only pay for certain accidents and are usually a secondary coverage, paying only what your regular health insurance does not. You cannot collect twice for the same malady, so what you are essentially insuring is part of your deductible which is a big financial no-no.

And finally, hospital indemnity is another insurance policy to avoid. This pays you a set amount per day—usually around $100—if you have to stay in the hospital. Premiums typically run a few hundred dollars a year. Adequate medical insurance should cover hospital expenses, so you won't need to pay for this as an extra expense.

After reading this chapter, hopefully you haven't gotten the impression that all insurance policies are unnecessary. That is not my philosophy at all. However, what I do want you to take from this chapter is to think carefully whenever you purchase an insurance policy and ask yourself if it is something that you really need. It's important to remember that there are other ways to protect yourself in addition to insurance.

For example, in a later chapter we will be discussing various strategies for protecting yourself in the event of a lawsuit. As you will see, our asset protection plans center around the effective use of business entities such as corporations, limited partnerships, and limited liability companies. A lot of people think that such planning is unnecessary if you obtain an errors and omissions policy to protect you in case of a lawsuit, and subsequent judgment against you or your business. Such a strategy is extremely dangerous because every insurance policy has a limit, and every insurance policy contains carefully drafted loopholes which relieve the insurance company of liability in certain situations.

The key thing I want you to take from this chapter is that insurance can in many instances be a tremendous value, but it should never be your only strategy for protecting your wealth. We'll cover much better ways for doing that later in the book.

The primary point in this chapter is to help you identify areas of insurance where you may inadvertently be wasting your hard-earned money. Insurance is something that always sounds good when it is presented, yet it must be effectively managed in order to give you the maximum benefit. By properly allocating some of your improperly allocated expenses, you will be much better able to begin your wealth creation and accumulation activities.

CHAPTER 9

MAKING YOUR LIFE LESS TAXING

*There's always somebody who is paid too much
and taxed too little- and it's always somebody else.*

Cullen Hightower

For most people, dealing with taxes is something that they seldom think about. Most wage earners never really think about taxes because they don't really see the actual amount of their income that goes toward paying taxes. Because of this, they simply look at the payment of taxes as just another expense that we don't really have much control over. The challenge with this mentality is that it is exactly what the government intended.

The reality of the matter is that if people truly thought about taxes on a regular basis, they would likely be outraged. As I've stated in some of my other books and in my seminars on the topic of taxes, I firmly believe that the best way to ever get true tax relief in this country would be to require people to sit down and physically write out a check for the amount of their taxes each and every year. If this were the case, people would take greater notice of the enormity and the impact of their tax bills. The government doesn't structure things like this because they undoubtedly understand the result. The smartest thing that they could possibly do is to establish a system where taxes are taken out of wage earners' paychecks before they ever receive them. This way, the impact is greatly softened and people simply accept their position.

For those people who want to build wealth and become financially independent, gaining control over the outflow of money from their lives is paramount. Few people realize that the amount that most people pay in the form of taxes is the single greatest expense that they will ever incur. The reason that they overlook this fact is that their taxes are taken out of their checks automatically. Small business owners and those whose incomes are structured outside of this automatic system recognize the importance of paying less in taxes. Many of the wealthiest people in this country fall into that category. By following the strategies that they have learned for reducing their tax burdens, anyone can get the same, or at least similar, results.

This chapter will provide you with strategies that you can use for legally reducing the substantial expense of taxes. While there are certain limitations for individuals trying to reduce their personal tax obligations, we've included a number of ways for you to do so. To really take a chunk out of your tax expenses, you need to take advantage of the tax benefits afforded to small businesses. We've included a lot of information for explaining how to do just that in a later chapter. For now, do what you can to cut your personal tax bill by taking advantage of the strategies that follow to make your life less taxing.

STRATEGY 107: *Do your tax planning early, often, and continually.*

Proper planning is the key to reducing or minimizing your income tax liability. Planning is a process, not an event, and therefore must be continual. No matter how competent your tax advisor, in most cases it is impossible to go back and "make it all better" after a transaction has occurred. In addition, there are several non-revocable elections that must be made by a certain date and once that date is passed, you cannot retroactively correct any mistakes or omissions. An example of this is that an Individual Retirement Account (IRA) must be established and funded by the due date of your return, not including extensions.

As important as tax planning is, you should first make sound economic decisions and then take into account the tax benefits or consequences of those decisions. You should not refuse to earn extra money in order to save on taxes nor should you spend extra dollars on things that you don't really want or need for the primary purpose of reducing your tax liability. No matter how oppressive you may consider the tax rates, they are still well under 100%.

In this chapter, we're going to provide you with some powerful strategies that you can apply to your personal situation to get some serious relief from the burden of taxes. These strategies will not apply to all people in all situations but you need to review them all to see which ones might work for you now and keep the others in mind in case your circumstances change.

STRATEGY 108: *Maximize your itemized deductions.*

One of the easiest things that individuals can do to lower their personal tax bill is to maximize their itemized deductions. Many taxpayers, because of home ownership, state and local income taxes, real estate taxes, and charitable contributions, will itemize their personal deductions rather than take the Standard Deduction. The Standard Deduction for 2008 is $10,900 for a married couple filing a joint return, $5,450 for a single individual, and $8,000 for heads of households. The Standard Deduction may be taken in lieu of itemizing your deductions. If you spend anywhere from $1 to $10,900 (for a married couple) on legitimate itemized deductions, then you should take the Standard Deduction. If the married couple wishes to deduct more than $10,900, then they must spend more than $10,900 and account for each dollar.

Since the government already gives you an automatic break with the Standard Deduction, a lot of taxpayers don't bother to keep up with their legitimate deductions. This can be extremely costly come tax time. By buying a home and itemizing your deductions, you will automatically lower your taxes through medical expenses, taxes paid, interest, charitable gifts, casualty losses and numerous miscellaneous deductions. These are expenses that you already incur and pay with money that has already been taxed. By itemizing, you will be able to lower your taxes and get some of that money back.

STRATEGY 109: *Take advantage of any potential medical deductions.*

When considering medical deductions, there are a lot of possible medical deductions that you and/or your tax preparer might not have ever considered. For instance, you can deduct all medical expenses for any person for whom you pay more than half of their support and pay their medical bills. This can be used for a spouse, former spouse, children and other dependents. Secondly, if you are self-employed you can deduct all medical premiums that you pay. Third, you can deduct premiums paid for Long Term Care insurance. The deductible amount varies with your age. And finally, you can even deduct home improvements if their main purpose is to provide a medical benefit. The general rule is that the amount that qualifies as a deduction is the difference between the cost of the improvements minus the fair market value that is added to your home.

To substantiate this deduction, obtain a written statement from a physician explaining the medical need for the improvement, as well as an appraisal showing the increase in the fair market value of the home because of the improvement. Costs to maintain or repair such improvements are also deductible. If structural changes are made to a home to accommodate a handicapped individual, since these changes do not normally increase the value of the home, the full amount of these changes would be deductible.

STRATEGY 110: *Maximize medical expense deductions by "accelerating" expenses into one year.*

Having just talked about some of the possible deductions available to individuals as a result of medical expenses, we should talk about exactly how, and when, you can make these deductions. In order to deduct medical expenses, there are a few items that need to be addressed. First, the medical expenses must be itemized. Secondly, the total of the medical expenses must exceed 7.5% of your adjusted gross income (AGI).

All too often, taxpayers will give up on taking a deduction for their medical expenses if they are close, but not over the 7.5% threshold. This problem can be easily cured. If you are close to exceeding this limit, you should consider prepaying some expenses to overcome that floor. You can even prepay expenses with your credit card. These expenses are considered to be paid when charged to your card, not when you pay the credit card bills.

STRATEGY 111: Don't forget to take real estate deductions.

We all know that owning real estate is one of the best ways to both earn immediate income and build long-term wealth. However, what a lot of people don't realize is that there are tremendous tax benefits from owning real estate as well. Did you know that you can deduct all real estate taxes actually paid during the year for all property owned? If your mortgage payment includes payments into an escrow account held by your mortgage lender, or their servicing company, only the payments made from that account by the lender are deductible, not the amounts paid to the lender.

Another great tax benefit of owning real estate is that you can deduct mortgage interest from your taxable income. A lot of people know that they can deduct the mortgage interest payments on their home but what a lot of these people don't know is that you can also deduct the money spent on mortgage interest on a second home as well. To qualify as a home, the structure (whether it is a "site built" traditional home, a manufactured home, a travel trailer or a boat) qualifies so long as it has eating, sleeping and toilet facilities. If you are considering purchasing a boat or travel trailer, make sure it has these facilities so you can deduct the interest paid. While it may cost more, it could be worth it when you consider the additional tax savings.

STRATEGY 112: Remember the "incidentals" when deducting mortgage interest.

Not only can you deduct money spent on mortgage interest, you can also deduct discount points paid on a mortgage as additional interest. One point is one percent of the mortgage amount and is prepaid interest. Points paid on a purchase money mortgage (the original mortgage used to purchase the property) are deductible in full in the year paid as additional interest. Points paid on a refinance are amortized (written off) over the life of the loan. For example, if you refinance to a 30 year mortgage, you would take 1/30th of the points paid every year. If you refinance again, you can deduct all the remaining points from the old loan.

STRATEGY 113: Deduct charitable contributions.

Without taking away any of the altruistic benefits of contributing to charities, there are tax deductions available for people who donate to charities. To deduct any charitable donation of money, a taxpayer must have a bank record or a written communication from the charity showing the name of the charity and the date and amount of the contribution. A bank record includes canceled checks, bank or credit union statements, and/or credit card statements. The old laws allowed taxpayers to back up their donations of money with personal bank registers, diaries, or notes made around the time of the donation. Those types of records are no longer sufficient. The key is to always document all of your charitable giving so that you can get the biggest tax deduction allowed.

STRATEGY 114: Take advantage of the deductibility of your home office.

Thanks to the advances in technology, more and more people today are able to work from just about anywhere- in a hotel room, on a plane, or even in their car. Yet the most popular place to work remotely is from home, and many people have established home offices for just that reason. Not only does a home office offer convenience, it can bring some tax relief as well.

In order to qualify for a tax deduction, a home office must be used "regularly" and "exclusively" under the following conditions:

1. As a principal place of business.

2. As a place where you meet with customers in the normal course of business, if that activity is required by your business.

3. As a place where income-generating activity takes place.

STRATEGY 115: Turn a negative event into a positive tax outcome by deducting casualty and theft losses.

Every day in the news it seems like there is some new natural disaster or crime wave that causes immeasurable pain and damage to Americans. Whether it is a hurricane, a fire, or identity theft, the notion that bad things happen to good people has never been more true. Yet our friends at the IRS have at least shown a little compassion by allowing us to take a deduction on casualty and theft losses.

A casualty is the loss of property (including damage and destruction) because of a sudden event. The event must be identifiable, unexpected, and unusual. Events that meet this criteria include:

- car accidents,
- disaster-related demolition,
- earthquakes,

- fires,
- floods,
- hurricanes,
- shipwrecks,
- storms,
- terrorist attacks,
- tornadoes,
- vandalism, and
- volcanic eruptions.

Loss of property because of theft may also be tax-deductible. According to the IRS, "a theft is the taking and removing of money or property with the intent to deprive the owner of it. The taking of property must be illegal under the law of the state where it occurred and it must have been done with criminal intent."

You may have a theft loss if you are the victim of

- blackmail,
- burglary,
- embezzlement,
- extortion,
- kidnapping for ransom,
- larceny, or
- robbery.

In order to claim a deduction for losses due to casualty or theft, one must first subtract $100 from the total amount of losses and then they must exceed 10% of your AGI. These losses are then reported on IRS Form 4684 to calculate your deductible losses. In a Federally declared disaster area you have the choice of which year to deduct the losses. For example, if your losses occurred in 2007, you can claim the loss on your 2006 or 2007 return, whichever benefits you the most.

STRATEGY 116: *Maximize your miscellaneous and "other miscellaneous" deductions.*

We've talked a lot about the various types of deductions you can take to reduce your personal tax bill, but there are two more categories of deductions we need to discuss: miscellaneous and "other miscellaneous" deductions. First, let's talk about miscellaneous deductions. These deductions are as follows:

- Unreimbursed employee business expenses
- Safety equipment
- Small tools
- Supplies you need for your job
- Dues to professional organizations and chambers of commerce
- Subscriptions to professional journals
- Fees to employment agencies and other costs relevant to looking for a job in your present occupation
- Certain educational expenses
- Tax preparation fees
- Certain fees for investment advice and Custodial fees

In terms of the amount of your deduction for this category of expenses, you can deduct their value which exceeds 2% of your adjusted gross income. If these expenses total $4,000, and 2% of your AGI is $3,000, then you would have a miscellaneous deduction of $1,000.

The second category of miscellaneous deductions, called "other miscellaneous deductions," is not subject to the 2% rule, thus 100% of these expenses can be deducted. These "other miscellaneous deductions" include:

1. Gambling losses up to the extent of gambling winnings.
2. Federal estate tax on income in respect of a decedent.
3. Amortizable bond premiums on bonds acquired before October 23, 1986.

4. Certain unrecovered investment in a pension.

5. Impairment related work expenses of a disabled person.

STRATEGY 117: Maximize your tax credits to lower your tax bill.

Tax credits are a more powerful tax reduction tool than tax deductions. If you are in a 28% marginal tax bracket, a $1,000 tax deduction would reduce your tax burden by $280 ($1,000 x 28%). By contrast, a $1,000 tax credit would reduce your actual tax bill by $1,000. In other words, a tax credit gives you a dollar for dollar offset on your taxes. Because they are so valuable, it's advantageous to seek out and take advantage of every tax credit for which you qualify.

STRATEGY 118: Use the Child Tax Credit to lower your tax bill.

One of the most popular tax credits which people claim each year is the Child Tax Credit. For purposes of the Child Tax Credit, a qualifying child is someone who:

- Is under the age of 17 at the end of the year.

- Is your son, daughter, legally adopted child, grandchild, stepchild, eligible foster child, brother, sister, stepbrother, stepsister, or a descendant of any of the above.

- Had the same residence as you for more than half of the taxable year, except for absences due to illness, education, business, vacation, or military service.

- Did not provide over half of his or her own support for the year.

Through the 2010 tax year, the credit for each qualifying child is $1,000.

STRATEGY 119: Obtain tax relief by paying for the care of dependents.

Another popular tax credit is the Child and Dependent Care Credit which is claimed for all eligible dependents. If you paid someone to care for a child under age 13 or a qualifying spouse or dependent so that you could work or look for work, you may be able to reduce your tax by claiming this credit. The credit is a percentage of the amount of work-related child and dependent care expenses that you paid to a care provider. The credit can be up to 35 percent of your qualifying expenses, depending on your income. Currently, you may use up to $3,000 of the expenses paid in a year for one qualifying individual, or $6,000 for two or more qualifying individuals. These dollar limits must be reduced by the amount of any dependent care benefits provided by your employer that you exclude from your income.

Eligible persons are:

1. Your children under age 13. If the child turns 13 during the tax year, the child remains a qualifying person for the part of the year that he/she was under 13.
2. Your disabled spouse who is unable to care for him/herself.
3. Any disabled person not able to care for him/herself, whom you can claim as a dependent (or could claim as a dependent except that the person has gross income of more than $3,500 in 2008).

STRATEGY 120: Claim a tax credit if you qualify as elderly or disabled.

Certain low-income individuals can claim a tax credit if they are at least age 65 or older before the close of the tax year, and to individuals under age 65 if they are retired with a permanent and total disability and have taxable disability income from a public or private employer. Persons wishing to claim this credit must be a U.S. citizen or resident or married to a U.S. citizen or resident and they both elect to be treated as U.S. residents (and taxed on their worldwide income).

STRATEGY 121: Lower your tax bill with the Adoption Tax Credit.

You may be able to take a tax credit for qualifying expenses paid to adopt an eligible child. The adoption credit is an amount subtracted from your tax liability. Although the credit generally is allowed for the year following the year in which the expenses are paid, a taxpayer who paid qualifying expenses in the current year for an adoption which became final in the current year may be eligible to the claim the adoption credit on the current year return. The adoption credit is not available for any reimbursed expense. In addition to the adoption credit, certain amounts reimbursed by your employer for qualifying adoption expenses may be excludable from your gross income. You may claim an adoption credit of up to $11,650 (for tax year 2008) per eligible child.

Eligible children include any child age 17 or younger, or a child of any age who is a U.S. citizen or resident alien and who is physically or mentally incapable of caring for himself or herself. Qualified adoption expenses are calculated by adding up all the expenses related to the adoption and then subtracting any amounts reimbursed or paid by your employer, government agency, or other organization. Adoption expenses include any and all costs directly relating to your adoption and that are reasonable and necessary for your adoption. Expenses include adoption fees, legal fees, court costs, and travel expenses.

Taxpayers who adopt a special needs child can claim the full amount of the adoption credit without regard to the actual expenses paid in the year the adoption becomes final. When to claim the adoption credit and what year you can claim the credit depends on when the adoption was finalized and whether the adopted child is a U.S. citizen, resident alien, or foreign national.

STRATEGY 122: Get credit for your educational expenses from the IRS.

Not only is money spent on education a wise investment for yourself and your family, it can earn you a tax credit as well. These tax credits are available to part-time students, full-time students, married students, and parents of dependent students. There are two tax credits available for such expenses: the Hope Tax Credit and the Lifetime Earning Tax Credit.

A taxpayer can claim the Hope Tax Credit for the first two years of an eligible student's postsecondary education so long as that student is enrolled at least half time in a program that leads to a degree, certificate, or other recognized educational credential for one academic period. Generally speaking, the taxpayer can claim the Hope Tax Credit if they pay qualified tuition and related higher education expenses for an eligible student. This eligible student can be the taxpayer, their spouse, or a dependent who is claimed on the taxpayer's tax returns.

The Lifetime Learning Credit applies to qualified tuition and fees for undergraduate, graduate and continuing education coursework to acquire or improve job skills. Students, or the parents of dependent students, may claim a credit of up to $2,000 for qualified education expenses paid for all students enrolled in eligible educational institutions. There is no limit on the number of years that the credit is available to a student. Taxpayers cannot take both the Hope and the Lifetime Learning Credit in the same year for the same student.

STRATEGY 123: Take your Earned Income Credit early.

The earned income credit (EITC) is a tax credit for certain people who work and have low wages. Unlike a lot of tax credits, the EITC is refundable, meaning that it can lead to a tax refund. In other words, any credit amount that exceeds the taxpayer's tax bill will be refunded to them. In some instances, an employee can receive part of their EITC early by filing an IRS Form W-5 with their employer. Employees are eligible to receive this advance on their EITC if they have a qualifying child, if their adjusted gross income is less than $33,241 ($35,241 if you expect to file a joint return for 2007), and if they expect to be eligible to receive the EITC.

STRATEGY 124: *Use exemptions to reduce your taxable income.*

Personal tax exemptions reduce your taxable income on your tax return. In other words, an exemption is simply a certain amount of money that is "exempt" from taxation. For 2008, the dollar amount of an exemption is $3,500. Since the exemption amount is indexed for inflation each year, it is subject to change. You may claim exemptions for:

1. Yourself. You may claim a personal exemption for yourself unless you are the dependent of someone else. This rule prevents your child or other dependent from claiming themselves, if you are entitled to the exemption.

2. Your spouse. You may claim your spouse as an exemption, if you file a joint return. If you file a separate return, you may claim your spouse as an exemption, if he or she has no income and is not a dependent of another person and does not claim themselves.

3. Children, parents and other dependents.

STRATEGY 125: *Get next year's tax refund this year.*

The latest statistics indicate that taxpayers receive over $60 billion in refunds each year. A tax refund is nothing more than a return of your own money, which you never owed to the IRS in the first place, and you do not receive any interest. By adding allowances to your W-4 form, you can get next year's refund in this year's paychecks.

STRATEGY 126: Whenever possible, be taxed as a business rather than an individual.

Our final strategy for reducing your individual taxes is not to be taxed as an individual, but rather, as a business. The IRS Code has two separate, but very unequal, tax systems: one for individuals and another for businesses. In almost every case, you're better off having your income taxed as being earned by your business rather than by yourself individually. We'll be covering this strategy in much greater detail in its own chapter.

When it comes to taxes, the key is to aggressively go after every deduction that you are legally entitled to take. The IRS plays fair. There are rules that they enforce and you need to become familiar with them. There is no need to become an expert but you must have a decent sense for how the game is played if you hope to come out a winner. By identifying and taking advantage of as many deductions as legally possible, you can free up some much needed cash that can be put to use in your wealth creation plan.

CHAPTER 10

MAKING MONEY WHILE YOU SLEEP ON THE INTERNET AND EBAY

*The secret of success of every man who has ever been successful
lies in the fact that he formed the habit of doing those things
that failures don't like to do.*

A. Jackson King

C reating wealth involves increasing cash flow. There are really two separate and distinct ways of doing this. One method for increasing cash flow is to apply defensive strategies such as identifying ways to save money. The other method is to go on the offensive and learn ways for making money. As you should know by now, this book is about utilizing both of these types of strategies. In this chapter, we're going to take a look at how you can maximize both offensive as well as defensive strategies by utilizing the power of the Internet.

Thanks to the Internet, we can now do a myriad of things that were once considered impossible. Today, virtually every aspect of our lives has become "logged on" and "connected" to the world via the World Wide Web. Be it writing a blog, social networking, communicating with friends and relatives across the country or overseas, working or playing online, or even conducting business online, the Internet has indeed paved the way for us to do the things we want to do without exerting so much effort. All you have to do is let your mouse do the surfing and you're just a click away from a brave new (virtual) world.

Many of the tasks associated with our lives have gotten much easier to a point that all we have to do is to "point and click" and things that used to take hours can now be accomplished almost instantly. The strategies contained in this chapter can enable us to use the power of the Internet to help us in our journey toward gaining control over our finances and escaping the "Artificial Wealth Trap." Specifically, we're going to focus on ways to generate income even while we sleep.

STRATEGY 127: Recognize the enormous potential which the Internet holds for your immediate income.

Despite all the differences the Internet has made in our lives, it still poses huge potentials and advantages that are waiting to be fully utilized. Once we recognize these potentials and possibilities, we can use them as advantages in whatever activity we are engaged. The key is that we must use our own creativity to identify potential beneficial uses for our personal and business endeavors. While the Internet offers great potential, it's up to us to recognize opportunities to maximize its use.

The Internet has become an enormous open market for conducting business. Nearly everyone can engage in some sort of business on the Internet and this has become a huge advantage for us all. Be it a large corporation, a small enterprise, or even an individual entrepreneur, we all can make the Internet a useful business tool. Never before has a market been so open to so many people with the opportunity to reach so many potential customers for so little money.

As another avenue for generating additional income, Internet marketing can be started with little capital and the action lies in how you will promote and advertise your products. This is the part where you try to get users to browse your site and of course, convince them why they should buy your advertised product(s).

STRATEGY 128: Evolve your business and life to take advantage of the Internet or get left behind.

The trend in our technology today is so fast paced that you need to continually think of potential advantages for making your business and personal life easier. Thinking ahead is the best leverage you can have to adapt to these fast paced changes. While life in general can be made easier with the use of the Internet, the potential for starting and growing a business is even greater. Since we're looking for ways to create income, we need to explore how to use the Internet to start our own business, and more specifically, as a way to make more money.

Evolving your business to utilize Internet strategies is the name of the game when it comes to Internet marketing. As the Internet grows every day, the number of your potential customers will also increase. Employing your business strategies online can set you on a path to creating quicker and easier access to more customers which can translate into quicker and easier income. Taking advantage of the growth opportunities that are available through the Internet will also prevent your business from being left behind. To keep that from happening, you must establish a plan for how to take advantage of this tremendous leverage device.

STRATEGY 129: Develop an Internet success plan for creating income.

As we've pointed out numerous times, planning is one of the most fundamental steps in every business endeavor that you will ever undertake. In every business venture, there should always be a solid plan or strategy that will provide direction for your business objectives. A solid business plan also helps you to keep up with tasks and increases the likelihood of generating profits or income from it. This is certainly the case when it comes to conducting business on the Internet.

There are a number of aspects unique to the Internet which you should keep in mind when devising a business plan for an online marketing business. These include:

- The type of online business you might want to enter.

- The target market in which you want to create your niche.

- Creating your own site and the possible costs that are included such as registering or buying a domain name, acquiring administrative accounts where customers can purchase and pay for your products with merchant accounts and shopping cart software, web designing, web hosting and search engine optimization.

- Promoting your site by directing traffic to your site and the means for how your site will emerge at the top of major search engines.

- Providing avenues for customer service for customers who patronize and frequently visit your site.

In devising a business plan for any Internet business, you have to work out the strengths, the ups and downs of your target market, fallback options to your weaknesses, and how much capital you are willing to invest into your business. Some of you reading this book may want to create a full-time business online while others of you would simply like to make a little extra money. The extent of your business will determine the necessary detail of your plans.

STRATEGY 130: Use the Internet to turbo-charge traditional forms of promoting a business much easier and much more affordably.

Regardless of the venture, the core elements of starting and running a business have always been the same, and this is no different when it comes to doing business on the Internet. As with any other business, if you want to make money on your own you must have a product or service that is valuable to others to exchange for something else that is of value to you, i.e., money.

Traditional forms of promoting your business may include printed advertisements on flyers, posters, yellow pages, magazines, and newspapers. The boom of advertisements over the Internet has increased the chances of entrepreneurs for how they will be able to market their products further into their own market. Viral marketing, or what is traditionally known as "word of mouth" advertising, is a powerful and conventional way to market your products. By providing high quality products and services, your satisfied customers will then refer your services and products to other potential customers. Nowhere is this more evident than with Internet marketing. The Internet gives customers a voice which is much more likely to be heard than ever before. This can be good or bad depending on what your customers are saying about you.

The Internet makes it possible to convey everything that all the previous media mentioned could only convey separately. Text, sound, graphics, etc., can all be combined into one convenient form of promotion. Best of all is how inexpensive this has become. The Internet has also allowed entrepreneurs to reach other market niches and the possibility of developing new products. Hence, the Internet has been used as an effective tool and opened new avenues in the field of marketing.

Another benefit of the Internet is the ability to add full color pictures without the high cost of printing. I recommend that you add pictures to your site but make sure it will not impede the loading time. Not all customers have up-to-date, state-of-the-art computers or high speed Internet access at home that can download graphics-loaded sites fast and easy, so you might simplify the pictures by having small or high-resolution pictures (thumbnail size). A great way to solve this dilemma is to display small easy to load pictures but provide the option of allowing your customers to click on the image to see a larger picture of your product in detail.

If you really want to take your online business' web content to the next level, consider using videos to provide other details about your product like instructions on how to use your product. You can also discuss in the video the various advantages and benefits of your product to convince your customers to buy it. Videos can be made in flash formats that allow faster loading time. The use of video content on your business' web site is one thing that we teach at our Internet marketing seminars that our students especially like. This enables them to offer top quality sites that anyone can access.

Lastly, your site can also have a forum containing articles and testimonials from other customers who have bought your product or service in the past. This further strengthens your product promotion as well as helps your site to convince prospective customers to buy your product or service. Reading testimonials from current and former customers has significant weight with persons considering your product or service.

STRATEGY 131: *Obtain the advice and wisdom of more experienced Internet marketers when devising your Internet success plan to avoid time-consuming trial and error.*

"If you build it, they will come" may be a great story line for a movie about baseball, but it doesn't always work as a success plan, especially with an Internet business. There are millions of dollars to be earned by doing business on the Internet but while many people have succeeded, just as many have not. Jumping blindly onto the Internet without a plan and without any guidance is like trying to drive a stick-shift automobile without receiving instructions. You could do it, but not without a heightened risk of wrecking the car. The way to lower our risk is by increasing our knowledge.

You may have a sound Internet marketing plan but you will never really know how it will fare until it's time to let it sail in the real world. To avoid the time-consuming trial and error approach, you can consult other Internet marketers to learn from their experience. You may also attend Internet marketing seminars conducted by experienced Internet marketers to help give you some necessary insights on starting your own Internet marketing business. Over the years, I've had the opportunity to work with and learn from some of the greatest Internet marketing minds in the world. I've taken this information and put it together in a way that anyone who wants to get started making money on the Internet can do so. If you'd like more information on how you can attend one of our seminars, visit our website at www. realwealthwithoutrisk.com/internet.

STRATEGY 132: Use leveraging strategies to maximize the impact of the Internet on your home-based business.

According to a 2007 survey of 1,972 online business owners, a little more than 92% reported that they were either making money or saving money by using the advantages of the Internet. When you consider that less than 20% of new businesses with traditional, physical storefronts ever survive their first five years in business, it is remarkable that over 90% of all new online businesses report making or saving money. Bill Gates, the founder of Microsoft and one of the wealthiest men in the world, once wrote: "Businesses of all sizes benefit from the Internet, but small companies are arguably the greatest beneficiaries."

Whether you already have a business presence on the Internet and are just looking for some new techniques to promote your existing site, or you are just beginning to learn about the possibilities of e-commerce online, you need to remember one valuable lesson from the online businesspeople who have gone before you: (*ordinary people are making extraordinary money with the Internet, and there is no reason why you can't join them.*)

One of the greatest benefits of the Internet is that it utilizes the law of leverage. Your product or service may appeal to only a small percentage of Internet users worldwide, but with millions and millions of people accessing the Internet a tiny percentage may be all you really need. Any person as a business owner now has the ability to market to tens of millions of potential consumers every day over the Internet. This wonderful advantage which the Internet has over any other form of commerce is the reason why every business needs to have some sort of a presence online. Since your business has the potential of reaching new customers twenty-four hours a day, seven days a week, you truly do have the opportunity to make money even while you're sleeping.

STRATEGY 133: Be creative in thinking of ways to increase your customer database.

Perhaps the most important goal of any business is to increase its customer base and the Internet is no different. There are a lot of ways to help you accomplish this goal through the implementation of innovative strategies such as blogging, video marketing and article publishing. You've got to put your primary emphasis on building your customer database. By thinking creatively of ways to increase the number of potential customers who are interested in your goods and services, you can ensure that your business will be around for a long time to come. Remember, a larger customer database translates into larger profits.

STRATEGY 134: Register your Internet site with as many online search engines as possible.

Building a large database doesn't just happen. You've got to apply a number of strategies. Registering your site with as many online search engines as possible is a great way to promote both your product and your site. This allows you to reach a wider audience through the help of online search engines like Yahoo!, MSN and Google. This step can be quite tricky so you want to make sure you do it correctly since it is crucial to achieve success in your online business.

There a few rules to follow when submitting your site to search engines. First, make sure that your site is fully operational. You don't want to submit your site if it is "under construction." Besides, if you drive people to your site when all of the links, content, etc. are not as they should be, chances are they won't be back. Secondly, make sure that you understand the cost for registering your site. Search engines will generally have a fee for registering your site and then a continuing charge based upon the number of customers that are driven there. Third, carefully select the category that your site will be listed under. Fourth, decide which keywords you think will direct people to your site. Typically, keywords are going to be the type of product or service offered. And finally, test the search engine once it has been registered.

STRATEGY 135: *"Affiliate" yourself with other companies to make money as the middleman if you have not yet developed a products or services of your own.*

One of the most common excuses that I hear from people for why they're not involved in Internet marketing is that they don't think that they have anything to market. People often tell me that they don't have the time, money, creativity, or ability to create their own product or service. I respond back to them that they can still make money by offering the products or services of someone else. If you're like most of the people I speak with, you may wonder what I'm talking about.

I'm sure that at some point or another over the course of your life you've been approached about a "tremendous opportunity" to set up your own home-based business marketing goods and/or services as a "distributor" for a marketing company. Rather than beating around the bush, what I'm talking about is often referred to as "multi-level marketing" or it's more recent name, "network marketing."

The pitch always starts off by telling you how much money you could make and how much better your life could be as a result of selling some sort of product or service as one of the company's independent distributors. Even better, they say, is that you don't have to do any selling. All you have to do is to set up meetings with your family and friends and the person that signed you up for the program will sell everything for you. While I am in no way saying that all of these programs are bad, the result is often disastrous.

What often happens in many of these situations is that a person winds up offending the people in their life to a point where their friends and family are afraid to see them coming out of a fear that the person is going to try to sell them something. This usually turns people off to the point that they don't want anything to do with any sort of sales and/or marketing business.

The good news is that this strategy is different. This one truly involves being able to market to people that you don't even know utilizing materials that you never had to design or create. It's called affiliate marketing and it can make you a lot of money.

Amazon.com CEO Jeff Bezos pioneered the affiliate program as an Internet marketing strategy in 1996. Since then, many sites have followed suit in promoting affiliate programs. The concept focuses on arrangements with online merchants and websites on how they will send traffic to the sites and the potential number of users who eventually buy the product from the site. The way these affiliate arrangements work is quite simple. If a link on an affiliate's site brings traffic or money to the merchant's site, the merchant pays the affiliate according to their agreement.

With affiliate programs, you essentially work as a broker selling other people's products for them and earn a commission for it after the sale. The first thing you must do is have your own web site and do everything possible to get people to visit it. Next, you need to have banners placed on your site for the affiliate programs. Every time someone makes a purchase because of an affiliate banner being on your site, you get to collect a commission on that sale.

Affiliate programs may seem an easy way to sell and a great way to generate income. However, what often happens that prevents people from making even more money with an affiliate program is that they tend to focus on a one-time sale. Yes, you do want to get as many new customers to your site as possible, but it's important to make your site exciting so that people will want to come back again and again. This will better position you to maximize your sales potential.

Becoming an affiliate for other websites' products and services is a great idea if you take the right steps. The following are things to look for and ways to plan out what you are about to do:

- Choose one or two affiliate programs that sell individual items, promote them well on your site, then follow up by offering other products and services. Your chances of success become much higher by focusing on just a couple of programs rather than too many.

- When choosing an affiliate program, choose programs that offer good profit margins. Amazon.com is the current leader in affiliate programs, because they were the first in the game. The challenge is that their program only pays 5 to 15% for each book sold off of your website. Many programs will pay their affiliates as much as 50% for each sale that the affiliate generates. My asset protection affiliate program starts at 50% and goes as high as 70% which makes it one of the most potentially profitable programs that you will ever encounter. If you would like more information about this program, send an email to info@ secretmillionaire.com to find out all of the details.

- When choosing an affiliate program, do your math and see which products sell the best, and remember to lead with an entry product that is not too expensive, and follow up with the more expensive products later, after you have built up the trust and name recognition needed for a more expensive purchase.

The bottom line is that you will have to market your website and the affiliate program product or service you offer. If you just put up a large number of affiliate programs, hoping that one will pull in the necessary business, you are simply taking the "magic dust" approach. This is very much like going to a casino or playing the lottery in hopes of building wealth. You may win, but the odds are stacked high against you. Take the responsibility to strategically promote your offers. Find out where your potential customers are and excite them to come and visit your site.

STRATEGY 136: Use leveraging strategies to maximize the impact of the Internet on your life.

Speaking of leveraging strategies, the Internet allows you to make money even if you think you don't have any products or services to sell. The Internet can still allow you to make money because it can enable you to work smarter, not harder, at your more traditional businesses and in your life in general. How does the Internet do this? It does it by using automation to free up your most valuable asset, time.

In business, you can use the power of the Internet to communicate with your customers for you so that you can focus on creating and marketing new products. By sending automatic emails regarding order confirmations, order status, "thank you messages," and information about new products, your customers will feel like you are giving them the "personal touch" when in fact you haven't had to even think about them, at least not in an individual sense. This is the type of leverage that enables a small business to make big profits.

Another way that the leveraging power of the Internet can free up your time is through more effective and more efficient marketing and advertising. I once had a client who was in sales, and he told me how twenty years ago whenever his company had a new product he would pull out his customer lists and tell his customers about the new products for sale. Looking back, he told me that the strategy was quite effective but the method took an incredible amount of time. He would sometimes spend a full day making phone calls, and most of the time he would either not get an answer, get a busy signal, or annoy someone by the unsolicited phone call. At the end of his efforts, he would be lucky if five percent of his phone calls generated real interest in the new products, and even less than that would actually result in a sale. Yet twenty years ago, what was the alternative to all this wasted time? Today we can use the Internet to effortlessly reach out to our customers and provide them with information on new products or services, and the amount of effort it takes is almost zero.

You can probably think of many more ways that the leveraging power of the Internet can make your business run smoother. Yet the point I want you to learn from this strategy is this: *(use the internet to automate your life.)* The less time and effort you spend on tasks which do not make you money, the more time and effort you will have for those that do.

Earlier in this chapter, I said that many of you might think that you have no chance of prospering from the Internet because you have no goods or services to sell. You may remember that I told you that such thinking was untrue. Over the next several strategies I'm going to be showing you how some of the goods and services that you already have can make you money.

STRATEGY 137: Learn to profit with online auctions.

Another great step in learning to make money on the internet is to familiarize yourself with how online auctions work and how you can gain profits from unused or unwanted things in your house. This is another way to earn money without spending a penny, going to a lot of effort, or being tied to a 9 to 5 job. In fact, one of the great things I love about internet auctions is that they are automatic, meaning that you can be earning money without even knowing it.

As both an entrepreneur and a consumer, I like online auctions for a number of reasons. For one thing, you can attract a large number of buyers and sellers to one place, thus making the opportunities to sell your products and find deals virtually unlimited. Second, you don't have as many geographical worries with Internet auctions. You can reach anyone, customers or merchants, with just a click of a mouse. Third, time is no factor with online auctions. Your online store doesn't have to keep any "store hours," and if you are shopping, you can do so from the comfort of your home after the kids have gone to bed. Fourth, from both a seller's and a shopper's perspective, online auctions are somewhat of a microcosm of capitalism. The factors of supply and demand operate on the Internet just like in the real world. If you are a seller with rare or hard to find products, online auctions allow the price of your goods to rise very quickly. And finally, with online auctions you don't have to worry about selling "niche" goods and services. Since the number of potential customers you can reach on the Internet is limitless, you can focus on your strong suits rather than peddling goods just because they may be in high demand.

In the next section, I will show you how eBay works and how you can earn extra cash from online auctions in general.

STRATEGY 138: Familiarize yourself with eBay and other online auctions.

EBay is undisputedly the largest online auction site in the world and has emerged as *the* marketplace of the twenty-first century. The founders of eBay had a pretty great idea back in 1995, and the world has certainly taken to the idea of shopping and selling online. It provides a safe and fun place to shop for just about everything, all from the comfort of your home. And eBay is no longer just the destination for collectibles and old china patterns, it is also a marketplace for new and/or mainstream goods and services. In fact, just about anything you can think of can be found on eBay or one of the other online auctions. Better yet, eBay is the perfect alternative to spending hours wandering through antique shops or swap meets looking for the perfect doohickey. It can even be your personal shopper for gifts and day-to-day items. The ability to browse through so many products in so much less time provides us with the type of leverage that we need in order to maximize our time and effectiveness.

STRATEGY 139: Identify disregarded items in your home or business which can be someone else's auction prize and your ticket to income.

Many people are familiar with eBay and other online auctions as buyers only. To create additional income, you need to become familiar with selling on eBay as well. The challenge for many people is that they don't know where or how to begin. Take a look around your house, what do you see? Nice toaster? Great looking old clock? Spiffy microwave? All these household appliances and collectibles are great to own, but when was the last time your toaster turned a profit? When you connect to eBay, your computer magically turns into a money machine. Just visit eBay and marvel at all the items that are just a few mouse clicks away from being bought and sold. If you've got some items that you'd like to get rid of, you can turn a profit by selling them online.

You should conduct your own personal inventory at home or even in your business to keep track of your items. By doing this you'll be able to check which items are not used but are still in good condition. These kinds of items can be sold over eBay or in other online auction sites and generate extra money for you. If you don't have any personal items that you are interested in selling, one great idea is to go to thrift stores where you can find items for extremely low prices that you can resell online for a profit. Many online sellers will purchase significantly discounted merchandise from places like Wal-Mart or other retailers and then sell them online. If you are a serious bargain shopper, you can turn this skill into a profitable business through the advent of online auctions.

We had one client who did this so well that she created a problem for herself that she had not experienced before. The "problem" was that she was now making so much more money than she was accustomed to making that she faced a serious increase in her taxes. We were more than happy to hear of her success and to help her to handle her "problem."

STRATEGY 140: Develop auction identification for your business and place continuous auctions for items in your inventory.

Online auctions such as eBay don't actually sell anything. Instead, these sites merely create a comfortable environment that brings people with common interests together. You can think of eBay like you think of the person who set you up on your last blind date, except the results are usually a lot better. Your matchmaking friend doesn't perform a marriage ceremony but does get you in the same room with your potential soul mate. Similarly, online auctions put buyers and sellers together in a virtual store and lets them conduct their business safely within the rules that it has established.

On online auction sites like eBay, you can sell almost anything, and better yet, people will buy almost anything. Since 1995, there has been a wide assortment of unusual and even outrageous items that have been put up for sale. Policies regarding what you are allowed to sell and what you are not allowed to sell are always stated in the policy section of the auction. For the list of items that can't be auctioned or sold on a particular online auction, check with the site's public policy or other "rules" section.

STRATEGY 141: *Continue to identify more efficient and effective ways for improving your personal and business effectiveness with the power of the Internet.*

My final strategy for making money on the Internet is a simple one: Be creative! The Internet and its related technologies are evolving at an unbelievable rate. You can expect that there will be many more innovations and new ways on how to market your products. And with that, it can lead you to a much wider range of your target market.

The bottom line when it comes to creating wealth with the Internet is best expressed by the slogan for the lottery: *(you've got to be in it to win it.)* If you never get started, you'll never profit. The Internet holds enormous potential but the only way for you to realize that potential is to get things going.

CHAPTER 11

CREATING INCOME WITH REAL ESTATE

Men are so constituted that every one undertakes what he sees another successful in, whether he has aptitude for it or not.

Johann Wolfgang Von Goethe

I firmly believe that any book that purports to teach people strategies for becoming wealthy has to include a section on real estate. Real estate has always been, and will continue to be one of the greatest, if not the greatest, wealth builders in this country. In fact, most of the millionaires in the United States have built their wealth in one way or another through real estate. And, more importantly to you, there is just as much profit opportunity in real estate right now as there has ever been. The only difference is that you have to be a lot smarter and have more information now to make money with real estate than you did even a few years ago.

Considering this, it seems somewhat inadequate to include only a single chapter on creating wealth through real estate in this book when I just mentioned that having an abundance of knowledge and information is necessary. The reason that it's ok, however, is that this is in no way intended to be a book primarily focused on making money in real estate. In this chapter, our focus is on how anyone can get started in real estate and profit from certain strategies that can jumpstart their quest to build wealth. We'll be covering some very basic information and some of the most common strategies for getting started. These strategies will prove beneficial to you as you go about the most important part of any real estate strategy, locating properties.

If you're an active investor who has been involved in real estate for years, chances are that you will already know a lot of the information contained in this section and I make no apology for that. This information is included primarily for those just getting started. My guess, however, is that there are a few strategies that will benefit even the most battle-scarred real estate veterans as well. If nothing else, the strategies will be a good reminder of things that you may already be familiar with so it's in your best interest to continue on.

STRATEGY 142: Learn why real estate is responsible for building so many fortunes.

There are a lot of reasons why real estate will continue to be the number one wealth builder in the United States. For example, personal use real estate is one of the few investments that has intrinsic value. This "intrinsic value" means that you can use real estate personally while you hold it for future profits. You can't do that with stock. Think of your home as a prime example of this. While enjoying a place to live and raise your family, you are also able to build equity as well as sheltering income from taxes. This is a very unique combination.

Additionally, by learning the right concepts, you can buy real estate even if you have no money to invest through mastering the strategy of 100% Financing. That's something that can't be done with stocks, bonds, precious metals or anything else. Using leverage, investment returns of 30%, 40%, and even 50% or more per year are not unusual. You can also leverage money with real estate because a small amount of investment capital can control a large amount of assets. What a $6,000 down payment on a $100,000 home means, for instance, is that for only a 6% risk, you can own a $100,000 investment. This leverage is the ultimate use of O.P.M. (other people's money). You may be familiar with this concept (O.P.M.) and the power that it provides. If you hope to create wealth through real estate, you must master it.

Another great reason for real estate is that almost everyone has at least lived in a house at some point in their lives, and therefore, has some experience with real estate, even if the house was rented. In comparison, few beginning investors have ever bought or used stock certificates and/or bonds. While living in a house does not prepare you to make wise real estate investments, the strategies in this chapter will.

Real estate also has the most proven track record of any investment, over the long haul. Since 1930, real estate has appreciated an average of almost 10% per year. Hanging on to real estate over time can allow even the least proficient investor to profit. Some stock market investors may contend that the stock market offers more potential, but my response would be that it also offers more risk. It's really unheard of for a piece of real estate to drop in value down to nothing whereas that's not the case with stocks.

The key point we want you to understand is that there are huge profits to be made in personal and investment real estate. The best way to tap into these profits is by following the five step method for building profit with real estate.

STRATEGY 143: Learn the five steps to earning income with real estate.

No matter how experienced you may be when it comes to real estate, there are five steps that all knowledgeable real estate investors take when making money. The reason why I love these steps is because they are universal and can be used in any type of economy. Better yet, these steps will aid you no matter what type of real estate investing you are interested in, from rehabbing properties to investing in tax liens.

The first step in succeeding in real estate is acquiring knowledge. Big profits from real estate almost always go to the most knowledgeable investor. People often think that learning the secrets of real estate investing is difficult. Believe me, it's not. Successful real estate investing can be put into simple rules and concepts that anyone can learn. We've taught thousands of people how to make millions of dollars by following the strategies. If you'd like more information on how you can do it too, visit www.realwealthwithoutrisk.com to download your FREE special report.

The second step to succeeding in real estate is to develop the ability to locate a good property. It's often been said that location is the most important profit element in buying real estate. As the saying goes, "it's all about location, location, location." Location means buying the right properties in the right areas at the right time. This may sound difficult but it just takes some plain old "ground pounding" and time.

Third, you need to learn how to evaluate the merits of each project or investment on a case-by-case basis. This is the process of determining the true value of a project. Before buying, you have to do some research to determine the market value or rental value of a property and whether a project is located in a neighborhood where values are going up or down. You also have to know how to inspect a property to determine if it is everything the seller says it is, how much additional work and cost will be incurred in getting it ready to occupy, and if the project has real financial merit.

After finding the right property, the right location, and evaluating the project, it's time for the fourth step in every successful real estate investment, negotiating the deal. During the negotiation process, the final price, terms, and method of financing will be determined. The process begins with your first inquiry and often continues up to the closing of the property. How good the "deal" ultimately turns out for you may be decided by your negotiating skills. Many of these finer points are learned as you practice them.

Finally, your road from real estate prospector to real estate millionaire ends with the exit strategy, which is to sell the property for a profit. At some point, you will want to cash in properties to reap the profits you have been accumulating, either to reinvest, or spend on something else. When selling your properties, you can turn these profits into immediate cash or long-term income, depending on which is the most important to you, and the most advantageous to you from a tax standpoint.

STRATEGY 144: Know the four kinds of profit in real estate.

Before tackling true real estate concepts, it is important for you to understand the four kinds of potential real estate profits and how each is determined. This strategy goes along with your ability to evaluate and negotiate a deal as we pointed out in the last strategy. By tracking your profits, you will be able to see at a glance how well your real estate investments are doing and whether the returns are worth the effort.

Appreciation
The first way to make a profit in real estate is through appreciation. This is the increase in the value of your property over time and can be measured as a percentage of cost. If you buy a $100,000 property, putting $10,000 down, and its value has increased to $120,000 at the end of 2 years, the total amount of appreciation is $20,000, computed by subtracting the total cost from the current value. The appreciation percentage is computed by dividing the appreciation amount of $20,000 by the total cost of $100,000 which equals 20%. The average appreciation per year is computed by dividing the total appreciation percentage of 20% by the number of years you have owned the property. In this case, the 20% is divided by two, and your average annual appreciation is 10% based on the original cost of the property.

You also need to know the return on your investment (ROI) from appreciation. The ROI for a project is the percentage of profit you have earned based on the down payment you made. Your return is computed by dividing the appreciation amount of $20,000 by the down payment of $10,000, showing that so far your return on investment from appreciation is 200%. When you learn to look at things this way, you can better appreciate what a great investment that real estate can be.

Principal Reduction
The second type of profit realized with real estate is reduction in principal. Principal reduction refers to the amount or percentage of the original mortgage that has been paid off. If this sounds to you a lot like "equity," good, that's exactly what we are talking about. On

201

your home loan, for example, a portion of your mortgage payment goes toward paying the principal with the balance going to interest, insurance and taxes. On a rental property, the tenants are making the payments through rent, a portion of which goes toward principal reduction. The mortgage company keeps the interest, for which you get a tax deduction, but the principal reduction increases your equity in the property.

Cash Flow

The third type of profit earned through real estate is cash flow. Cash flow is related primarily to rental properties and is the difference between the total amount of money a property takes in each year and the total amount it costs to operate. Cash flow can be either positive or negative. Your goal is to keep negative cash flow as low as possible. One of the biggest investor mistakes is acquiring real estate without regard for how easily negative cash flow can increase from vacant properties, non-collected rents, and unexpected maintenance costs. Investors with good intentions who cannot cover the negative cash flow can lose properties in foreclosure or end up sinking lots of money in a black hole of repairs. To avoid this, you need to understand the mathematics of real estate investing and make sure your investment plan includes contingency funds for unexpected negative cash flow. Your long-term goal is to increase rents faster than expenses.

Tax Deductions

Our last type of profit through real estate is the acquisition of tax deductions. By achieving tax deductions, what we're really achieving is a tax shelter. For example, if your Adjusted Gross Income (AGI) for tax purposes is under $100,000 a year, then real estate is probably the best tax sheltered investment you can find. For instance, if you're in a 30% tax bracket, the government returns to you 30 cents for every dollar of tax deductions you can create. Every $1,000 in tax deductions will return to you $300 in cash either in a refund check or in reduced taxes. Most tax deductions create cash flow in the current year, whereas appreciation and equity are long-term. We discuss tax reduction strategies in much more detail in a later chapter.

STRATEGY 145: *Increase your profits through leverage.*

One of the things that first attracted me to real estate both as a way to generate income and create wealth is the concept of leverage. The secret behind leverage and why it is so great for real estate investors is that you can contribute only a fraction of the cost of an investment (or even none at all through 100% financing) yet reap all of the benefits. Think about how remarkable the power of leverage makes real estate investing when compared to other forms of investments. If you want to buy 100 shares of a stock, is your broker going to put up the money for 90 shares? No way. And can you imagine finding a partner who will loan you money to start a new business but not want to share proportionately in the profits? With real estate, thanks to leverage, other people's money can lead to your income and wealth.

STRATEGY 146: *Create a cushion for negative cash flow.*

No matter how well you plan or how good a project may look on paper, there will be times when you are unable to rent your property or to collect the rents which you are owed. That's just a fact of life when dealing with tenants and real estate. If you have no cushion for this, you can easily become real estate rich, but cash poor. You may be able to show a million dollars in assets on your financial statement, and not have enough cash to buy lunch. To eliminate this problem, you need to maintain a minimum of three months' worth of mortgage payments in cash or credit for each property you own.

If a property has a mortgage payment of $800 a month, you want a cushion of available cash or credit totaling $2,400 for that property. You can achieve this cushion in two ways, either with cash or by lining up available credit to be used when you need it. A great way to have credit lined up is to have identified an "equity partner" who can invest in your property when you need help rather than by going into debt with a more traditional loan. This is not as good as having a reserve, but it is much better than getting caught without having the money to service your mortgage debt.

STRATEGY 147: Buy only the "right kind" of residential properties when getting started.

When first getting started in real estate, I always recommend beginning with residential properties. However, you must understand that all residential properties are not created equally. You've got to find the right ones. The kind of residential property you choose and where it is located will have a great bearing on future appreciation, the initial cost of the property, and, if the property is to be rented, the amount of rent you can ultimately charge. As we've already discussed, location is important, but don't rule out a project that looks good to you just because it happens to be in a less than desirable location. By using the right concepts, even a marginal location can sometimes be turned into a profitable investment. Still, as a general rule, the better the location, the better your chances of success. As a novice investor, you need to pay particular attention to location. This means choosing the right property in the right neighborhood in the right price range and in the right condition. This may sound a bit like trying to time things for the perfect opportunity but that's not the case. It's not as difficult as it may sound.

No matter what sort of investment you are pursuing, follow these steps to finding the "right kind" of property. First, try and purchase three or four bedroom properties. Three quarters of all the people in this country live in three bedroom homes or larger. That keeps three bedroom homes and condos in greater demand and easier to sell than any other size. As a general rule, you should never buy anything smaller than three bedroom properties for rentals. Secondly, buy only properties that are in good condition. For the novice investor or for investors who do not have a lot of carpentry skills, this is especially true. Third, avoid buying properties that are newer than 20 years old. A lot of investors try to look primarily for old properties which may be "diamonds in the rough." All too often, these projects turn into money pits rather than money trees.

The fourth strategy for buying "the "right kind" of properties is to only buy properties which are in the "average" price range. What is "average" will vary quite a bit across the country. By buying properties which are extremely cheap or incredibly expensive it will be harder to rent or sell them later on. Nobody wants to buy or rent a cheap house from you, and if the property is too expensive to buy or rent you may be stuck with it for a long time. Also, be sure to only buy properties that are on paved streets. I can assure you that you may be able to find some great deals on properties that sit on undeveloped roads, but the challenge is that I can also assure you that you will likely have a harder time renting or selling that property.

STRATEGY 148: Look for properties in appreciating areas.

Investing near, or in the path of progress has been a winning real estate concept for a long time. Essentially, property appreciates for two primary reasons: increased demand and the effects of inflation. Demand appreciation is when there are more buyers than sellers. The price of any commodity, including real estate, rises in direct proportion to the amount of excess demand. Most real estate goes through a buyer's and seller's market cycle at one time or another. During seller's markets, demand outstrips supply and the price of property rises. Demand appreciation can be far greater than inflation appreciation and in some cycles can reach 10%, 20%, or even more per year for short periods of time.

Like increased demand, inflation increases (appreciates) the value of property because the replacement cost of any property increases with time and is also affected by the value of the dollar. Inflation (or replacement cost appreciation) drives up the cost of a property an average of 3% per year, whether you make any improvements or not. Inflation appreciation is essentially the amount of money it would take to exactly duplicate an existing property at some point in the future.

STRATEGY 149: Buy multi-unit properties when possible.

Multi-unit properties are a great way to acquire a home for yourself and some tax-deductible rental units at the same time. The IRS allows you to apply the tax deductions for a personal residence to the unit you live in and tax deductions allowed for a rental property to the other units. If you're looking for a personal residence, a two to four unit property can be a great investment. The upside is that you live in the property so you can manage it effectively, you have other people making a portion of your mortgage payments for you, and you control a larger amount of assets, giving you a greater chance for future profits.

You also need to be aware, however, that living in your own multi-unit property can have a few downsides. First, your tenants will be right next door and will not hesitate to bother you about every little thing that goes wrong. Second, you should avoid properties with more than 4 units, unless you have investment partners with the expertise to handle bigger projects. And finally, be leery of friends, relatives, girlfriends and boyfriends who suddenly want to move in to your new multi-unit property. They might turn out to be the worst tenants you could ever have.

STRATEGY 150: Don't hesitate to employ the help of a realtor or other professional if you need it.

There are a lot of advantages and disadvantages in working with other real estate professionals, such as brokers or agents. Generally, the less experience you have in real estate, the more important that professional help can be. The problem is that few agents have any real experience putting together good real estate deals. The test to get a real estate license does not require knowledge of how to help investors and home buyers get good deals on homes. The test covers rules, regulations, real estate concepts and mathematics, but not investments. Many real estate agents own no investment real estate themselves, and have no interest in doing so. They are little more than commissioned sales people in that sense.

A good clue that an agent is not prepared to help you buy properties is when you hear one of them make the statement, "No, sorry, that can't be done," with no explanation of how you can accomplish what you want. The truth is that there is almost always a way around problems in this business, if you are motivated and knowledgeable. If you do decide to work with a Realtor, be prepared to spend considerable time and frustration locating one who is on your side and who will follow your guidelines. The good news is that once you find a good one they can be an invaluable member of your master mind team.

STRATEGY 151: Buy properties for sale by owner (FSBOs).

"For sale by owner" (FSBO) properties are not listed with real estate brokers. That can be both good news and bad. FSBOs are harder to find, but are usually the best properties to concentrate on if you have decided to work on your own. Around 20-25% of the real estate properties for sale at any given time are FSBOs.

There are generally three ways to find FSBOs. First, always read the Real Estate Section in the Sunday paper. Most states require that the words "Agent" or "Broker" appear in all real estate ads for properties listed with real estate professionals. Therefore, even if an ad does not specifically state "For Sale By Owner," you can usually assume that it is unless the words "Agent," "Broker" or "Realtor" appear in the ad. Second, look for homes with FSBO signs. If you find a specific neighborhood you're interested in, spend some time driving around and you'll spot properties that have FSBO signs in the yards. Make a list of the addresses and major features of these properties, then call the owners. If you have a cellular phone, call while you're there and ask the owners if you can see the property right away. Most of the time, they will agree, particularly if they are anxious to sell. If not, set an appointment to come back. And finally, let all of your friends and business associates know that you are looking for FSBOs. You'll be surprised by how many FSBOs you can find this way. Keep a notebook handy so you can write down any leads you are given.

STRATEGY 152: Find motivated sellers and maximize your profits.

Motivated sellers are what every investor looks for. Those are sellers that have *a need* to sell quickly, not just a desire. You don't want to go out looking to take advantage of someone else's problems, but you are looking for a flexible seller who is willing to work with you. Motivated sellers sometimes even identify themselves in their newspaper ads or listings. If an ad reads, "Owner Must Sell" or "Make An Offer" or "Price Just Reduced," it's a good bet the owner is in a hurry to sell and will at least consider almost any reasonable offer you make. Be aware, however, that there's a difference between being motivated and being desperate. Just because a seller may be motivated does not mean that they are willing to practically give away their house. You've got to be reasonable if you hope to be successful.

STRATEGY 153: Avoid raw land for investments.

As a final strategy regarding choosing the right type of property, I almost always steer new investors away from raw land. Raw land (no buildings, houses, or other structures on it), acreage or vacant property, has until recent years been considered a good long-term investment. However, there are considerable financial drawbacks that make raw land a risky area for an investor (particularly a novice).

For one thing, you're not going to earn any income from raw land. A raw land provides you with no type of tax shelter other than deduction for the actual interest or property taxes paid on it. By contrast, residential and commercial buildings are depreciable, meaning that the actual cost of development becomes tax deductible. Over time, tax deductions become a significant part of your profits. Third, the appreciation of raw land can be painfully slow. With other types of property, your money can grow much more quickly. And finally, you will have a much harder time obtaining funding when purchasing raw land. We talked earlier about the benefit of using leverage to purchase properties. With raw land, your power of leverage is severely weakened.

STRATEGY 154: Decide what type of real estate is best suited to your personal situation.

Now that we've covered some of the basic real estate information that you need to know if you plan on getting involved in this tremendous investment arena, it's up to you to decide what type of investing that you'd like to get involved with. There are almost as many ways to invest in real estate as there are people investing in it. The key to being successful is to identify the top few strategies that you are most interested in and focus your efforts on being the best that you can be in those strategies. That is a decision that you will need to make for yourself and one that will require more in-depth research on your part.

We teach a number of different real estate trainings covering a variety of different topics including foreclosures, wholesaling, commercial real estate, multi-family real estate, OPM real estate, tax liens, and creating a real estate retirement plan. Each of these courses covers strategies that have proven enormously beneficial for investors of all backgrounds from beginners all the way through to long-time professionals. If you'd like more information regarding how you can get involved with one of these programs, visit our website at www.realwealthwithoutrisk.com to speak with one of our enrollment counselors.

Part IV:

ACCUMULATE

CHAPTER 12

ACCUMULATING REAL WEALTH

In investing money, the amount of interest you want should depend on whether you want to eat well or sleep well.

J. Kenfield Morley

The only way that you will ever become wealthy is if you begin to *accumulate* wealth. This may sound pretty basic but it's something that people apparently don't understand, at least if their actions are any indication. Many people simply don't understand why they find themselves continuing to live from paycheck to paycheck when there are others who are able to accumulate enormous levels of wealth. The biggest challenge that these people have is that they've never taken the time to truly consider the process of accumulating wealth. This is what keeps them in the "Artificial Wealth Trap."

STRATEGY 155: Learn the difference between making money and building wealth.

It's really quite simple. The reason that most people aren't wealthy is because they don't know *how* to build wealth. To be a bit more specific, they don't really even know what it means to build wealth. What eludes most people is that *building wealth* is different than *making money*. To ever build real wealth for yourself, you've got to learn the difference between the two.

Most people think that the key to financial independence is to simply increase their income. While this is certainly important, so much so that we've dedicated an entire Part of this book to focusing on strategies to do this, you've got to understand that *simply making more money, in and of itself, will not make you wealthy.* The only way to become wealthy is to continually increase the gap between the amount of money that comes in and the amount that goes out. That's it. Those who fail to learn this lesson are doomed to a life of financial frustration and will never become financially independent.

In this Part of the book, we will be covering specific strategies for how to increase the gap between what comes in and what goes out so that you can indeed build the type of wealth that you have set yourself up to attain through the previous Parts of the book. There are a number of incredible strategies for making this happen, but the key is that you've got to put those strategies to work for you. If you don't do that, you will end up like the vast majority out there who never build enough wealth for themselves to ever become financially free. *It's up to you which group of people that you will be a part of, the group that achieves their dreams or those who merely dream of achieving.*

STRATEGY 156: Establish a wealth accumulation mindset.

The first step in any endeavor should be to get yourself into the proper frame of mind. This is especially true when dealing with the topic of wealth accumulation. Perhaps the single greatest difference that I've observed between my most successful clients and those who simply want to live the affluent lifestyle is in their approach to accumulating wealth. This all comes down to a difference in their mindset. An important lesson that I've learned is that once you are mentally ready for a task, achieving it will seem a much smaller hurdle to overcome.

The wealth accumulation mindset looks to the long-term building of wealth rather than merely seeking methods to create enough income to buy more "stuff." It is not about constantly looking for the latest, greatest investment to expedite the process. A proper wealth accumulation mindset looks into the future and determines ways in which the cash flow that you have today can be put to work building wealth for a prosperous financial future. This is not to say that you will not participate in a number of tremendous opportunities for making great money in the process. The difference is that your future will not be dependent on these opportunities immediately paying off. This requires a mindset that is different from others.

The wealth accumulation mindset will help you work to ensure that your future lifestyle is the one that you want, not the one that you are forced to have due to a lack of proper planning. This is difficult for many people because the world around them continually seeks to pull them into the "Artificial Wealth Trap." To become wealthy, you've got to overcome this temptation for instant gratification and realize that the financial freedom that you will experience down the road will be well worth any delay that accompanies the wealth accumulation mindset.

One of my favorite sayings that I learned from a mentor of mine is that you should "live like no one else so that you can live like no one else." In other words, the wealth accumulation steps that you take today, impact your wealth and your lifestyle not only for today, but also in the years to come. Getting into the right mindset is a big step in the right direction.

STRATEGY 157: Set your investment objectives before you invest.

As you've undoubtedly discovered if you've read completely through the book to this point, one of my favorite strategies is to "plan your work and then work your plan." This holds true in the field of wealth accumulation more than perhaps any other field. The reason is that the *plan* is the key to building long-term wealth. Without a plan, it is highly likely that you will find yourself in the same boat as many other hard-working families who end up without the means necessary to provide for themselves after they leave the working world. Establishing a plan keeps this from happening.

Before you invest the first dollar, you should always ask yourself, "What do I want to accomplish with this money?" Without setting investment objectives, you could make the wrong investment and ultimately not accomplish your goals. In my experience with clients, those who failed to ask this question from the very beginning experienced frustration, fear, and failure because they bounced around from investment to investment looking for the so-called "magic pill." What I've learned by working with the most successful of my clients is that the "magic pill" does indeed exist. It exists in the formation and following of a plan for long-term wealth accumulation.

In formulating your plan, you've got to first decide what it is that you hope to accomplish. Some of the things that you may need to consider include:

- Will you need access to your investment money as an emergency fund?

- How long can you invest this money or these assets before you need them for your budget or for reinvestment?

- What kind of return would you like to see on your investment?

- How much are you willing to risk?

- Are the invested assets necessary for your current operations, or is this discretionary cash?

If you don't have the answers to these questions, you could find yourself in a serious financial bind. Those people who make it big in the long run are those who had the foresight to formulate their plan and then stick to it. The people who end up losing their money are the ones who find themselves with short-term cash needs that require them to abandon their plans and liquidate their portfolios at times that are, shall we say, less than ideal. These short-term cash needs are especially prevalent in the lives of those who have fallen into the "Artificial Wealth Trap."

STRATEGY 158: Decide on a particular investment area and develop a fundamental understanding of that area.

One of the reasons why so many people fail to see the profits that they might have otherwise realized is that they end up bouncing around in different investment areas looking for what they think are better opportunities. If they had simply focused on one area in particular, they would have found themselves in a much better position. I've had plenty of people tell me that this is contrary to what they have always heard about investing since it seemingly disputes the strategy of diversification. This is not the case at all.

I certainly believe that you should diversify. The reason that most people end up losing money, however, is that they are *too* diversified. It sounds strange to a lot of people when I first point out this difficulty. It seems to fly in the face of conventional wisdom. Well, if there's one thing that I've learned from working with extraordinarily wealthy clients, and from my own experience as well, it is that *conventional wisdom yields conventional results.* If the conventional wisdom was correct, more people would end up retiring wealthy. Instead, the conventional wisdom leads people down a deceptive path to the "Artificial Wealth Trap." *To get different results, you must do things differently.*

A quote that has had a major impact on me in my financial life is one that I came across in my research by one of the wealthiest people to ever live in America, the steel magnate, Andrew Carnegie. The quote read:

Put all good eggs in one basket and then watch that basket.

When I first read this quote, I had a bit of a challenge with it. In fact, as an asset protection attorney and a personal financial strategist, I've taught thousands of people to *never* keep all of their eggs in one basket. From an asset protection standpoint, this would violate every strategy imaginable. However, the quote was focused primarily on business principles rather than on traditional wealth protection measures. I guess the thing that I like best about the quote is that it actually serves

217

as a tremendous wealth protection strategy as well in that it keeps wealth protected from loss caused by not following a plan.

The way that this concept protects wealth is that it reminds people to stay out of investments that they are not familiar with. A lesson that I learned years ago from a very successful mentor of mine has helped me to avoid a great deal of calamity. Unfortunately, I've found myself having to relearn the lesson a few times as well. In fact, anytime that I've violated this principle, I've regretted it. The principle is summed up in a simple statement as follows:

Make money in my business, lose it in yours.

This is a strategy that many people have a difficult time following. The reason is that it's a major part of the "Artificial Wealth Trap." When you look around and see people making money in an endeavor, it's extremely tempting to try to do the same thing for yourself. What you may not have seen was that they were following a plan and had a level of understanding in the endeavor that others, including you, did not. Because you went into it without a plan and without the requisite knowledge of the business, you probably ended up losing money.

This is the lesson that Andrew Carnegie was teaching with his quote. I'm sure he knew the temptation of going after profits in areas where other people had profited rather than sticking to one's own area of expertise. I've heard this referred to as the "bright, shiny object syndrome" since it refers to the allure of chasing after something that pulls your attention away from your primary objective. By chasing after a bunch of bright, shiny money-making opportunities it's easy to become distracted from the task at hand, the thing that you're good at. There are a lot of ways to make a lot of money. The key is to find the ones that you want to develop a skill in and stick with them.

STRATEGY 159: Develop a plan for your investment capital that is in accordance with your objectives.

Plain and simple, you need to have a plan for your investment capital. This will involve the establishment of specific goals for what you want to accomplish with your money. You may even have multiple goals. For example, if you want money to reap financial rewards now, but you need some of the excess cash to use for future investments, then this must be taken into consideration when choosing your investment strategies. You can allocate a certain portion of your investment dollars to short-term strategies and another portion to longer term options. The key is to recognize the purpose of your investments and have them stay on target. Don't get side-tracked from your plan by throwing money at investments that do not fit in with your plan.

Many people liquidate assets at inopportune times banking on a prospective profit from a "better" investment only to guarantee a loss that wasn't necessary. Chasing after these "better" deals to pay for dips in asset values can end up costing you a lot of money. You can't always rely on one investment to pay for another one, and no investment or investment strategy is guaranteed. By setting specific investment objectives, you can have a clearly defined path upon which your investment money can travel.

STRATEGY 160: Work to increase your "wealth sustainability level."

Something that I've always been fascinated by is the difference in the attitudes of those who are truly wealthy and those who fall into the various phases of the "Artificial Wealth Trap." The truly wealthy seem to be a great deal happier than those who continue living a life of affluence that they can't financially sustain. Now, I understand that many people who read that sentence will feel like I've got an incredible grasp on the obvious. Some may go as far as to say that it's a waste of their time to read something so readily apparent. Well, those people would be wrong.

First of all, let me explain what I mean when I refer to those who are "truly wealthy." If you're like most people, you've probably got a different definition from mine. When I sit down to meet with someone who wants my help in planning their financial affairs, I always want to take a look at a few things to give me a snapshot of their lives, their lifestyles, and their lifetime objectives. By reviewing this information,

I can better assist them with putting together a personalized plan that will ensure long-term wealth.

What I learn about people by looking at this information is quite telling. Early on in my career, I was quite shocked at the enormous disparity between the wealth levels of those clients who I would have guessed were "rich" and those who I would have guessed were more "modestly positioned." More often than not, the ones who were the most financially independent were those who didn't seem the part.

One thing that I've got to point out, however, is that these people who were more financially independent did not necessarily have a higher net worth than some of the others. The difference was in what I refer to as their "wealth sustainability levels." This is a much different measuring device and my guess is that this is a term that you've never heard until now. By "wealth sustainability level," I am referring to the ability to sustain the level of wealth that a client enjoys over an extended length of time.

Some of the clients that I've worked with have had a very high net worth but disproportionately low wealth sustainability levels. While they seemed to be living the good life at the time, they were operating in a way that they simply could not afford to maintain over the long haul if they ever hoped to retire. It's important to realize that *there is no amount of money that you can't outspend.* For this reason, it becomes imperative that we gear our standards of living to ensure the highest wealth sustainability level possible.

The clients who I view as "truly wealthy" are those who have had these exceptionally high wealth sustainability levels. They are the happiest because they don't have to worry about going backwards financially. They've structured a plan for themselves that will virtually guarantee a comfortable standard of living for the rest of their lives. This doesn't mean that they live a life of destitution. On the contrary, it means that they are able to live a life of financial freedom. Their lives are not governed by money needs so they are able to do whatever it is that they most want to do. The only way to do this is to follow a well-thought out plan for long-term wealth accumulation.

STRATEGY 161: *Adopt an attitude of wealth inevitability.*

In formulating my overall concept of the E.S.C.A.P.E. Plan from the "Artificial Wealth Trap," I've come to realize the incredible importance of mindset. Not only did I come to realize that a positive attitude was important, that was covered in the initial ENVISION portion. What I've found is that the proper mindset is actually a key ingredient for success in each of the other components as well.

In my meetings with clients over the years, I've often found myself asking the most successful ones if they would be willing to share some of their secrets with me. I remember meeting with one client in particular who shared something with me that really hit home. He told me that early on in his business life, he came to the realization that he would someday be rich. It's important to note that he said *realization* and not just *belief.* There is a big difference between the two. When I asked him how he came to that realization, he told me something very important that I now strive to follow personally and share with my clients as much as possible.

He said that most people would equate the discovery of what he referred to as "inevitable wealth" with some sort of monetary event that put a great deal of money into their pockets. He told me that his discovery, however, came one day when he was sitting down running some numbers on financial projections. The thought struck him as he ran a calculation of how much money that he would end up with if he simply stuck to his simple plan of setting aside a certain amount of money each and every year into a long-term accumulation plan. After seeing that chart, he said that he had a conscious feeling of enlightenment as if the weight of the world had suddenly been lifted off of his shoulders. All of a sudden, he felt an easing of pressure that gave him an amazing feeling of happiness.

He told me that right then and there he realized that he could stop feeling so much pressure to work himself to death because he knew that he and his family were going to be just fine. The thought of building wealth was no longer just a possibility, *(it was inevitable if he simply continued following his plan.)* By adopting an "attitude of wealth inevitability," he was able to enjoy himself much more than he had ever allowed himself. He said that he also developed an air of confidence about him that made him feel tremendous. The key to adopting this same attitude for yourself is to establish your plan of strategies and then to follow that plan.

STRATEGY 162: Implement "the most powerful force in the universe" into your wealth accumulation plan.

The most important factor in adopting the attitude of wealth inevitability is to utilize what Albert Einstein purportedly referred to as "the most powerful force in the universe," compound interest. Once you understand the phenomenal power of this mathematical miracle, you will see that building wealth for yourself can indeed by inevitable. In fact, it's almost impossible not to become wealthy if you can abide by the strategies that take advantage of the miracle of compounding interest. The key is that you've got to put this fundamental financial strategy to work for you. The sooner you do so, the better off you'll be in your quest for inevitable wealth.

It's highly probable that you've at least heard about the concept of compounding interest. We've all been exposed to it at some point. The best part about the concept is that it is so amazing and yet so simple. Despite this simplicity, far too few people ever take the time to utilize this simple wealth building power tool. While it may be simple to understand, it is apparently difficult to implement judging by the lack of those following the strategy. However, if you will take the time to put this tool to work for you, you can virtually guarantee yourself that you will escape the "Artificial Wealth Trap" and set yourself on the road to wealth.

In working with clients, I've found that the concept of compound interest is easiest to explain by using an example. Suppose you have $100 which you would like to invest. Let's say that you decide to put that money into an account which offers 10% annual interest. This means that the bank will pay you the value of 10% of your money for the right to use it. After one year, your $100 will have grown to $110. This may seem modest, but consider what happens the next year. At the end of the second year your account will have grown to $121.00

($110 plus 10% of that, which is $11.00). Now, what is important in this example is not that you've only earned $21 after two years. What I want you to see is that the amount of growth *compounds* every year. In other words, the amount of money made increases every year. The reason for this is that *your money makes money that then makes even more money.*

Let's look at another example to show you how setting this plan in motion can make the accumulation of wealth virtually inevitable. This time, let's look at a hypothetical 401(k) retirement plan. We'll talk quite a bit about this and other types of retirement plans in one of the chapters in this Part of the book. Suppose a 35 year old man sets out his retirement strategy and decides that he wants to retire by age 65. He starts out by investing $333.33 per month into his 401(k) plan. This is a total of $4,000 per year. Let's also suppose that he invested the money in the stock market and averaged a 10% annual rate of return. In the 30 years between ages 35 and 65, our young investor would have contributed a total of $120,000. Yet thanks to the miracle of compounding interest, at age 65 he will have amassed $759,016! This is the type of growth that begins to get people excited.

However, let's take a look at what could have happened if he had started earlier than at age 35. To see the difference, let's take a look at the man's younger brother who started investing with the same type of plan, except that he started investing at age 25 and contributed $250 per month for a total of $3,000 per year. In the 40 years between ages 25 and 65, our young investor would have contributed the same total as the older brother of $120,000. However, when the younger brother reaches age 65, his 401(k) will total $1,594,197!

This vast difference baffles many people. Why is it that just ten years difference equates to more than double the amount generated with the older brother? Once again, the answer lies with the power of compounding interest. You see, the earlier you begin, the greater your ability to maximize the benefit of compounding growth. Hopefully, from the above illustration you understand my main point which is the earlier you start saving, the greater the force of compound interest will have on your inevitable wealth.

Let's take our same numbers, but this time our new investor is the brothers' uncle who begins when he is 45 years old. Since he too wants to retire at age 65, his retirement saving window is cut to 20 years. To make up for this, he is going to invest $500 per month so that he will still be contributing the same overall total investment of $120,000 into his retirement account as the two brothers. While he contributes the same overall amount, the end result is quite different. When the 45 year old reaches age 65, he will only have accumulated $382,848. Now, don't get me wrong, this is still a great deal of money but far less than in our other examples because of the later start. The reason for this is that he didn't maximize the power of compounding interest.

The bottom line when it comes to harnessing the power of compounding interest is that it's just simple math that affords you the possibility of accumulating virtually inevitable wealth. What is hard about compounding interest is that you have to start using it now. In other words, you should start investing as soon as you can with as much money as you can. The way that I often explain this concept is to tell people to increase their wealth workforce, which leads us to our next accumulation strategy.

STRATEGY 163: *Increase your wealth plan workforce.*

One of the first steps in implementing any plan is to identify the strategies necessary to make the plan happen. In a wealth accumulation plan, the key strategy is to have income-producing assets. As we learned in the CREATE Part of the book, income is to wealth what gas is to an automobile; without it, you cease to be able to operate. We must have income in order to have anything to accumulate.

The difficulty that most people have is that they've never done anything to increase what I refer to as their wealth plan workforce. Increasing your workforce means to put more things to work building wealth than just yourself. As an employee of a company, you are earning a salary, but you are also making money for your employer. You are part of that employer's workforce. Ideally, the greater the number of active participants in an employer's workforce, the greater the potential output. From a business standpoint, if you aren't doing something that makes money for your employer, you probably won't have that job for very long because you'll be replaced by someone who is more productive.

You need to consider your plan for accumulating wealth in the same manner. As part of your plan, you need a greater number of "workers" whose job it is to produce income or value for you and your portfolio. When considering which assets to keep or which new ones to add to your asset list, you need to bear in mind which assets will continue to produce income for you both now and over time. Those assets can become a "workforce" that will act as employees for you, the employer, to continue to build your wealth. This is the secret that the most financially successful people know and apply.

Part of your job will become managing your workforce. As with a business, if an asset costs you money, or doesn't bring in income for you, you need to really think about that asset and whether you want it included in your overall wealth plan. Like an unproductive employee, you may need to replace any unproductive assets with those that may be more profitable for you. To make the determination, ask yourself if the asset really fits into your goals and if it will help you achieve them. The asset may be important enough to you to keep it even if it isn't producing income, but you definitely want to weigh the pros and cons of the assets in your wealth plan workforce when deciding on which assets to keep and which ones to re-employ elsewhere.

STRATEGY 164: Develop a basic understanding of stocks, bonds, mutual funds and money markets.

When it comes to investing your money, you really need to have at least a basic understanding of the markets in which you are investing. Major mistakes have been made and fortunes lost when investors just put their money into an investment without really knowing how that investment vehicle actually worked. Once people get burned in a particular type of investment arena they often make the mistake of abandoning that area altogether when all they really needed to do was to improve their knowledge level in that area. To generate the type of long-term growth that you will need if you are to achieve financial independence, you need to be invested, at least partially, in the financial markets.

Serious money can be made in stocks, bonds, mutual funds and money market accounts. In the same vein, major money can be lost in them as well. When you don't understand what it is that you are getting yourself into, you are especially vulnerable to the risks inherent in any type of investment. Even beyond facing a loss in an investment, you may be faced with unexpected situations such as having your money tied up for a prolonged period of time in certain types of investments. If you need that money for living expenses, or you come across a better deal in another type of investment, you may find that your cash is unavailable to you, or unavailable without substantial penalties, until the time period is up. Knowing the rules of the game before you begin playing can keep you from experiencing a devastating loss.

It's important to understand that I am not saying that you need to become an expert in trading the stock market, or in commodities or bonds, or any other type of investment. This may be something that you decide to do, but becoming an expert isn't essential. While you don't have to become the world's leading authority on your investment areas, you really must have at least a basic understanding of the risks and characteristics of each type that you decide to utilize for your wealth accumulation plan.

STRATEGY 165: Develop a base level understanding of real estate investment concepts.

Real estate can be one of the hottest investment tools around for those people who know how to benefit from it. It's been said that there have been more millionaires made through real estate than from any other type of investment activity. I like real estate a lot as a tool for accumulating wealth so long as you're involved in the right type of real estate. It seems like there are almost as many ways to invest your wealth in real estate as there are people investing in it. To effectively utilize this arena for building your wealth, you've got to learn how to make sense of the ins and outs of it.

All too frequently, I see people who have made major mistakes by venturing into real estate investments before they truly understood the deal that they were getting themselves into. Like any other investment vehicle, you need to have, at minimum, a basic understanding of the type of real estate deal you are getting involved with. Coming into a real estate investment blindly is just asking for unforeseen problems to arise. Real estate can be a highly profitable venture, with many, many strong benefits for those willing to put their money into the deal. It can also be confusing, and for the uneducated, it can be very risky and costly when entered into incorrectly, or with unreasonable expectations.

When investing in real estate, you need to educate yourself on a number of issues.

- What are your risks?

- What return can you expect to receive?

- When can you expect to start receiving that return?

- How much of your time, both initially and on an ongoing basis, will you need to put into this investment?

- If this investment no longer suits you, can you get out of it and how?

Be sure to answer these, along with a number of other questions that we will point out specifically in the chapter on real estate wealth building, before you take the steps to make that investment is critical to your investing success. Do what it takes to understand just what it is that you are getting into, how to go about getting out if necessary, and the process of how the money flows. This will help to keep you from falling into the real estate area of the "Artificial Wealth Trap."

STRATEGY 166: Understand risk and its role in the investments you consider.

One of the most universally recognized investment lessons is that along with risk comes the potential for reward. While this may be a valuable lesson, it has also caused a large number of people to lose a great deal of money. The biggest reason for this is that many people view the risk vs. reward balance as an absolute measuring device. Some people take enormous risks banking on the fact that the reward will be just as enormous if the risk pays off. More often than not, these people fail to properly gauge the amount of risk in comparison to the potential reward and end up losing the bulk of their investment. Risk is a fact of life. It is certainly present in any deal that you will ever encounter.

A crucial part of any investment or investment strategy is to understand exactly what is at risk in the investment, how much is at risk, what those risks are, and ways to minimize, or perhaps even eliminate certain risks.

Minimizing risk is a way to ensure a greater likelihood of success. Perhaps the reward may not be as great if you strive to continually look for as much of a way to build wealth without risk as possible but in the long run, you'll be much better off.

Always take the time before entering into any investment to assess the risks involved and whether they are worth it. You should always ask yourself the necessary questions in making this assessment. These can include:

- What is at risk?

- How much cash or other capital is at risk?

- Are you just risking your money or are you risking your time as well?

- If you're risking your time, how much?

- Could that time be better spent elsewhere?

- Is it worth the rate of return?

If the asset is too precious to you for you to put it at risk, don't get involved in the deal.

STRATEGY 167: Keep the minimum required balance in your checking account and the rest of your cash in a money market or other interest-bearing account.

An essential key to rapidly accumulating wealth is to *make certain that your money is working for you instead of you working for your money*. To make sure that this is happening, you've got to take steps to put your money to work. Even small steps can add up to big rewards in the future and shouldn't be overlooked in your overall plan. You need to step back and look around you for whatever changes that you can make to help you to accumulate more and more wealth all the time.

Everywhere I go, I tell people that they need to begin thinking as much like a business as possible. A great way to do this is to keep your money from going on vacation. What do I mean by this? If we continue to look at our money as a member of our workforce, we will want to keep it working on a full-time basis. One way to do this is to check with your banking institution to determine if they have a checking or savings account that can earn interest on the money that you have invested with them. When you do this, be sure to ask for an account without a bank surcharge.

Make certain that you also ask about any minimum balance requirements that might be associated with these types of accounts. If they charge too much of a fee for this, the interest earned may not be worth the service charge to keep your extra cash in this type of account. It may turn out that your money could be better invested elsewhere if you don't need it right away, but you'll never know until you look into it. As the saying goes, looking into this type of a benefit doesn't cost, it pays.

STRATEGY 168: *Contribute to your retirement plan now rather than later.*

The whole point of our wealth accumulation plan is to get us to a point where we can do what we *want* to do with our lives rather than what we *have* to do. If you're like most people, the job that you have today is not the one that you most want but the one that you've got to have. Accumulating wealth frees you up from this modern day involuntary servitude and enables you to spend your time as you would like rather than making a career out of doing work that you'd prefer not to do. The only thing that makes the process tolerable is the potential reward at the end of our careers, the dream of living a worry-free retirement.

To make this dream a reality, we've got to save enough money to make it happen. According to statistics, however, Americans aren't saving anywhere near enough money for retirement. Retirement is something that most people like to dream about doing sooner rather than later. Our actions, however, tell me that we really don't want to retire at all. What I mean by that is that the vast majority of people certainly aren't doing anything that would help them to retire early. Rather than utilizing what is perhaps the greatest wealth-building tool available, most people are just thinking and dreaming about it. That alone won't work.

The sad thing is that a retirement plan is one of the most powerful ways available for the accumulation of wealth, but according to all of the statistics, many people just aren't taking advantage of it. A retirement plan is so powerful because it can take advantage of two of the most amazing concepts in investing: the power of compound interest that we looked at earlier, and tax-deferred growth. In a tax-deferred or tax-free retirement plan, your money grows at an almost exponential rate since taxes aren't being taken out of the earned interest. This has astonishing potential.

The reason that more people don't take advantage of this is because it does not provide immediate results. Most people see retirement as something far off in the future. Unlike creditors calling about current bills, or deals that can be put together to make money within a relatively short period, many see the process of saving for retirement as something that can easily be put off until tomorrow. Unfortunately, they don't see that "tomorrow" will be here much sooner than expected.

One of my favorite advertisements is for a money management firm that shows a car window with the reflection of a billboard bearing the word, "Retirement." On the bottom of the mirror is the statement, "Warning: Objects in mirror are much closer than they appear." This is the message that people seem to be ignoring when it comes to their retirement.

A lot of people learn an unfortunate lesson when they find that they have fallen into the "Artificial Wealth Trap" by using what could be their retirement money today to fund their enjoyment of the affluent lifestyle. Down the road, they may realize that by not investing in a properly structured retirement plan they missed out on one of the most powerful wealth accumulation tools available. Don't let this happen to you. Do it now, not later.

STRATEGY 169: Learn and apply the secret of cash disgorgement.

Once again, thinking like a business is a huge part of gaining control over your finances and implementing a wealth accumulation plan. By applying the strategies and principles that businesses utilize to your personal financial situation, you can accumulate wealth more assuredly and much more rapidly. One of the strategies that businesses employ on a regular basis is the secret of "cash disgorgement." I first encountered this strategy several years ago while reviewing one of the Corporate Finance textbooks from one of the courses that my wife took in earning her M.B.A. in Finance. While the book explained it as an important concept for business, I found it equally, if not more, intriguing as a strategy for personal finance.

Cash disgorgement is simply the principle that large accumulations of cash in a business should be spent, or reinvested, to insure their greatest level of effectiveness. If your money is just sitting there, in the best case scenario, it isn't working for you as efficiently as it could be. Worst case scenario, you are neglecting the opportunity to reduce bad debt, missing out on investment opportunities, or spending the cash frivolously on things that aren't necessities. This is the whole concept that most people have heard about as cash burning a hole in their pocket. To keep this from happening, you should disgorge yourself of the cash. Let me explain what I mean.

Successful businesses often use cash disgorgement to counter these negative scenarios. These savvy business owners realize that their money needs to be put to work for them in one way or another. By moving the cash into a more lucrative investment vehicle by redirecting it or to minimize debt, they can use their surplus money in a positive manner to more rapidly accumulate wealth. Cash just sitting there in a non-interest bearing account, or even a low-interest account, is not building wealth. In fact, it could be counter-productive to your long-term wealth accumulation goals. To build wealth more quickly, apply the secret of cash disgorgement by immediately allocating any unused cash into a long-term wealth-building plan.

STRATEGY 170: Use the 10% Solution to go from paycheck to prosperity rather than paycheck to paycheck.

I can't tell you how many times I hear clients tell me that they have "too much month at the end of the money." Even worse, it seems like this is happening to more and more people all the time as they find themselves drawn down into the "Artificial Wealth Trap." Every day when you turn on the news or pick up a newspaper, you hear that a majority of Americans, now more than at any other time in our economic history, are living from paycheck to paycheck and that we are spending, on average, more than we earn. The more that people listen to this rhetoric, the more helpless and hopeless they feel caught in this trap. In some ways, it's become somewhat of a self-fulfilling prophecy.

Feeling helpless and hopeless can lead to apathy and despair. People often just decide that there is nothing that they can do to better their situation, so why even bother to try? When the financial landscape looks bleak, many feel like a plan is a waste of time. What the financial experts and reporters aren't telling us, however, is that there are simple steps that most anyone can take to lessen their financial burden and move from paycheck to prosperity.

The first step in this plan is to take 10% of your income right off the top and pay yourself first. By paying yourself first, I mean that you need to invest this 10% in your future by depositing it directly into a wealth accumulation plan. Whatever you do, don't just pocket the money and buy a big screen TV or some other wasteful item with this money. If you want to buy the TV, buy it with money that you generate outside of the 10% wealth accumulation money.

This is a way to put the cash disgorgement plan that we talked about in the previous strategy to work. By taking the first 10% of your money right off the top and committing it to your investment plan, you will be forced to make ends meet with the remaining 90%. While this may seem impossible if you're currently living paycheck to paycheck, it can be done if you put your mind to it and realize that this 10% is the cornerstone upon which to build your prosperity. This strategy will be covered in much greater detail in the next chapter. For now, simply remember that *if you'll do what most people won't do, you'll be able to do what most people can't do.*

STRATEGY 171: Put your wealth accumulation plan on auto-pilot.

Many people, after initially hearing about the 10% solution, find that it is simply too tempting to spend the 10% rather than allocating it directly into their investment plan. To overcome this temptation, the biggest favor that you could ever do for yourself is to put your wealth accumulation plan on auto-pilot. Some of you may have enough discipline when it comes to saving money to just do it on your own. Statistics, however, show that the vast majority of people don't.

They begin their savings program with the best of intentions. After starting off well, an unexpected expense comes up, or an item that they just can't resist goes on sale, and all of a sudden they find themselves sucked right back into the "Artificial Wealth Trap." Another temptation for people attempting to implement the 10% solution is that they think they will use the money this week and promise themselves that they will pay it back out of next week's check. Whatever the reason, the result is that their plan for wealth accumulation just never happens.

To overcome this challenge, put your plan on auto-pilot. Once your plan has been put into place, you simply turn on the auto-pilot and it handles things for you. The temptation to spend your savings money is eliminated because you never see it. Since you don't expect to receive it, it shouldn't figure in with your expected income. Believe me when I tell you that this automatic wealth accumulation plan has created its fair share of millionaires and it can do the same thing for you.

The saying "out of sight, out of mind" definitely applies to this concept, and it's a powerful method to help you accumulate real wealth for an amazing retirement plan. The auto-pilot function takes the work out of your hands and frees you to tackle your daily concerns. When you're ready to access your accumulated wealth, your auto-pilot system will have helped greatly in achieving the smooth landing that all of us would like to have. Do what it takes to set it and forget it.

Over the course of the next several chapters, you will learn the specific strategies associated with a variety of ways for accumulating long-term and long-lasting wealth for yourself and for your family. By following these strategies, you will see an amazing difference in your life and in your attitude. Once you begin to see some growth, things begin to really get exciting.

Accumulating wealth is like growing a tree. It all begins with the smallest sapling. If you will set the plan in motion, you will soon find yourself covered by the shade of an enormous tree that provides you with shelter, security, and beauty. If you keep cutting down your small saplings to give yourself instant gratification, you'll never see them grow into colossal trees. Follow the strategies in the following chapters and you can have the type of trees, and the type of life, that you want and deserve for yourself.

CHAPTER 13

REAL ESTATE WEALTH BUILDING

Few enterprises of great labor or hazard would be undertaken
if we had not the power of magnifying the advantages
we expect from them.

Samuel Johnson

In the chapter on real estate in the CREATE Part of the book, we mentioned that there have been more millionaires made through real estate than through any other investment arena. In that chapter, we took a look at some basic real estate principles for identifying the type of properties that can make us money through the application of real estate income strategies. In this chapter, we're going to focus our attention on ways to accumulate wealth through the development and application of a long-term real estate investment plan. Remember, however, that our focus in this book is not to provide an all-inclusive look at real estate. To do so would require much more room than we have available. We provide in-depth materials on the topic through our home study courses (CDs, DVDs, workbooks, etc.) and live trainings. For now, we're going to introduce you to the long-term investment view of real estate since it is something that must be explored as part of any successful wealth accumulation plan.

Over the years, real estate has proven to be one of the best possible vehicles for building long-term wealth primarily for two reasons. First, everyone is familiar with real estate because we have to use it personally for housing and most people work in an office building or some other type of real estate property. This affords everyone the opportunity to see firsthand how real estate works whether they ever truly take notice of it or not. Second, real estate investment offers everyone the opportunity to get involved with it due to the concept of leverage. Were it not for leverage, very few, if any, people would ever be able to afford to purchase real estate, especially larger properties. While we looked at this first point in plenty of detail in the previous chapter on real estate, this chapter will be focused primarily on the second point (leverage).

STRATEGY 172: *Adopt a real estate wealth-building accumulation mindset.*

As you should undoubtedly know by now, I believe that the first step involved in any endeavor is to develop the proper mindset. When it comes to real estate wealth-building, the mindset that we need to adopt is far different than the mindset that we've been trained to exhibit in being drawn into the "Artificial Wealth Trap." Far too many people display the attitude of requiring instant gratification in nearly every aspect of their lives and real estate is no different.

If you hope to build lasting wealth in real estate, you've got to change your mindset and accept the delayed gratification that comes from establishing a plan, putting it into action, and then waiting for it to pay off until sometime further down the road. This method has created a number of fortunes and can do so for you if you will follow the strategies.

When I was growing up, my Dad always taught me that the key concept was to not wait to buy real estate but to buy real estate and wait. It took me a while to understand what he meant but once I learned the power of this principle, it has helped me to adopt the mindset of wealth inevitability that I mentioned in the introductory chapter to this Part.

You see, what he was explaining to me was that real estate almost always goes up in value over the years if you simply have the patience to wait for that to happen. He explained to me that the reason that more people never utilize the long-term wealth-building strategy for real estate is that most people are too impatient to ever see things through to fruition. He used the example of how few people ever maximize the use of retirement plans even though they have the potential to ensure financial freedom and said that real estate is the same way. What really impacted me, however, was that he promised me that if I would follow the strategy, the strategy would follow through for me and allow me to generate the type of wealth needed to become a millionaire. The best part of this is that his promise has been fulfilled, not only in my life, but in the lives of the numerous students who I've shared this strategy with as well. The key to seeing this come true in your life is to first begin with the proper mindset.

STRATEGY 173: Utilize real estate as the IDEAL accumulation investment.

One of the earliest lessons I learned with regard to real estate is that it is what is known as the "IDEAL" investment. The reason that it's referred to in this way is that it meets the criteria laid out in the acronym for the word "IDEAL." The acronym looks like this:

I ncome

D epreciation/Deductions

E quity buildup

A ppreciation

L everage

To give you a better understanding of each of these concepts, let's take a look at each one individually.

Income

The first thing that you should look at when considering a piece of real estate to purchase is the income that it either produces currently or has the potential of producing. In looking at any investment, the generation of income is obviously a desirable component. The great thing about real estate is that, unlike many other investments, it can actually generate income while at the same time going up in value through appreciation, which we'll address in just a moment. The key to finding the right type of properties is to find the type that will generate sufficient income to service the debt required to purchase the property along with being able to pay for the other expenses involved as well.

Depreciation/Deductions

The second thing to look at when evaluating real estate is the availability of depreciation and other forms of tax deductions. Real estate has long been considered one of the best tax shelters available due to the fact that you can take a tax write-off for the so-called, "wear and tear" on the building part of the property. This can provide a great way to shelter part of your income so that you can reduce the amount of what otherwise would be due in taxes.

In addition to depreciation deductions, there are numerous other deductions available through the ownership of real estate. These would include nearly all expenses that are "ordinary and necessary" in the maintenance and operation of your real estate business. This enables you to deduct against income the expenses of your real estate. In most instances, this can negate almost all of the income generated so that you are able to build up wealth without having to pay the overwhelming bulk of the income to the government through taxes.

Equity Buildup

The third thing to focus on with your long-term real estate wealth accumulation plan is the building up of equity. In economic terminology, equity is defined as "the difference between the market value of a property and the claims held against it." These "claims" are the mortgage on the property and any other liens thereon. For the purpose of our discussion on wealth building, equity equals wealth. The greater the equity a property holds, the greater our wealth becomes.

One of the things that I teach my clients and students regarding real estate is that the beauty of it is that it offers us the ability to accumulate wealth in not just one, but two great ways. First of all, as mentioned previously, the value of real estate almost always increases in value over the long haul. This helps us to increase the spread between the value of the property and the amount of debt. Second, as the debt is decreased in the property, the spread increases. This is something that most people have experienced through home ownership. With rental real estate, you have the opportunity to have someone else pay the debt off for you. This provides the type of opportunity that you need if you hope to continually build up more and more wealth.

Appreciation

The fourth quality of any potential real estate investment which makes it IDEAL is appreciation. As we just stated, appreciation is the increase of a piece of property over time. The amount of time necessary for appreciation to occur is different for every property, in every market. Of course, the higher a property's rate of appreciation, the faster the owner of the property can build equity, and in turn, wealth.

Learning how properties appreciate in value is the key for finding properties which will help you build the most equity over time. The first way that properties appreciate is inflation. Since this occurs as a result of market forces and applies the same way to all properties, inflation deserves little of our attention. The second way that properties can appreciate is because of urban growth. Many people accumulate wealth simply by purchasing a property on the outskirts of an urban area and then watching the city or town grow toward their property. As the edge of an urban area gets closer to a property, the higher the property can appreciate.

Another way that appreciation can occur is through redevelopment. Over the last ten to fifteen years, many city planners across the country have begun implementing projects to "reclaim" dilapidated urban areas. As a result, people who have held on to run down properties in high-crime areas have seen the value of their properties appreciate dramatically as cities start to build entertainment districts, sports complexes, shopping malls, and business centers in areas which were once considered urban wastelands.

A fourth way that properties can appreciate is through zoning changes. In many instances, shrewd investors will purchase properties with little or no value and then cause the property to appreciate overnight by successfully petitioning for a change in how the property is zoned.

Leverage

The final quality of any IDEAL property is leverage. As we have already learned, leverage is when we use only a fraction of our money to purchase property but get to enjoy 100% of the benefits of ownership. Examples of these benefits are keeping 100% of a property's rental income, appreciation, and tax deductions. The benefit that the bank who loaned you the money to purchase the property receives is the interest on that money. You'll recall that leverage is a quality which is somewhat unique to real estate. So in finding our IDEAL property, we must make sure that we maximize the power of leverage.

Of course, not all types of property qualify for a mortgage. Many banks have requirements for which types of properties they may finance, and a property which does not meet these requirements would not be IDEAL. Another instance where it may be hard to use leverage is when the property buyer is unable to obtain a mortgage because of poor credit. If you find yourself in this category, you might want to re-read the chapter in this book on repairing credit. In the meantime, you do not have to sit out of the real estate market if you can come up with some creative ways to finance property. For more information on strategies for buying property using other people's money, visit www.realwealthwithoutrisk.com/opm.

STRATEGY 174: Only invest in properties that fit the IDEAL formula.

Now that we know what we mean by "IDEAL" properties, we should make it a point to only purchase properties which follow this formula. In fact, learning how to put the IDEAL formula into practice is what separates people for whom real estate is an expensive hobby and those who successfully use real estate as a tool for building lasting wealth over time.

Now it's time to really focus on becoming skilled at using the IDEAL formula. You will recall from our other chapter on real estate that we said to never invest in raw land. Let's think about raw land and long-term wealth in light of our IDEAL formula. First, we know that the raw land will not be producing any income. Secondly, we know that our tax benefits such as deductions and depreciations will be very little as well. There may be some equity buildup in the raw land, but since the property generates no income, any equity that results from making mortgage payments will be coming entirely out of our own pocket. You may be able to purchase the property with no money down and use the bank's money, but this isn't much of a benefit considering the raw land's less than optimal income, tax benefits, and equity building qualities.

From what we've said so far about raw land, it sure doesn't seem IDEAL, does it? But let's think about the part of the formula we skipped over, appreciation. Is the property in the path of urban sprawl? Have you heard rumors that a shopping mall is going to be built nearby? If so, then this piece of raw land may be a pretty good investment after all.

My point for this strategy is this: our IDEAL formula isn't an "all or nothing" tool for selecting properties. One quality, such as appreciation, may outweigh all of the other factors. However, for new investors who are not as experienced in the real estate market, my advice would be to stick with properties that follow most, if not all, of the components in our IDEAL formula.

STRATEGY 175: Determine your long-term real estate wealth accumulation goals.

As important as choosing which properties to purchase, you also need to determine what your goals are for accumulating long-term wealth with real estate. You might say simply that your goal is to make as much money as possible. Unfortunately, that is not exactly a goal.

In determining your long-term real estate wealth accumulation goals, you need to decide exactly how much money you will need in order to live comfortably. Determining your long-term real estate accumulation goals also means deciding for yourself the types of properties and activities with which you are most comfortable. When I say "comfortable," what I mean is to decide your acceptable level of certain factors such as risk, types of properties, mortgage amounts, etc. Let me give you an example.

Early on in my real estate career, I decided that I would focus my investing on commercial properties rather than residential. You may think that I based this decision strictly on monetary factors, and I'll admit that was part of my decision-making process. The real reason why I was not interested in owning a lot of residential properties is because I know that I would have an extremely difficult time evicting a family out of one of my properties if they were delinquent in their rent. I don't feel that way when dealing with commercial tenants. For me, residential real estate is simply too emotional to get involved with personally. That being said, I do own several residential properties but they're all managed by a separate property management company so that I don't have to handle them personally.

STRATEGY 176: Formulate your plan for accomplishing your real estate accumulation goals.

As important as it is to set your long-term real estate goals, you also need to formulate your plan for getting there. You've already read many times in this book where I've said to "plan your work and then work your plan." Well, it should be no surprise that this applies to accumulating wealth through real estate as well.

Through the strategies in this book, I've already given you the plans for accumulating wealth with real estate. Deciding which strategies work best for you, like deciding what your goals are, is something that only you can decide.

In formulating your plan, there is one concept that I want you to have in mind. Your plan is going to have two phases: pre- and post- accumulation. I like to call the first phase the "pre-millionaire phase." This is the phase when you plan to become, for example, a millionaire through real estate. The steps in this phase are actually quite simple. First, you should purchase one million dollars' worth of property. This can be one single property, but I would recommend diversifying among many properties initially. Second, you need to borrow the money to make these purchases. Here we are putting the power of leverage to work. Finally, you need to pay back this money, (by paying off the mortgages). You do this by earning income from the properties that you can then use to repay the mortgages. Of course, until each property is paid for, you want to produce a short-term income. However, even if you break even or are a little short some months, you are still building equity. If you can follow this plan, you are virtually guaranteed to become a millionaire which is why I refer to this as "pre-millionaire" status.

In the "post-millionaire" phase, as you could probably imagine, your job is much simpler. At this point, you need to decide what to do with your real estate. Are you earning sufficient income? If this is the case, then you might want to hold on to the properties. If your wealth is strictly tied up in the properties, however, then you will need to decide which properties to sell and how best to hold your income. Of course, we've included numerous strategies for how to hold assets and/or safely invest your cash in this book. These next strategies will provide you with a way to sell your properties without having to pay taxes.

STRATEGY 177: Utilize §1031 tax-deferred exchanges to avoid costly tax implications when selling properties.

A §1031 exchange is a method by which a property owner trades one or more relinquished properties for one or more replacement properties of "like-kind" while deferring the payment of income taxes on the transaction. In everyday language, when a §1031 exchange occurs it means that the seller of some sort of "investment" property reinvests the sale proceeds into another property and therefore no "ascension of wealth" is realized in a way that generates taxable income. In other words, the potential taxpayer's investment is still the same, only the form has changed (e.g. vacant land exchanged for an apartment building). Therefore, it would be unfair to force the taxpayer to pay taxes on such a change in their investment.

One of the things I like most about §1031 exchanges is that they allow you to invest in real estate and allow the asset to produce both income and appreciation. While the income will be taxable, there is no tax assessed on the appreciation. Therefore, as the value of your property grows, your buying power for your next piece of property grows as well, and best of all, it is tax-free. You are increasing your buying power by electing to avoid the drain of capital gains taxes.

Be advised that there are a number of requirements involved in taking advantage of §1031 exchanges. This is not an area to attempt a "do it yourself" approach. You should always seek professional assistance with this strategy. If you are interested in learning more, send us an email to info@artificialwealthtrap.com.

STRATEGY 178: *Use a self-directed retirement plan to turbo-charge your wealth-building efforts.*

We spend a great deal of time in this book talking about retirement plans, taxes, and, of course, real estate. One of the greatest benefits of retirement plans, next to their use of compounding interest, is the fact that our money can grow free of capital gains taxes. As a real estate investor, you're going to be paying a lot of attention to capital gains taxes, especially once you are in the "post-millionaire" phase of your long-term real estate wealth accumulation plan. Many people ask me if there is a way to get the tax-free growth of a Roth IRA and combine it with the amazing wealth-building abilities of real estate. I'm often asked this question in almost a joking manner, but people quickly turn serious when my answer is "Actually, yes."

So, how do we achieve the best of these two worlds? Through a self-directed retirement plan. With a normal IRA, for instance, the brokerage firm, which is typically the custodian of the IRA, often has a great deal of influence on the assets held in the account. Usually, these assets are the ones which make the most money for them. With a self-directed IRA, you control the assets. Believe it or not, these assets can include real estate.

Now, you can't just go out and create your own IRA. You'll still need the help of professionals, such as an attorney or financial planner, to get things off the ground. Once the IRA is established, you, and only you, will control the investments which are made with the money you place into the IRA. If you invest this money into real estate, by holding the real estate in a Roth IRA it can appreciate in value free of capital gains taxes just like any other asset. Of course, all of the usual rules concerning IRAs still apply, such as withdrawal penalties, so you'll need to keep these rules in mind when using your IRA to turbo-charge your real estate wealth accumulation plan. Once again, you've got to be extremely careful with these strategies and transactions. For more information, send us an email to info@artificialwealthtrap.com and we'd be happy to assist you with the process.

STRATEGY 179: Always consider cash flow and leverage tolerance levels when executing your real estate wealth accumulation plan.

Earlier in this chapter we discussed your comfort level with the various factors that go into deciding to invest in real estate such as property types, risk, debt, and so forth. With this strategy, we're not talking so much about your comfort level, but rather, your ability to withstand, the normal fluctuations in the real estate market. Just because a property will appreciate over the course of, for example, twenty years, that there will always be short-term swings in the market. When deciding your goals, you need to keep two things in mind, cash flow and leverage, and how to survive them when the market is having a slow spell.

More to the point, when I talk about tolerating cash flow and leverage levels, what I am referring to is your ability to earn sufficient income (cash flow) to make your mortgage payments (the source of your leverage) when times are slow. How many months can you go without earning income from a property while still being able to afford making the mortgage payments? Your answer to this question, and the final consideration you should make when deciding how much you can tolerate, depends on your cash reserves. As a general rule, you should have at least three months' worth of mortgage payments (six months is better) stashed away so that your overall plan can survive the little bumps in the road on your way to wealth. By effectively managing your cash flow and leverage tolerance levels, you'll be better situated to weather the storm when times get tough.

STRATEGY 180: Review your long-term real estate wealth-building plan and adjust accordingly.

The principle of periodic review should be applied to most areas of your life, and this includes your plan for long-term real estate wealth building. Market forces should be a chief concern and you should readjust your real estate investments to take advantage of, and protect yourself from, these types of changes. Your progress in building wealth should also be reviewed. Are you where you need to be? Is it time to cut back, or increase, the level of risk according to your progress?

You should always look at how your real estate plan is doing so that you can make any necessary adjustments. In particular, you should always keep an eye on cash flow, debt ratios, and equity. You can learn a lot by effectively managing these measurements. Even better, you may be motivated when you see your progress.

When it comes to using real estate as a wealth accumulation tool, remember that it is not meant to be a way to "get rich quick." Many of my most successful clients have been quite content in getting rich slowly. Remember, when all is said and done, our goal is to get rich period. You can make that happen with a well-structured and properly followed real estate wealth accumulation plan. As my Dad taught me years ago, *don't wait to buy real estate, buy real estate and wait.*

CHAPTER 14

MANAGING INVESTMENTS
AND BUILDING WEALTH

There are two times in a man's life when he should not speculate:
when he can't afford it and when he can.

Mark Twain

As you've learned, I am an avid supporter of using real estate as the primary tool for building long-term wealth. My experience has been that the opportunity for using leverage and utilizing the power of OPM (other people's money) to create and accumulate wealth for ourselves is greater in that arena than any other. However, one of the most essential rules for mastering money management skills is to diversify one's assets. One of the best ways to do this is by taking advantage of the stock market.

When it comes to investing in the stock market, I was taught as I was growing up to stay out of the market because it was simply too risky. The thought was that this type of investing was best left to those who specialized in this area. You've got to remember, when I was growing up the availability of information and the ability to trade securities was cost prohibitive for most people. It wasn't until fairly recently that small investors had the ability to track stocks, place trades, and manage their own accounts without having to pay exorbitant fees.

Changes in technology and the market place have made things much easier, much more affordable, and much less risky. I've got to explain what I mean when I say "much less risky." Make no mistake, the stock market can be every bit as risky today as it has ever been. The reason that I say that things are much less risky is because of the availability of information and the knowledge necessary for trading successfully. This availability notwithstanding, I always caution investors to steer clear of investing in things with which they are not familiar. You have the potential to make a fortune in the markets if you will take the time to learn the strategies for doing so.

In this chapter, we've included several of the strategies that you need to know and to follow in order to build wealth in multiple areas. The stock market can indeed be risky but as we've mentioned repeatedly throughout this book, the level of risk decreases as your knowledge level increases. By following the strategies, you will position yourself to gain the benefit of investment diversification without putting your assets at undue risk.

STRATEGY 181: Set your investment objectives before you invest.

Before you put your money into investments, you must determine a few details. First and foremost, you must determine what type of investment(s) you'll be acquiring and willing to pay for with your hard-earned cash. Also, you must determine what types of returns you will be seeking on the investment capital. Information beforehand could help you in making wise decisions on how you'll be able to invest your money. By following a well thought out plan, you'll be surprised that through investments, what was once a small investment can multiply into thousands or potentially even millions of dollars. Aside from this, you must also determine your objectives before making an investment. Assess your overall objective in making any investment and develop both short-term and long-term plans for how you will accomplish your goals.

You should determine these details before putting your money into prospective investments. In this way, you'll be able to save money in a more efficient way while expecting your desired returns. This can also help prevent you from getting into the wrong type of investments. Remember that investing has risks. You must prepare yourself in taking these risks and plan some possible fallback options. This way, you'll be better able to avert the situation of being caught in the eye of the storm or being the captain of a sinking ship.

STRATEGY 182: *Always focus on goals that fall into 3 key areas: preservation of capital, income, and growth.*

No matter what type of investment you want to make, your goal for the investment should always fall into one of three categories:

- Preservation of capital

  This pertains to protecting your investment capital (amount to be invested) from the risk of loss. One clear example of this scenario: An individual may have saved $10,000 for a down payment on a house they plan to buy in less than 12 months' time.

- Income

  Income is the process of generating a consistent stream of cash payments. An example of this objective is a retired couple who wants to have a means of continued income after they retire.

- Growth

  Growth is simply increasing the value of your investment capital. This is the objective whenever an individual invests on a long-term basis to meet a specific goal such as retirement, acquiring a dream home or even pursuing college education.

By taking the time to determine your primary objectives for your investment capital, you'll be better situated to obtain the results that you seek on an overall basis. These objectives can keep you on target in determining what types of investments are best suited for your participation.

STRATEGY 183: Use your computer as a tool for smart investing.

Back when our parents were young and investing in the stock market for the first time, their only source of information about the market came in the form of advice from their broker or the final numbers that were reported in the newspaper. Today, however, thanks to personal computers and the internet, the amount of research available to you is virtually endless. There are hundreds of websites out there designed to assist you in becoming a successful investor by giving you a connection to the two things every investor needs: information and a way to buy and sell stocks. There are many online brokerage web sites that handle both of these functions. When you are ready to actually begin your investing, one of your options is to bypass full-service brokers and do it yourself online. These brokerages generally charge a flat commission of between $7 and $25 a trade, as opposed to the percentage-based commission that full-service brokers charge. These websites also provide much of the information that you need to do your research. Additionally, there are several good websites out there that are for informational purposes only, such as The Motley Fool (www.fool.com), and the websites for both NASDAQ (www.nasdaq.com) and the New York Stock Exchange (www.nyse.com). You can use these sites and others to gain valuable knowledge for making more informed decisions.

STRATEGY 184: Develop the investor mindset.

I get asked all the time, "What is the single most important step one can take to be a successful investor?" My answer often surprises people. A lot of people think that the most important thing to being a successful investor is to know how to accurately evaluate stocks or how to time the market. These skills are certainly valuable, but it's my experience that the most important step one can take in becoming a successful investor is to develop what I call the "investor mindset."

The investor mindset is nothing too difficult to accomplish, it simply means having a comfort level with, and emotional detachment from, the process of investing. After you accomplish that, everything else will fall into place, provided you follow a sound fundamental system. By achieving that comfort level, you will almost guarantee yourself of not making the kind of bad decisions that trip up many investors.

The first step in developing the investor mindset is developing a solid understanding of the stock market. I'm not talking about becoming an expert on beta values and support lines. I'm talking about the kind of knowledge that allows you to sit down with a list of stocks, evaluate a handful of them, make a selection and then purchase your shares with the feeling that you know what you're doing. I can guarantee you that, by understanding the process you're following instead of following it blindly, you'll be less likely to stray from it as the stakes get higher or as occasional downturns in your portfolio pop up. That's why it is critical to develop an understanding of what you're doing. The enthusiasm and confidence you acquire by learning how to invest will ensure that you execute your plan effectively.

The second key element of developing the investor mindset is to set your objectives effectively. We've already discussed investment objectives in this chapter but we can't emphasize their importance enough. Clearly defined objectives are the road map you use to complete the investment journey. It is essential in the decision-making process to know exactly how the options before you can help you to accomplish your goals. It's not always enough to simply evaluate different opportunities in terms of which one will make the most money. Some investments may provide a solid short-term return, but might be a terrible decision if you're investing for your retirement in thirty years. Other options may be great for the long haul, but too risky if you know you'll need your money in just a few years. Unless you know what this money is for, you'll have no idea why you're even doing it.

The third element of developing the investor mindset is to invest safely. In other words, don't bet the farm on the stock market. Ideally, you should have your basic financial needs met before you consider putting money into the stock market. And when I say basic, I mean that you should not use your mortgage payment on a stock that you think is the greatest thing since indoor air conditioning. While it's

251

important to recognize opportunities, it seldom makes sense to "bet the farm" on the latest, greatest "sure thing."

Finally, developing the investor mindset means making a commitment to working your plan for investing and to not let emotions get in the way. You can't allow yourself to get "wowed" by some new investment opportunity and abandon your objectives for investing. Emotions are exactly the kind of pitfalls that trip up many beginning investors. These people begin investing either based upon fear, desperation, or greed, none of which is a sound way to plan your future.

STRATEGY 185: *Practice your investing skills on paper before you invest.*

For new investors, another way to achieve a comfort level with investing and thus develop the "investor mindset" which we just discussed is to practice your investing skills with "play money" before you actually begin investing. If you're in the position of having to save up a few hundred dollars before you can invest, the time it takes to save is the perfect time for you to do a practice run.

A great way to get this practice in is to give yourself $10,000 of imaginary money and invest it in stocks, bonds, mutual funds, or other investments. Then you can track your investments and see how they perform over the next year. Chances are you'll end up with seven to ten stocks, most of which will go up over the course of 12 months. You may have one or two that don't do so well, and that's fine, because if you take a look at your total earnings in your portfolio, you'll most likely see a positive number, assuming you've followed all the strategies I've laid out for you in this book.

Another great benefit of practicing before you start to actually invest is that by the time you are ready to invest real money you will already be familiar with the process of researching and tracking your investments. In fact, I wouldn't be surprised if you put some real money into some of those investments you had in your Fantasy Portfolio.

STRATEGY 186: Understand stocks, bonds and money markets.

After you have set your objectives for investing, you must understand these terms: stocks, bonds and money markets. Your knowledge of these terms will allow you to evaluate different investment opportunities and this will also allow you to select the investment option that is right for you.

First, let's talk about stocks. Stocks represent a unit or piece of corporate ownership. If you own a stock, it means you have a share or a piece of a certain corporation. There are two ways to acquire shares of stock: original issue or via the open market. Original issue stock is a type of stock that is issued when a corporation is initially formed. For example, an entrepreneur may want to engage in a new business but may not have enough capital. In order to raise money, he or she can incorporate their business and then sell shares of stock to investors. By contrast, stocks acquired via the open market are purchased and sold on structured exchanges or via private offerings. This is the type of market where most individuals and institutions buy and sell stocks or shares via different exchanges such as the American Stock Exchange and the New York Stock Exchange.

Next, let's discuss bonds. A bond is a certificate which represents the money lent to a certain corporation or government by an investor. The bond will state how much the issuer will owe the investor in return for purchasing the bond and when the investor is scheduled to receive their money. In essence, buying a bond means that you are lending your money for a specific period of time at a generally fixed interest rate. Commonly, investors purchase bonds for income since the majority of bonds pay interest on a periodic basis, whether monthly, quarterly, semi-annual or annual.

For investors interested in bonds, the choices are virtually limitless. Corporate bonds represent money that is being lent to a corporation. Like any other loan, these types of bonds can be either secured or unsecured. Secured bonds are usually backed by different types of assets of the corporation while unsecured bonds are backed only by the corporation's reputation, good credit standing and financial stability.

Then there are government bonds. These types of bonds are issued by municipalities, states, and the federal government. In fact, the federal government is the nation's largest issuer of bonds. Federal bonds include treasury bonds, treasury notes, and treasury bills. Treasury bonds are the type of bonds that have a long-term maturity date of ten to thirty years after they are sold. These bonds pay semi-annual interest as a percentage of their stated value. By contrast, treasury notes are held for a much shorter period of time, generally one to ten years. They can also pay semi-annual interest as a percentage of their stated value and are issued in $1,000 denominations. Treasury bills are debt securities that have maturities of 13, 26 and 52 weeks. These types of bonds do not pay any interest and are usually issued in $1,000 denominations. Instead, they are issued on a discount basis and the investor will receive the full value of the bond at maturity. As an investor, you may purchase this type of bond if you are looking for a safe and short-term (less than a year) investment.

And finally, let's take a look at money market investments. Money Market mutual funds are similar to bank accounts, but instead of the money being used by the bank, it is invested into short-term debt issues (bonds). The type of bonds that money markets generally invest in are T-Bills and other short-term corporate bonds that will mature in less than 90 days. Since you can pull money out of these accounts almost as easily as bank accounts, they are considered cash. One of the highest yielding "cash" investments is Money Markets accounts.

STRATEGY 187: Decide which type of broker you need to make your investments.

Just as there are different styles of investing and types of investors, there are also several different types of brokers. Which one you work with depends mostly on your needs, especially how much advice you want from your broker. If you feel confident in your ability to research and select stocks, you may not want any advice. In this situation, there are many discount online brokerage firms that might be a good fit for you. On the other hand, if you feel more comfortable having an expert on your side, you may want a lot of advice. If that's the case, you'll probably want to work with a full-service broker. Just remember there's no such thing as free advice in the investment business. You will pay for that advice in the form of higher commissions on your transaction.

A lot of people make the mistake of shying away from those brokerages that charge higher fees when they really do need the extra service. This is an example of a lesson that I learned years ago that has helped me tremendously over the years. The lesson is to never trip over pennies on your way to dollars. The money that you spend on good help can yield the greatest returns. The key is to make sure that the help is actually good.

STRATEGY 188: Choose low tax-free yields over larger yields which are taxable.

Municipal bonds are great for investors who want to receive a tax-free yield. These bonds usually will be structured similar to the bonds we discussed, with one major difference, the interest is tax-free. Even if you find the interest paid on municipal bonds to be lower than other bonds, the earnings are not usually taxed. For example, suppose you and your spouse are in the 35% marginal tax bracket and are trying to choose between purchasing a bond producing 7% taxable interest or a tax free municipal bond paying about 5%. Because of your high tax bracket, your yield on the 5% municipal bond will actually be greater than the yield on the 7% bond *after taxes*. This is something that has to be considered when evaluating an investment's true rate of return.

STRATEGY 189: Invest in money market mutual funds if you need the money in less than a year.

A great way to achieve returns from your investments in less than a year is to invest in money market mutual funds. Money market mutual funds are similar to bank accounts, but instead of the money being used by the bank, it is invested into short-term debt issues (bonds). The types of bonds that money markets generally invest in are treasury bills and other short-term corporate bonds that will mature in less than 90 days. Since you can pull money out of these accounts almost as easily as you can with bank accounts, they are considered cash. And remember, as a general rule, money you need in less than one year should not be risked by investing in anything but cash.

STRATEGY 190: *Understand the risks of any opportunity before you invest.*

To effectively manage risk, you have to get a handle on the nature of the risk. For investment purposes, risk is the uncertainty of whether an anticipated return will be achieved when compared to the possibility of loss of the initial investment. Since nothing is truly ever "guaranteed" in the investment world, you need to understand the concept of risk so you can knowledgeably choose an investment with the risk level best suited to you. The biggest risk of all, though, is doing nothing. If you hope to become financially free, that's not a risk that you can take.

The one thing every investor must realize about risk is that there are many sources of risk. All the different risks fall into two categories: systematic risk and unsystematic risk. Systematic risks are the kind of risks that you cannot avoid by diversifying. These types of risk are already associated with investing and are therefore unavoidable. Examples of this type of risk include market risk (fluctuation in a particular market), interest rate risk (fluctuation with interest rates), and reinvestment risk (the risks associated with reinvesting your earnings to take advantage of compound interest). By contrast, unsystematic risk is the kind of risk which you *can* avoid by diversifying. Examples of unsystematic risk include business risk (as an entrepreneur, you can avoid this by investing very little or none of your money in a particularly risky or unproven business) and financial risk (as an investor, you can evaluate the financial statement of a corporation and avoid placing all of your investment dollars in a company with a shaky foundation). As mentioned earlier in the book, the key is not to avoid risk but to focus on taking *calculated* risks. By doing this, we maximize the potential for increased returns and decreased downsides.

STRATEGY 191: Do not invest in collectibles.

A collectible is a non-financial asset which may have value or could appreciate in value. Examples of collectibles are rare coins, baseball cards, postage stamps, Hollywood memorabilia, works of art, or musical instruments owned by famous musicians. Owning these types of assets could be seen as an enjoyable hobby, but should never be viewed as an investment . This is because the value of collectibles is subjective. The markets for these kinds of assets can rise or fall overnight. As a result, the risk involved in such investing is too unpredictable to make it a reliable part of any portfolio.

STRATEGY 192: Do not invest in commodities.

Commodities are termed as basic goods that are interchangeable with other goods of the same type. Commodities are also inputs in the production of other goods and services. Examples of commodities include wheat, soybeans, sugar, coffee and livestock. People have been trading commodities for hundreds of years because they have value, yet because of the laws of supply and demand, the weather, or other factors, the fluctuating prices of commodities make them an ill-advised investment choice.

Since long-term investors cannot purchase a bushel of corn and keep it in a safe until the market rises, there is also a market for commodity futures. Commodity futures are defined as investments that refer to the purchase or selling of a contract to deliver a commodity in the future. It usually indicates a specific commodity in a specific quality to be delivered in a specific month. A buyer then accepts the contract and the seller (the investor in the commodity future) agrees to sell the commodity as agreed in the contract on the designated month at an agreed upon price and quantity.

Because of the sudden influx in the commodity prices in both local and international markets, investing in commodities is considered a risky or speculative investment. You are never guaranteed a stable return from your commodity investment because of these fluctuating prices. It is therefore not recommended to invest in the commodities market because of its risky or speculative nature and there is never a guarantee of a steady return from your commodity investments. While you may have heard stories of people who made fortunes in this market, the fact remains that this is an investment area that is too risky for most people to participate.

STRATEGY 193: Take advantage of a DRIP account when purchasing single stocks.

One of the biggest reasons why many people never start investing in the stock market is because they think that they need to first save several thousand dollars to begin investing. With a DRIP (dividend reinvestment program) you can start investing for as little as $10 or $20 dollars a month. All of the dividends earned are reinvested in additional shares of stock, which explains the name dividend reinvestment plans.

A DRIP is a program run by a publicly-traded company for its shareholders. In other words, a DRIP is a program where an individual is allowed to purchase stock directly from the company rather than through a broker. This eliminates the need to open a brokerage account which means that you'll no longer have to worry about saving a large amount of money before you can start investing. Instead of sending dividend checks to shareholders enrolled in a company's DRIP, the company reinvests those dividends by purchasing additional shares (or fractional shares) in the shareholder's name.

One of the things about DRIP accounts that I really like is that the DRIP program at most companies allows for automatic withdrawals from bank accounts. Another thing that I really like about investing through DRIP programs is that it allows for "dollar cost averaging". Dollar cost averaging occurs when you invest smaller amounts over a long period of time instead of a large sum of money all at one time.

Dollar cost averaging provides you with protection from dramatic swings in the price of the stock you are buying.

Another great method for utilizing this is to hold your DRIP account in an IRA. There are many banks which will allow you to open up IRAs with your DRIP account. Additionally, there are some companies, such as Chrysler, Exxon-Mobil, and Lucent Technologies which have DRIP-sponsored IRAs, including Roth IRAs. By using an IRA to hold your DRIP account, you'll receive some positive tax benefits which you wouldn't have received otherwise.

STRATEGY 194: Invest in mutual funds.

The number of investment choices available to the individual investor is immense. Because the average investor has difficulty managing and/or does not have enough money to start their own diversified investment portfolio, mutual funds were created. A mutual fund is a professional money management company that invests an individual's money for a fee. The fund is a collection of securities, usually stocks, the type and quantity of which is selected by a professional fund manager according to the investment objective(s) of that mutual fund. There are thousands of funds available with numerous investment objectives. Some funds invest only in stocks from a particular industry, from companies that are socially conscious, or from companies which are a certain size, just to name a few of the possibilities. There are even mutual funds that invest only in other mutual funds. Another advantage of mutual funds is that they are liquid, meaning that they can be cashed out whenever the investor desires.

In addition to the variety of choices, mutual funds also allow the individual investor to construct a portfolio that fits their particular needs simply by buying into the fund. Each unit of the fund represents a collection of different stocks, which means that diversification is automatic. Mutual funds also allow individuals to start investing with little money, even as little as $50.00. By using mutual funds, the average investor can obtain diversification, professional money management, liquidity and multiple investment options in a simple one-stop process.

STRATEGY 195: *Invest only in "open end" mutual funds.*

In getting started with mutual funds, a good rule to follow is to stick with *open end* funds. In simple terms, this means that the fund does not have a set number of shares. Instead, the fund will issue new shares to an investor based upon the current net asset value and redeem the shares when the investor decides to sell. Open end funds always reflect the net asset value of the fund's underlying investments because shares are created and destroyed as necessary.

On the other hand, a *closed end* mutual fund issues a limited number of shares that are bought and sold on the secondary market. This means that if an investor in a closed end mutual fund wants to sell, the fund must find a buyer or the investor cannot redeem the shares.

STRATEGY 196: *Invest only in "no load" mutual funds.*

In order for an average investor to build a substantial portfolio of investments, it is recommended to invest only in *no load* mutual funds. A no load mutual fund is one in which shares are sold without a commission or sales charge. The reason for this is that the shares are distributed directly by the investment company, instead of going through a secondary party. By contrast, a loaded mutual fund is the kind of fund that entails commissions to a particular salesperson or corporation who sold the fund to you. This load or fee has nothing to do with how your fund will perform in the market and does not guarantee any advantage over no load mutual funds.

By investing in a no load fund, all of the money invested goes to work for the investor. For example, if you invest $10,000 in a no load fund, all $10,000 has the potential of earning a return. By contrast, if that same $10,000 was invested in a loaded fund which charged a 5% sales commission, only $9,500 of the investor's money would go towards earning a return.

STRATEGY 197: *Avoid investing in individual stocks and bonds if you are a new investor.*

Based upon my experience in working with clients, buying 100 to 1,000 shares of a single company's stock or pumping $1,000 to $25,000 into one or two bond issues is much riskier than investing in stocks and bonds through mutual funds. This trend is even worse for new investors. Besides, buying individual stocks and bonds also means paying commissions. As we've already learned, you will pay no commission by using no load mutual funds. If you insist on investing in an individual stock or bond, only do so with money you can lose. Remember, the reason for this tip is because of the level of risk involved. As we've mentioned, the level of risk decreases as the level of knowledge increases. Once you begin learning more about investing in individual stocks, this then becomes more of an option for you.

STRATEGY 198: *Ride the upswings in the market.*

A great strategy for building wealth in the stock market is to identify trends of particular stocks and then capitalize on their upswings. If you take a look at some blue chips you can likely find one. Once you find such a stock, you should ask yourself how you can take advantage of it.

Suppose you find a stock that fluctuates between $24 and $35 dollars on a consistent basis. I always allow myself a $2 cushion on a stock's highs and lows. You should get in the habit of watching the stock and take notice when it gets to around $26. When the stock hits $26, purchase your desired number of shares. Then, monitor your stock and as soon at hits $33 a share, sell it.

Just because you've sold all of your shares does not mean that you should quit watching the stock. In fact, you should do just the opposite and watch the stock as it goes back down. Then, simply repeat this process. Over time, you'll build a repertoire of stocks with which you can consistently use this technique to build a nice amount of wealth.

STRATEGY 199: Take a chance on a stock's redemption.

Another specific for generating wealth from the stock market that my clients have used is by investing in companies which have suffered a sudden media crisis. The strategy is to find a company that has shown long-term stability but whose price has dropped suddenly due to some sort of negative press. Examples of such press would be reporting quarterly earnings which were far below expectations, an accounting scandal, or a product recall. Once this otherwise winning stock has dropped, some investors will buy the stock at its lowest value in hopes that it will rise back to its normal price once the media storm has passed.

Let's look at an example of this strategy in action. In 1985, the Valdez, an oil tanker for Exxon, ran aground off the Alaskan coast, creating one of the biggest, man-made natural disasters in history. For months, the negative publicity for Exxon was intense as the Federal Government got involved in efforts to make sure Exxon shared in the cost of cleaning up the mess and making sure that the company was punished for the accident. During this period, Exxon's stock price plummeted. Still, despite the media fallout Exxon was still a very strong company from a business standpoint. Not surprisingly, within a year Exxon's stock price had recovered completely to its pre-Valdez level. As a result, investors who recognized the long-term worth of Exxon and purchased stock during the height of the Valdez scandal were handsomely rewarded later on.

This may sound simple, but it can be extremely risky and should only be used after you have put the rest of your investment strategies into place.

STRATEGY 200: Take advantage of "two for one" stock splits.

Very often a company will meet and decide that their stock price has gotten too high, and that the small investor perceives it as too expensive, so they will split each share into two shares and thereby cut the price in half. For example, let's say a company has 10 million shares trading at $150 a share and they want to do a 2-for-1 stock split. They simply file the necessary paperwork with the SEC and then they would have 20 million shares trading at $75 a share. If you already own 100 shares of that stock, you'll receive a notice that you now own 200 shares. What usually follows is that the stock will suddenly become affordable to many more investors, and in turn, the stock price begins to rise.

Investors can quickly increase the size of their portfolio and watch an increase in the value of their stocks if they look for stocks which are about to split. Lists of stocks which are soon expected to split are published frequently in the Wall Street Journal and Investor's Business Daily, or you can log onto many of the financial websites out there. Look for companies that have been doing well leading up to the split. One of the major splitters of the last decade has been Microsoft, which seems to split about once a year or so. And historically, their splits have tended to trigger quick upswings. By following this , you will have the potential to make some very good returns without taking on a huge level of risk.

While our primary focus in this chapter has been on the stock market and related investments, I also want to provide you with some non-stock related investment strategies.

STRATEGY 201:   Never invest in vacant land without plans to develop the property.

Real estate is one of my favorite investments, but you should never invest in vacant land without some sort of plan to develop the property in the future. Unless leased, vacant land leads to negative cash flow, meaning you'll never earn investment returns from a vacant land. However, if you purchase vacant land with the intent to build upon or otherwise develop the property, this will help you generate future returns from your real estate investment.

STRATEGY 202: *Never hold your money hostage in a timeshare.*

A lot of people have heard of the term "timeshare" but do not actually understand its meaning. Timesharing is not simply renting a vacation getaway. Instead, purchasing a timeshare is a real estate investment, usually in a condominium unit, which is co-owned by other investors. Each investor may personally use the unit during designated weeks which are chosen as part of the timeshare purchase agreement. Normally, interests in timeshares are sold for between $8,000 and $25,000 or even much more and enable the owner to use the property for two weeks a year.

Timesharing is not a good investment. For one thing, timeshares usually do not appreciate in value. This means that your money is not working for you. The other problem with investing in timeshares is that when you try to sell the timeshare you will be competing with sellers with newer timeshares which are easier to sell. A good indicator of how well timeshares work out is to take a look at the abundance of timeshare resale outlets. This is not a good use for your money and should not be viewed as a wealth-building option.

STRATEGY 203: *Never use a life insurance policy as an "investment."*

When it comes to investing and life insurance, my motto is to purchase life insurance as if you were going to die tomorrow but invest your money as if you are going to live forever. What I mean by this is that life insurance should be seen as a guarantee that your loved ones will be cared for in the event of your sudden death. Investing, by contrast, should be done with the mindset of watching your money grow. In other words, life insurance and investing are both necessary parts of a good financial plan but they have little in common. Accordingly, your should be to buy some term insurance but to otherwise use your money to build investment wealth by choosing the correct investments and strategies for yourself.

STRATEGY 204: Use the 10% solution to fund your plan for retirement prosperity.

Many Americans are living paycheck to paycheck and believe that there is never enough money left over after their expenses to invest. The biggest challenge is that they fall into the "Artificial Wealth Trap" and never learn how to escape. In other words, these people will never achieve a level of income they cannot outspend. You do not, and should not, have to live this way. As we've mentioned numerous times, there is a way out. Take 10% right off the top and pay yourself first. Take the next 10%, even before you pay your rent, mortgage, car or any other bills, and put it to work for you in some type of retirement account. Do the same with every paycheck you receive from today forward.

Let's discuss this concept a bit further. Instead of blowing the money on what may seem like necessities, your 10% should be invested in a savings account until you have accumulated the equivalent of two to three months of living expenses. Once you have accumulated your cash savings, continue to pay yourself the 10%, but now make the payments (see "attitude money" below) into long-term investment vehicles such as mutual funds. Qualified plans such as 401(k), 403(b), SEP-IRA, SIMPLE plans and other employer sponsored retirement plans are a great way to apply the 10% Solution since the money is put aside for you before you ever receive it in your paycheck.

I know we've touched on this many times but let's look at another example of the 10% at work. Suppose you paid yourself first, the amount of $100 a month from an annual salary of $12,000 and then invested that sum for 40 years. With an average return rate of 12%, your $100 will grow to about $1,176,477. Later on, this significant amount of money will help you invest in other investments which may help you gain more returns (and more cash savings). The biggest point to glean from this illustration is how powerful it can be even on a small salary. It's highly likely that you already make far more than this example so it should be that much easier for you. The key is to remember to always pay yourself first. The less money you think you have, the more important this becomes. Make the 10% solution a personal challenge and get started today.

STRATEGY 205: Save 20% of your annual salary as "attitude money."

This next strategy is one that I learned from a mentor many years ago. It has helped me immensely and can do the same for you. It's a strategy that you'll never see in a financial book but one that is tremendously effective. It all has to do with your attitude. Whether it is right or wrong, have you ever noticed how directly your attitude is related to your bank account balance? You probably have if you are still on the paycheck to paycheck treadmill. A positive attitude and financial self confidence are two of the most important wealth building tools. The easiest method for maintaining the winning attitude that comes from cash in the bank is never to be without it.

Using the 10% Solution which we discussed above, continue making deposits into your mutual fund account until the balance is equal to 20% of one year's take home pay. Promise yourself that you will never touch the money, not for overdue bills, emergencies or any other logical reason. The reason for this is that as soon as the money goes, so does your attitude. You will find it far easier, from an attitude standpoint, to have overdue bills with money available to pay them if you wanted to, than to have your bills totally paid and be back in the paycheck to paycheck rut. You will always encounter tough months when the money goes out faster than it comes in. Your 20% cushion is your attitude money, your dependable shelter during financial storms. Never, never touch it no matter how tough it gets. Your new, more stable attitude will propel you past your short-term financial dilemmas and provide you with a sense of freedom that you will love.

Once you have reached the 20% quota, you won't have to deposit another dime into that account. If your goal is to double your income every four years or so, your 20% account invested correctly also will double in the same amount of time. Open a separate account for your future 10% deposits to make sure that you keep this money separate.

The key point to remember when it comes to investing is to pay attention to things and follow a well thought out plan. Millions of people have become financially independent by establishing and following the strategies contained in this book and you can too. Investing is like the story of the tortoise and the hare, slow and steady wins the race. If you can maintain this strategy, you can find yourself a winner as well.

CHAPTER 15

RETIREMENT POWER PLANNING

*The secret point of money and power in America is neither the things
that money can buy nor power for power's sake,
but absolute personal freedom, mobility and privacy.*

Joan Didion

The information in this chapter covers one of the most exciting areas in the world of finance, retirement plans. No, I'm not being sarcastic when I describe retirement planning as being one of the most exciting things that you could possibly be involved in if you hope to someday become wealthy. Retirement plans offer something that few, if any, other money-making endeavors are able to provide and that is the combination of the two most powerful tools in the financial universe: *compounding growth* and *tax-free growth.*

In my seminars, I often point out the power of these incredible forces with an illustration that I first learned from Warren Buffett. While I'd like to tell you that I personally know Mr. Buffett and that he taught me this lesson personally, that is not true. I learned this lesson from reading some of the materials that Mr. Buffett once wrote on the concept of compounding and tax-free growth. His illustration really made the point hit home for me and I know it will do the same for you.

Basically, Mr. Buffett mentioned a comic strip that he had read years earlier in which the main character wanted to marry the object of his affection. The challenge that this character had was that the young lady would only marry a millionaire. Unfortunately, this poor fellow only had a single dollar to his name. Needless to say, he was far from millionaire status. Nonetheless, he decided to speak with the richest man in town to find out how to turn his single dollar into a million dollars. The wealthy man told him that he needed to learn how to double his dollar. Once he could figure out how to double his money, the man told him that he would only need to double that dollar, along with the profits from each transaction, twenty times to end up with his million dollars.

To illustrate this concept, take out a calculator and start with that dollar, multiply it times two, and then continue to do so until you've doubled the money twenty times. At the end of this exercise, you will find that your total adds up to $1,048,576! This is the phenomenal power of compounding. Not only does your dollar go to work for you but the dollar that it generates goes to work for you as well. This is the same concept that we talked about earlier in the book when I mentioned the strategy of increasing your wealth work force. If you can increase your income-producing assets, you will find out that wealth can be built quite rapidly.

The next part of the illustration that I learned from Warren Buffett has to do with taxes. Specifically, it details the devastation that results from having to pay taxes each and every time you generate profits. To demonstrate this destruction, go through the same exercise as before but insert an additional step. This time, after each of your calculations of doubling your money, subtract 30% of the newly created money to account for the taxes that will be taken out of your profits. The results are astonishing. After these taxes are taken out, you end up with far less. The end result is that you end up with just $40,642.31! That equates to over a million dollars in potential revenues gone due to the imposition of taxes.

Well, many people would tell me that taxes are just a fact of life and something that we've just got to deal with. While that may be partially true, the whole truth is that there are ways to legally get around having to pay so much in taxes. One of the best ways to get the growth that we need to build wealth without being subjected to the devastation of taxes is with the implementation of a retirement plan. That's what this chapter is all about.

STRATEGY 206: Start contributing to your retirement now.

When it comes to retirement planning, the best piece of advice that I could ever give you is to start now. The sooner you begin, the greater your potential for building wealth for yourself and your family. In fact, you need to realize that the most important bill for you to pay each month is the one to yourself and your family. The reason for this is because of the opportunity to maximize the potential of tax-free growth. If you were to invest $2,000 in a tax deferred retirement account each year between the ages of 20 and 26, and never invest another cent, you will have more money when you reach age 65 than if you wait until you are 26 and invest $2, 000 every year for the next 40 years. The reason for this is that you are maximizing compounding growth. Time is the key. Start today, even if it requires a short-term setback on other expenses or credit. It is better to retire with bad credit and money, than with no money and great credit.

STRATEGY 207: By reducing your current living expenses you can afford to plan for retirement.

One of the greatest impediments for most people when it comes to starting their retirement plan is that they think that they do not have enough money to begin to invest. In other words, they think that after paying all of their other bills they will not have enough left over at the end of the month to save towards retirement. As we just talked about, the bill you pay first each month should be to yourself. The reality is that most people can afford to start saving for their retirement simply by cutting some of their expenses. If you want to get ahead financially, you need to make some tough choices about your spending habits. We've covered this concept extensively in this book already. If you haven't begun to implement the changes necessary, get started now.

STRATEGY 208: Decide how much savings you'll need to live comfortably in retirement.

Once you begin contributing money into a retirement account, you need to set some targets for yourself. The first target needs to be focused on the amount of savings that you'll need for a comfortable retirement. When deciding how much money you'll need to live off of during retirement, there are several factors to consider. Most financial advisors estimate that everyone needs to have between 75% and 95% of their pre-retirement income available to them, per year. This way, the retiree won't be forced to deal with a drastic drop-off in the way they live.

Another consideration to make is how long you expect to live after you retire. Thanks to healthier lifestyles and advances in medicine, people are living longer than ever before. This is great but it also presents a challenge in that we've got to be able to pay for these extra years. Calculating the amount that you'll need is essential. Of course, you'll want to take inflation, medical costs, travel, and other expenses into consideration too.

So, how do you determine how much you will need to live on during retirement? Unfortunately, there is no exact formula that fits everyone, which is why everyone should first educate themselves as much as possible on retirement planning basics. You can at least decide the type of retirement lifestyle that you have in mind and determine the minimum amount that you'll need in order to fund it.

STRATEGY 209: Determine what the right retirement age is for you and plan accordingly.

One of the most important decisions you can make when it comes to retirement is deciding on the right time to retire. Most often, this decision is based on two considerations:

1. how much a person has saved; and

2. what type of standard of living they want to maintain during retirement.

Additionally, this will depend on what you want to do during retirement, whether you have a diverse portfolio that will be safe during retirement, and factoring in known expenses as well as unexpected ones such as medical care or repairs to one's home.

One of the easiest ways to decide when you can retire is to calculate your monthly expenses and then compare that to your sources of income after you retire. These sources of income are usually made up of Social Security, accumulated assets, and other sources such as company pension plans or post-retirement employment. The key is to not allow your lifestyle to outpace your retirement income.

After preparing financially, one consideration that many people fail to consider is what in the world they will do during retirement. For many people, retirement can be mind-numbingly boring. Most of us are used to having a structured life that revolves around work, and when that structure is taken away, the void can be depressing. If your plans for retirement include traveling, going back to school, or starting a new business you must make sure that you have made financial arrangements to provide for these plans.

STRATEGY 210: Start saving for retirement as soon as possible to maximize the effects of compounding interest.

As mentioned earlier, the sooner you begin saving for retirement the larger your nest egg can grow thanks to the miracle of compounding interest. This makes it less likely that you will have to play catch-up when you are nearing retirement age. Stated another way, the longer you postpone saving, the greater the difference will be between where you are in your retirement savings and where you could be.

Let's look at a simple example of how waiting to begin planning your retirement is really a plan to be behind. Suppose you save $200 a month for ten years at a return of 6%. At the end of this time you would have accumulated $32,653. However, suppose you postponed saving for two years. In that case, at the end of the same period of time you would have only $24,519. By waiting to begin saving for retirement, you've cost yourself over $8,000 in compounded interest. This also means that you would have to save more money in later years to catch-up to where you need to be. For people who already think that they can't afford to save money, this derails their retirement planning even further.

STRATEGY 211: *Learn to enjoy life in some way other than going into debt and jeopardizing your retirement.*

No financial adviser would ever intentionally counsel his or her clients to live an unhappy existence for the bulk of their lives simply for the sake of saving for retirement. If this were the case, very few people would actually save anything for their retirement. However, this is all too often the message that many clients inadvertently receive. It is true that you must learn to make some sacrifices, or at least have a little discipline, in order to save for retirement and enjoy your golden years. The good news, however, is that through working with my clients over the years, I've developed three principles for how one can enjoy their life while still saving plenty of money for their future.

The first principle for living life and saving for retirement is to spend less than you earn. Stated another way, as your income increases your standard of living must remain the same or increase less than your income does. It is sound advice to let your standard of living remain at its original position as your earning increases so you can have ample amounts to save. The prelude to saving is earning money first and then to see to it that you reduce overhead and pay for all of your needs on a cash basis to avoid excessive interest surcharges. I firmly believe that if you maintain a simple standard of living as your income is increasing it will afford you the ability to have a comfortable retirement.

My second principle for living your life while still saving money for retirement is to use any and all excess money to invest. Now, in saying this, I don't mean that you should never reward yourself for working hard, raising your family, paying your taxes, etc. Obviously, you should treat yourself every now and then to remind you why you're working so hard in the first place. By getting in the habit of seeing extra money as more money that you can invest instead of more money that you can waste, your retirement outlook will be that much brighter.

And finally, you should never, ever borrow money from your retirement nest egg simply to enjoy life today. Taking a vacation today at the expense of your future security would be one of the most foolish decisions you could ever make.

STRATEGY 212: Do not rely on Social Security to be a critical part of your retirement planning.

This will surely come as no surprise to most people who read this. Simply stated, depending on your age there are no guarantees for how much you'll receive from Social Security when you retire or even if it will still exist. To make matters worse, there is also no way to predict what the age limits will be for collecting Social Security when you get ready to retire. Accordingly, any retirement plan that relies too heavily on Social Security is a plan for failure.

STRATEGY 213: Decide to start receiving Social Security benefits at age 62.

In the event that Social Security does exist when you get ready to retire, many people ask me when they should start receiving benefits. If you are near retirement age, you have the choice of receiving benefits at age 62 or 65. Don't listen to financial experts who advise that everyone should wait until they reach full retirement age (age 65) to begin receiving Social Security benefits. These so-called "experts" reason that by taking Social Security benefits at age 62, you will only receive 80% of the benefits you would get at age 65. Based upon this fact, these experts advise everyone to wait until age 65 to start receiving benefits if they can afford to do so.

However, there are a couple of problems with waiting until age 65 to begin receiving Social Security benefits. For one thing, there are no guarantees that Social Security will be around long enough for you to wait until age 65. Secondly, there are no guarantees that you will be around when you reach age 65, especially if you have health problems. And finally, the best reason for taking your Social Security benefits when you reach age 62 is because you can invest that monthly check and the interest you'll earn on that money over the course of three years will more than offset the fact that you're receiving smaller payments by not having waited until you were age 65. In fact, the interest can be enough to where the person who waits until age 65 would never catch up.

STRATEGY 214: Familiarize yourself with the different types of Individual Retirement Accounts so that you can choose the IRA which is right for you.

You might be surprised to learn that there are many forms of Individual Retirement Accounts (IRAs) from which you can choose. The most common type of IRA is a "contributory IRA" which means that any person with employment earnings may contribute to an account. Other types of IRAs are "rollover IRAs," SEPs, Simple IRAs, and Roth IRAs. Let's go over these various types and define them.

Contributory IRA- This type of IRA is available to anyone who has earnings or business income (earned income). Because of the tax advantages of the various IRAs, our good friends in Congress have placed limits on the amount of money we can contribute annually. How much can you contribute? The answer to this question depends on two things: the year in which the contribution is made and the IRA participant's age. For 2008, a person who is forty-nine years old and younger may contribute up to $5,000 each year to his or her IRA. This limit is $6,000 if that person is age 50 or older. Contributions and earnings are taxed when withdrawn after age 59 ½. Withdrawals before the age 59 ½ are taxable and subject to a 10% penalty with

276

certain exceptions. Withdrawals must begin by the year after you reach 70 ½ to avoid penalties. With a traditional contributory IRA, if you are not covered by an employer's retirement plan, you may take a deduction on your tax return in the amount of your contribution. If you are covered by an employer's plan, then your IRA contribution may be deductible in whole, in part, or not at all depending on your gross income.

Rollover IRA-This is a type of IRA which is categorized separately because of the source of your contribution into the IRA. "Rollover" means to move money from a qualified retirement plan such as a 401(k) into an IRA. If you receive a payout from your company-sponsored retirement plan, a rollover IRA could be to your advantage. It is important to note that you will continue to receive the tax-deferred status of your retirement savings and you will avoid penalties and taxes. Contributions and earnings are taxed when withdrawn after age 59 ½. Withdrawals before the age 59 ½ are taxable and subject to a 10% penalty with certain exceptions. Withdrawals must begin by the year after you reach 70 ½ to avoid penalties.

Roth IRA-With a Roth IRA, if you meet certain requirements, all earnings on your contributions into the IRA are tax-free when you or your beneficiary decides to withdraw them. Other features of Roth IRAs include avoiding the early distribution penalty on certain withdrawals, and eliminating the need to take minimum distributions after age 70½.

Simplified Employee Pension- A simplified employee pension, or SEP, is a special type of IRA that is established by an employer for the benefit of its employees or by small business owners for their own benefit. Under a SEP, each participant in the plan will have his or her own retirement account into which the employer contributes. These contributions are excluded from the employees' pay and are not taxable until the funds are distributed. For persons who are self-employed, a SEP can be established even if they have zero employees.

With a SEP, contribution limits are higher than with other types of plans. In fact, an annual contribution to a SEP can be as much as 25% of an employee's compensation, up to a maximum amount of $40,000.

There are some disadvantages to using a SEP, however. From an employer's perspective, the participation and vesting rules are not as favorable as other plans. Participation rules will determine which employees must be covered by the plan and who must receive compensation to their plan accounts. Regarding vesting, the rules for SEPs determine how much an employee is able to receive if he or she becomes employed elsewhere or passes away. The results of these rules can be quite costly for small businesses.

SIMPLE IRAs- A "Simplified incentive match plan for employees (SIMPLE)" is an IRA designed to make it easier for small business owners to establish a retirement plan for their employees. A SIMPLE IRA is a salary reduction plan, like a 401(k), and it allows employees to divert some of their compensation into retirement savings. Like the SEP, contributions to SIMPLE IRAs are made into a separate account for each participating employee. The participant/employee is allowed to select any percentage of compensation to be contributed to his or her account, up to certain yearly limits.

STRATEGY 215: *Maximize contributions to your employer retirement plan only up to the amount matched.*

Many employers offer retirement plans to their employees as a way to compensate, motivate, and reduce employee turnover. If your employer offers a plan and matches some or all of your contributions, maximize your contributions up to the amount your employer matches, and then use any amount over that to fund a Roth IRA if you qualify. For example, if your employer matches 6% of your salary, defer at least that amount and put the remaining amount of your 10% solution into a Roth IRA or other type of IRA if you do not qualify for a Roth.

For example, assume that you are paid $4,000 per month and you want to contribute 10% per month to your employer's 401(k) plan, which the employer matches at the rate of 6% ($240 = 6% of $4,000). You could reduce your contribution to 6% and put the remaining 4% of the 10% Solution into a Roth IRA. Since matching contributions are essentially free money and tax-deferred, your first retirement money should always be invested here first.

STRATEGY 216: Fund a Roth IRA first if your employer does not match contributions to the employer plan.

If your employer does not match any of your contributions, fully fund the Roth IRA first and then the employer plan. For example, if you make $60,000 per year and want to apply the 10% Solution, you need to invest $6,000 (10% of $60,000) per year. You should invest $5,000 into your Roth first, then put $1,000 into your employer plan to maximize the 10% Solution.

Since there is no matching in the plan, you have greater investment choices in the self-directed Roth IRA and greater flexibility for college funding, house buying and estate planning. Also, the tax-free advantages of the Roth outweigh the tax-deferred advantages of the employer-sponsored plan.

Let's take a look at two different scenarios: Suppose that you invested $6,000 annually into an Employer plan for 20 years at 12% interest. After 20 years, this would have grown to $468,010. However, when the money is withdrawn there would be a tax of $142,400, which would leave $325,610 for retirement. By contrast, let's suppose that we invested $5,000 into a Roth IRA for 20 years at 12% interest, and $1,000 in the Employer Plan for 20 years at 12% interest. At the end of 20 years we would have $390,008 in the Roth IRA with zero taxes when the funds were withdrawn. In the Employer Plan, we would have $78,002 and owe $15,844 in taxes. Together, after taxes these two accounts would total $452,166. So, by investing part of our money into the IRA we increased our overall retirement funds by $126,556.

As you can see, the difference is substantial. Even if an individual faithfully invested the tax savings from the employer retirement plan, he/she would still not earn as much because of the taxes owed when you take the distribution

STRATEGY 217: *Use the IRA rollover rules to minimize the taxes on your employer's retirement plan lump sum distribution.*

When you change jobs or retire, your objective is to get control of your 401(k), 403(b), 457, SIMPLE or SEP money without paying taxes. The rollover rules allow you to move your entire company retirement plan to any IRA without the $5,000 ($6,000 if age 50 or older) IRA contribution restriction and without paying taxes. Since the rollover allows you to move your money without tax consequences, it is your best alternative for getting control of your retirement money, keeping the money totally tax sheltered, and achieving greater earnings through self-directed investments.

STRATEGY 218: *Never request a check directly from the employer plan.*

If you receive a check from your employer plan directly, by law your employer must withhold 20% of the money and send it to the IRS. Even if you want to roll the money into an IRA, you would have to come up with the additional 20%. Accordingly, you should always do trustee to trustee rollovers. A "Trustee to Trustee" transfer is when the money is never sent directly to you, but directly to a new qualified plan such as an IRA. You can withdraw the money from the IRA without the 20%, just not directly from the plan.

STRATEGY 219: *Make your own retirement plan, if your employer does not offer one.*

Since no one is going to care about your plan for retirement more than you, you should create your own plan by using IRAs. As we stated a little earlier, there are traditional IRAs, Roth IRAs, SEP IRAs and SIMPLE IRAs. All of these are available for you to build your own plan. Use the Roth IRA if you qualify because of the tax-free advantages and multiple withdrawal choices. If you are self-employed, use the SEP or SIMPLE IRAs in addition to the Roth IRA, to fund your retirement plan.

STRATEGY 220: Choose a Traditional IRA versus a Roth IRA based upon your age.

When counseling with my clients, one of the most asked questions I receive is whether to invest in a traditional IRA or a Roth IRA. The answer depends on one's personal situation and on the assumptions they are making about the future. I always tell them that they have to look at how long they have before they withdraw money from their IRA and what their tax bracket will be at that time. Also, we've got to look at the amount of earnings they expect to generate between now and when they retire. Deciding which type of IRA is better is somewhat of a gamble considering the uncertainty of these determining factors.

In spite of this, there is a good rule of thumb for choosing between the two IRAs which works for most of my clients. As a rule, if you are near retirement age and do not expect your IRA earnings to significantly increase by the time you retire, then you might be better off just accepting the immediate deductions you'll receive from contributing to a traditional contributory IRA.

However, for most people, especially younger people who have many years to save for retirement, a Roth IRA is a better choice. The chief reason for this is that the Roth IRA is effectively bigger than a regular IRA because it holds after-tax dollars. If you can take advantage of this feature of the Roth IRA by maximizing your contributions, you'll add greater tax leverage to your retirement savings over the duration of your retirement-saving years.

***STRATEGY 221: Take advantage of the new phase-out
levels for deductible IRAs for persons covered by a
qualified retirement plan through work, if you need a
tax break.***

Active participants whose income is below a "threshold level" may make deductible IRA contributions. The maximum $5,000 deduction available to active participants is reduced proportionately over a "phase-out" range. Active participants with incomes above the phaseout range are not entitled to any IRA deduction. If an active participant's income falls within the phaseout range, their deduction will be reduced by $300 for every $1,000 of income above the minimum threshold.

Starting in 2008, the phaseout range widens to $83,000 $103,000 for married couples filing jointly. The maximum deductible IRA contribution for an individual who is not an active participant, but whose spouse is, will be phased out at Adjusted Gross Incomes between $159,000 and $169,000.

***STRATEGY 222: Rarely should you convert a Traditional
IRA into a Roth IRA.***

The Roth IRA offers tax-free buildup as opposed to current IRAs which offer tax-deferred buildup. The maximum contribution to a Roth IRA is the lesser of $5,000 reduced by deductible IRA contributions, or the individual's compensation for the year. Although Roth IRAs are more beneficial, rarely use the rollover option that would allow you to convert your Traditional existing IRA into a Roth unless you have little or no taxable growth in your Traditional IRA. As soon as the money is rolled over, all earnings and tax-deductible contributions are taxable.

An example of the type of IRAs that are favorable for rollover are those that are newly created, especially non-deductible IRAs. Rolling a regular IRA with substantial tax-deferred growth into a Roth IRA would create a huge tax liability at a time of your earning life when your tax rate is at its highest. Leave regular IRAs alone until retirement when your marginal tax rate is usually at its lowest. Rolling a regular IRA into a Roth IRA would be to your advantage only if you are currently in a low tax bracket but expect to be in a higher tax bracket at retirement.

STRATEGY 223: Do not fall for the Roth IRA conversion "hype."

The conversion from a traditional IRA to a Roth IRA is being marketed heavily by the financial services industry and the government, because this will raise fees and tax revenues for them. Many people are falling for this "hype" and rushing to convert their traditional IRAs to a Roth without taking into consideration all of the ramifications of doing so.

Because of the potential traps and additional taxes you will pay from a Roth conversion, you should avoid it. The conversion rarely makes sense for the majority of people, but if you still wish to do the conversion, wait until December to withdraw the money. At this time, you can calculate your Adjusted Gross Income and how it affects your phaseouts, tax brackets, state taxes, and other personal financial issues. If the conversion turns out to be too costly, then roll the money back into the traditional IRA within the correct time limits and your taxes will not be affected.

STRATEGY 224: Take money out of your IRA as an absolute last resort if you face a financial emergency prior to retirement.

Ideally, assets in your nest egg will remain intact and grow well into your retirement. Then again, life is never perfect, and there will be times when you're tempted to tap into your retirement accounts. If you find yourself in this situation before you retire, you should take money out of your IRA only as a last resort.

Taking money out of your IRA before you retire to pay for emergencies is a bad idea for a number of reasons, and not just the fact that you'll cut into your overall balance. You reduce future savings potential too. For example, say you had $10,000 earning 10% annually. If you kept the money intact, you'd have $11,000 by the end of the year. Now, let's say you raid your account and reduce it by $1,000 to $9,000. It would earn $900 by year's end leaving you with a total of $9,900. That's a $100 earnings shortfall on top of the $1,000 you took out. Additionally, IRAs generally levy a hefty 10% penalty for cashing in before your full retirement age in addition to income taxes you may owe.

The upshot: You may need money badly, but consider other options before turning to retirement savings to bail you out. A home equity loan that comes with certain tax breaks and less rigid repayment terms may be a better choice. If it's college you need to fund, consider low-priced college loans, a work grant or going to a cheaper institution. Even a second job can wind up being a far better way to address today's expenses while preserving your savings for tomorrow. We've given you a number of strategies throughout the book to help you free up improperly allocated money. Don't mess up your plan by getting into the money that you've properly allocated.

STRATEGY 225: Take advantage of pre-tax savings through a 401(k) plan.

A 401(k) is a type of qualified retirement plan that allows employees to save and invest for their own retirement. Through a 401(k), you can authorize your employer to deduct a certain amount of money from your paycheck before taxes are calculated, and to invest that money into the plan. Your money is invested in investment options that you choose from the ones offered through your company's plan. The federal government established the 401(k) in 1981 with special tax advantages to encourage people to prepare for their own retirement.

With a 401(k), you decide how much money you want deducted from your paycheck and invested into the plan during each pay period, up to the legal maximum. The maximum limit you can contribute each year into your 401(k) is determined annually by the IRS. There are several different limits that apply to a 401(k) plan in addition to the overall contribution limit. These limits, your salary, and the type of 401(k) plan to which you are contributing may limit your 401(k) contributions to a lesser amount. For an exact answer to how much you can contribute to your 401(k), it is best to speak to your plan administrator. Another benefit of using a 401(k) is that you usually have several options for how the money in your account should be invested.

There is also a tax benefit to contributing to a 401(k). The money you contribute to your account is deducted from your paycheck before income taxes are taken out. This means that by contributing to a 401(k), you can actually lower the amount you pay each pay period in current taxes. For example, if you earn $1,000 each paycheck, and you contribute, say 5% ($50), you are only taxed on $950. You don't owe income taxes on the money until you withdraw it from the plan, when you could be in a lower tax bracket.

STRATEGY 226: *Enjoy your retirement money.*

It is alright to spend the money from your retirement account for pleasure, after you retire. Then you can withdraw all you want since that's what it is for. Too many successful retired people spend too much time trying to preserve capital instead of spending and enjoying it. You can't take it with you. So far no one has discovered a way to attach a bank vault to a hearse. The important thing to remember is that you've worked hard for your retirement so you need to enjoy it and reap the fruits of your labor.

Retirement planning is a process that can help you to achieve the life of your dreams. However, it's not the only aspect to your overall financial plan. You've got to remember that the key to our overall E.S.C.A.P.E. Plan from the "Artificial Wealth Trap" is to follow a system. Establishing and following a plan for how you will be able to provide for yourself during your retirement is just one component of that overall plan. Do what it takes to put your plan in place and then set it on auto-pilot so that you can live the life that you want. As I've mentioned before, the time to get started is now. Remember, if you will live like no one else, you can live like no one else. Following the E.S.C.A.P.E. plan can help you do it.

Part V:

PRESERVE

CHAPTER 16

AVOIDING THE BIGGEST THREATS
TO YOUR WEALTH

It requires a great deal of boldness and a great deal of caution to
make a great fortune, and when you have got it,
it requires ten times as much wit to keep it.

Ralph Waldo Emerson

I f you were to ask most people what they believe to be the key to wealth, their answer would probably be to make more money. This is definitely part of it but there's a lot more. It takes more than simply focusing on one part if we hope to build real wealth. That's where most books and programs fail to truly assist people in getting their financial lives in order. There are several different aspects to the art of wealth and it takes all of them in order to ever become wealthy.

I view this in a similar manner to looking at a championship sports team. The best teams have both offensive as well as defensive skills that position them to win. It's the same way with building wealth. If you are ever to win at the game of personal finance, you've got to employ both offensive as well as defensive strategies into the process. The "Artificial Wealth Trap" E.S.C.A.P.E. Plan is designed to provide all of the required aspects for you to emerge victorious.

As you should have learned in the CREATE section of this book, making money is to building wealth what gasoline is to an automobile. It is the fuel that powers the engine. However, this "fuel" alone will not guarantee that someone will become wealthy.

Over the course of my career as a wealth protection attorney, I've encountered and worked with numerous high-income individuals who have never built up any type of meaningful wealth. In fact, for many of these people, they're not any better off than anyone else who is living from paycheck to paycheck, their paychecks are just bigger. If they ever hope to become wealthy, they've got to put the fuel that these paychecks provide to work generating more. It's the same process regardless of the size of the paycheck. That's what the information that we covered in the ACCUMULATE section of the book was designed to assist you in accomplishing.

In this Part of the book, we turn our focus to the PRESERVE portion of the plan. For the majority of my professional life, I've dedicated my career to assisting people with this important task. Using the sports team analogy that I mentioned earlier, I guess I've spent the bulk of my time serving as a defensive coordinator. Through this work, I've been able to assist thousands of people in saving millions of dollars from taxes and lawsuits. I've been privileged to work with a number of individuals and organizations in helping them to keep more of their money so that they could grow it for themselves and their families. In this Part, we'll take a look at how you can utilize these same strategies for your own personal situation.

You've got to realize that the more money that you begin to accumulate the greater the threats to your assets. The analogy that I give people to illustrate this point is that the threat to your assets is similar to water flowing down a stream. When the water is flowing at a steady pace, things can easily be contained. However, when the flow of the water begins to drastically increase, it becomes harder and harder to contain the water and it eventually begins to wear away at the foundation. It works the same way when money comes into your life.

This may sound like a positive situation but I can assure you that it can destroy your plans for accumulating long-term wealth. Think about pictures that you've seen of flood waters. As the water level continually gets higher and higher, it becomes harder for the levees to contain all of it. With enough force, the levees will break and all of the water leaves the contained area. This is how things can happen to your wealth if you don't take the preventive steps to plan for the increased flow.

In the previous Parts of the book, we've shown you tremendous money-making, money-saving, and money-growing strategies for increasing the flow of money into your life. If you don't prepare yourself for the increased flow, you will find that you will end up losing a good portion of it. It is when the flow is at its greatest that it is the most difficult to gain control over. That is when those who would like to sue you begin coming around. It is also when the government begins to increase its pressure in the form of taxes by imposing a higher tax rate on your income. Even worse, it's also when you begin to face issues such as losing a big chunk of your money in probate fees and/or death taxes associated with your estate. The bottom line is that if you don't do something to contain your wealth, you will end up losing it.

The information in this Part of the book will help you to keep that from happening.

STRATEGY 227: Identify the threats to your wealth.

When it comes to protecting things that are near and dear to us, such as our homes, we're most often reactive instead of proactive. Think about it. When do most people typically put in an alarm system? They put it in *after* their home has been broken into. When do they buy fire extinguishers? That's right, after they or someone close to them, has experienced a fire. Many of the most difficult situations that people face could be prevented with a little bit of forethought. It's the same way when it comes to avoiding threats to your wealth.

When it comes to avoiding these threats, most people take a more reactive approach in their strategies than a proactive one. They are reactive because they may simply hear about threats to their assets, but they may not really comprehend the significance of those dangers until they go through the experience personally. More importantly, they often do not realize just how likely they are to be under attack by these threats until it's too late. The goal of this chapter and this Part of the book as a whole is to help you to identify the various threats to your wealth so that you can put into effect strategies and safeguards for protecting against them.

Make no mistake about it, your assets are indeed at risk. The perils are very real and are much more common than you may believe. In fact, many of you may be experiencing some of these threats right now. Our goal in this Part of the book is to help you to realize that there are things that can be done to reduce, or even eliminate, the impact of these threats. We will be covering dozens of strategies that can help you with this important task.

The first step in being proactive in our approach to protecting ourselves from the threats to our wealth is to identify them. In today's world, the biggest dangers to your wealth are lawsuits, income taxes, death taxes, and catastrophic health care expenses. The good news is that there are some outstanding *proactive* strategies that can be put in place to protect against these threats. The first thing that you must do is to "know your enemy" by identifying the things that can be hazardous to your wealth. Each of these "enemies" will be addressed individually along with powerful strategies for defeating them.

STRATEGY 228: Develop a battlefield mindset.

In order to protect your assets, you must learn to be more aggressive in your strategies. What this means is that your plan must be put in place before you need it. You see, once you need it, it's already too late. Once you find yourself battling a catastrophic illness, health insurance is no longer an affordable option. Similarly, once a lawsuit has been filed, it is too late to set up protection. The best plan is to put preventive measures in place before any sort of wealth-devastating event occurs.

An essential step in implementing this proactive approach is to develop a battlefield mindset. Simply put, you must become consciously aware of the threats and set proper defenses in place to protect you from attack by these threats to your wealth. More specifically, you must do it *before* you are attacked. This requires a different mentality from the norm.

The mentality required is similar to that of a military leader. A good battlefield commander will make certain that his troops are well placed and fortified against the enemy *before* there is any engagement. The commander will also have strategies in place and train his troops in drills so that they are ready when the conflict takes place. Notice I said *when*, not *if*. This is the mindset that you must develop if you intend to keep your assets safe. It may sound a bit like paranoia to you but I can assure you that it's necessary.

You must fortify your assets, before they are attacked, and you must have an ongoing plan in place to make certain that your fortifications are at full strength against the enemy. In the chapter on protecting yourself from frivolous lawsuits, you will learn some statistics that are downright scary. To protect yourself from this type of threat, you must develop a battlefield mindset.

STRATEGY 229: Establish a personalized financial fortress system for your assets.

When I speak about protecting assets, I often use the example of building a fortress around them to keep them safe. This "fortress" concept is a good example because it's analogous to each of our personal situations in that not every castle has the same structure or defenses. Each is built with defenses that suit the particular needs of the lord or lady of that castle and the potential enemies surrounding them. Similarly, your personal situation is at least slightly different from that of others so you will need to construct your own personalized fortress around your assets.

Your personalized financial fortress system should be built to suit your personal needs and goals. By looking at where you are, as well as where you're going, you can set into place the cornerstones of your financial fortress. Like a real castle, yours may start out relatively small, with the financial equivalent of only a wall and perhaps a gate as protection. But as the needs for your fortress grow, you will add on additional components to your protection plan to protect what is inside.

Regardless of the size of your fortress, if you don't build it, if you don't establish it, you will never have the protection that the fortress can give you. You absolutely must put your personalized fortress into place before you need it rather than waiting until it's too late. This Part of the book will show you exactly how to do that through the use of legal entities and other strategies for safeguarding your hard-earned wealth.

STRATEGY 230: Create an estate plan regardless of your total net worth.

When most people think of estate planning, they usually think of the super wealthy. Names like Vanderbilt, Carnegie and Rockefeller typically come to mind. What you must realize, however, is that estate planning is not just for the super-wealthy, it's for anyone who has assets. You don't have to own multi-million dollar houses and private jets or have millions of dollars in the bank to need an estate plan. Basically, *everyone* needs an estate plan of some sort.

Depending on your situation, your estate plan may be as simple as a few documents and directives that can ensure a smooth transition of your assets upon your death. It doesn't necessarily have to be made up of reams of paper and require the work of dozens of lawyers or the fees that accompany their work. It simply needs to outline the way that you would like for your estate to be handled upon your death. When I refer to "your estate," you've got to realize that essentially, whatever you own is considered a part of your estate. How that is handled upon your death depends on what type of plan you have in place. The key is that you actually have some sort of plan.

There are many reasons for you to have an estate plan in place other than detailing the transition of your assets. One is to provide for yourself and your loved ones in the event that you become incapacitated. If this were to occur, your estate plan can provide directions for the handling of your medical care and also for how your family should carry out your wishes if and when you are unable do so. Additionally, if you have minor or special needs children, or dependent parents, an estate plan can be drafted which will provide them with the care that you would want them to have, not the care that the courts decide for them.

Since an estate plan is about carrying out your wishes for how to handle your estate upon your death, it becomes apparent that everyone needs one. This can only be done if you've taken the time to create that estate plan.

STRATEGY 231: *Operate your activity as a business, not as a hobby.*

I often hear people telling others that they need to get a hobby. The attorney in me immediately wants to inform them that "no, they don't need a hobby, they need a business." Fortunately, the practical side of me knows when to simply say nothing at all. The truth remains that you need to start a home-based business to take advantage of the many benefits that this can bring you.

I often get the question, "so what kind of business should I start?" There is no easy answer for this question and I certainly wouldn't want to make a suggestion without knowing someone fairly well. I could spend all day suggesting potential home-based business ideas and have the other person saying that it just really isn't something they could do or would ever even want to do. A potential business venture is something for you to decide for yourself. The key is to get it started.

One of the easiest ways to start a home-based business that you know you will enjoy, and often already have a head start on, is to look to your current hobbies and interests for ideas. For many of you, you may already be well into a hobby. This could be things such as woodworking, photography, web design, handcrafted fishing lures or all sorts of activities. Even things like renovating houses, cars, or buildings can be a great way for you to turn your passion or one of your current hobbies into an incredible business opportunity. Whether this becomes something that takes the place of your current employment or simply supplements it, there are a large number of benefits available for those people who operate a business. We covered quite a few strategies on ways to gain income from this business over the internet and with online auctions in an earlier chapter. Over the next few chapters, you'll see some great ways to capture many of the tax and legal benefits for yourself.

STRATEGY 232: Form a legal entity for operating your business.

Once you make the decision to begin operating a home-based business, it is essential that you take the next step and establish a legal entity in order to take advantage of the tremendous benefits that businesses are entitled to under the Tax Code. When you begin operating your own business, you can then begin to reap the same huge rewards that major companies enjoy if you will simply take the time to structure your business in a similar manner.

The primary legal difference between your small, start-up home-based business and the big boys is that their legal team structured them to operate their business within a legal entity. These legal entities are able to maximize the advantages of operating a business venture by receiving additional tax benefits, greater asset protection, and even some built-in estate planning benefits. What types of benefits that you are able to take advantage of depends on what type of entity you choose to set up. We'll talk about the various types of legal entity options in greater detail in the next few chapters in this Part. However, a quick overview can be helpful.

Legal entities come in many forms, but for businesses there are generally three types: corporations, limited liability companies, and limited partnerships. Which type you want to form for your business depends on several factors that are unique to your situation and your type of business. Since there are many factors involved, selecting the type of legal entity which best suits you should only be done with the guidance of an entity specialist.

An entity specialist can inform you of the advantages and drawbacks to each type of entity and can help you to avoid any unforeseen pitfalls. This powerful knowledge can help you to make an educated decision about which type of entity is best suited for your particular needs. It is an investment that will produce huge returns for years to come. For more information on legal entities or to speak with an entity specialist, visit our website at www.secretmillionaire.com.

STRATEGY 233: *Change the type of dollars that you spend for maximum tax savings.*

I always tell my clients and students that one of the best ways for them to get the most benefits out of a home-based business, as well as their lives in general, is to continually act and think like a business rather than as an individual. The reason for this is that businesses do things differently. Part of this approach is to learn to spend your money more like a business, rather than spending it like an individual. One way to do this is to learn to change the type of dollars that you spend.

That doesn't mean that you should run out and exchange your U.S. dollars for Euros or Yen or anything like that because that isn't what we're talking about here. What we are talking about is the fact that businesses, by law, can spend their dollars differently than we can as individuals. They can spend their money *before* taxes take a significant chunk out of their income. This means that they can deduct a lot of their expenses against their taxable income. You need to do the same thing by learning to change the type of dollars that you spend from after-tax dollars to before-tax dollars. To take advantage of this, however, you've got to learn the rules for doing it correctly. We'll be getting into this in more detail a few chapters from now and we'll be showing you some incredible strategies for significantly reducing your taxes.

When you operate your home-based business, and spend before-tax dollars, you can save yourself extraordinary amounts of money each and every year by lowering your taxes. How much you can save depends on many factors, not the least of which is how much you are, or are not, thinking and acting like a business. Businesses, if operated properly, have the ability to pay significantly less of their gross income in taxes than do individuals. However, the amazing tax benefits don't just take care of themselves. To reap the rewards, you have to do something to make it happen. You must learn to think and act like a business and you must learn to change the type of dollars you spend from after-tax dollars to before-tax dollars.

STRATEGY 234: Change the nature of your income from earned to unearned.

A complaint that I hear over and over in my practice and my teaching is that people are paying too much in taxes. My response to this statement is always, "so what are you doing about it?" It seems like just about everyone wants to legally reduce their tax burden, but they simply have no idea as to where to start. In fact, in talking with a lot of people on this topic over the years I've come to the realization that they are completely overwhelmed by the idea. It doesn't have to be so hard. Reducing your taxes doesn't have to be difficult, but you do have to do things differently.

Little steps can take you a long way toward reducing your taxes. Enough of these little steps can add up to a pretty significant chunk of tax savings. One relatively simple step is to change the nature of your income from "earned" to "unearned." If you can change earned income (like your salary or W-2 income) to unearned income (like rents or royalties), you can save big bucks. For example, by simply changing the type of income you receive, you can cut over 15% in taxes on that income. If you think about that, 15% of even $50,000 per year would add up to $7,500 of extra money in your pocket. What could you do with an extra $7,500? The best part about it is that it can be yours with no additional work. You simply have to make some changes.

This is a great way to put your money to work without the risk associated with investing. Think about it. If you could get a guaranteed 15% return on an investment, say a mutual fund, or a stock, chances are that you would be pretty happy. But it gets even better because that 15% savings is not just for this year, but for each and every year that you continue to employ this strategy and best of all, it's risk-free. One simple change in the type of income that you receive can bring about powerful tax savings and put more money in your pocket. This is why it is so important to change the nature of your income.

STRATEGY 235: Use only legal tax strategies, never tax evasion.

It seems that a pretty universal sentiment among people out there is that everyone wants to pay the least amount in taxes that is legally possible. I'm all for it but there's one word in that statement that I want to especially emphasize and that is "legally." Defrauding the government by cheating at the tax game is called tax evasion. Tax evasion is a high-risk move and one that has brought down many wealthy and powerful people who thought that they could play outside the lines. You need to be sure that you aren't one of them.

We all make jokes about the IRS but in truth, they can be quite savvy. They know just about every legal (and illegal) way that one can use to reduce taxes. Remember, these are the people who brought down Al Capone when no one else could. The folks at the IRS know what they are doing and they have been doing it very successfully for years. Basically, the lesson I teach people is to not fall into the trap of trying to outsmart them. There's no need for this type of foolishness. With all of the perfectly legal ways to dramatically slash your taxes, evading or illegally denying the government its due isn't just dangerous, it's downright dumb.

Doing things properly and employing strategies for legally avoiding taxes can save you enough money to create the wealth and lifestyle that you have always wanted. Illegally evading your taxes, on the other hand, can buy you a government sponsored, all-expense paid, extended, mandatory vacation, and a new wardrobe of orange jumpsuits. In the chapter on taxes in this Part of the book, we'll show you how to make wise tax choices so that you can be sure to keep not only your wealth, but also your freedom.

STRATEGY 236: Protect your wealth by protecting your health.

In addition to lawsuits, income taxes, and death taxes, one thing that can wipe out all of your hard-earned wealth is a major health challenge. The most important gift that any of us can have is the gift of good health. In this day and age, we're living long, healthy lives, and we're fighting and winning the battle against many diseases and illnesses that were once fatal. Today in this country, we have the opportunity to do more to protect our health than our ancestors could ever imagine.

However, this world-class health care certainly isn't free. Someone has to pay for it. Whether that payment is made through higher taxes, or higher insurance premiums, there is always a cost involved and that cost can be sky high. Even with insurance or assistance, one catastrophic illness or accident can wipe out your hard-earned wealth and leave you in a sad state of affairs.

Like your taxes, my question for you regarding your health is, "what are you doing to protect it?" Whether you realize it or not, when you protect your health, you are protecting your wealth. It's been said that good health is like money in that people only talk about it to the extent that they don't have it. Because of this, many people mistakenly believe that having a good health preservation plan is something that they can put off until later. Well, like a lawsuit, a health care catastrophe can blindside you and hit you when you least expect it.

Taking the initial steps to put a health preservation plan into place, can prevent nasty surprises in your future in the event of a major health crisis. Taking care of your health is one of the most important aspects to your overall wealth preservation plan. Like anything else in the wealth escape, if you fail to plan, you plan to fail. Part of this planning will include an evaluation of different health care planning options including insurance and health savings accounts. We've included an entire chapter on the topic because of its importance.

It's been said that the only constant in the universe is change. A wise man may have made this statement, but it doesn't take a genius to know that this is an absolute truth. Sometimes people may feel as if things never change, but in truth, life is just the opposite. Our lives are in a constant state of change. Whether you realize it or not, your situation changes substantially on a regular basis. Obviously, we all age each year. As we age, we enter different phases of our lives that necessitate different planning strategies. Just as we change individually, our families change each year as well with births, marriages, deaths and divorces. We change jobs, cars, houses, and many people may even change spouses or significant others. Each of these changes requires us to evaluate whether our wealth preservation plan is in need of change as well.

As people stop to reassess whether or not their life changes cause them to need a different vehicle, house, or job, they often ignore other crucial parts of their life. They never consider that as their life changes, their personal preservation plan may need changes in order to keep up with the speed of life. Waiting until it is too late to make any adjustments to your plan can have catastrophic results. An out of date plan may be nearly as bad as having no plan at all. To avoid any challenges that may arise from an outdated plan, you must assess your plan on a regular basis to make sure that it is still a proper fit. Just as a suit that had previously been tailored for your dimensions may not fit you so well anymore, your wealth preservation plan can lose its fit over time as well. For this reason, you must continually assess your personal preservation plan every other year at an absolute minimum.

Over the next several chapters, we will be detailing specific strategies to assist you in the PRESERVE portion of the "Artificial Wealth Trap" E.S.C.A.P.E. Plan. The value of these strategies will vary depending on where you find yourself in the wealth planning process. The best part about the layout of these strategies is that they work extraordinarily well for everyone regardless of their position in the wealth planning continuum. If you find yourself needing some strategies more than others due to your current situation, remember to utilize those that may not be as applicable currently as a resource for future needs.

The task of preserving wealth is one of the most valuable endeavors that you could undertake. Since small leaks have the potential of sinking even the largest ships, you absolutely must learn how to identify and fix them. The information contained in the chapters that follow will enable you to do just that. Take the time to learn them, but more importantly, *do what it takes to apply them.*

CHAPTER 17

PROTECTING WEALTH FROM FRIVOLOUS LAWSUITS

*Lawsuit: A machine which you go into as a pig
and come out of as a sausage.*

Ambrose Bierce

In this chapter, we're going to take a look at how unscrupulous plaintiffs decide to target you with their frivolous lawsuits. In doing so, we're going to discuss some alarming statistics about these frivolous lawsuits and we'll also introduce a new term, "catastrophic lawsuit." Finally, and most importantly, we'll look at some real-world strategies for protecting yourself from these frivolous lawsuits and, when they can't be avoided, how to survive them.

Before getting too far into this chapter we need to familiarize ourselves with the term "asset protection." Asset protection is an area of the law which deals with various strategies for owning personal and commercial assets so that the detrimental effects of a successful lawsuit against us can be mitigated. In my years as an attorney, I've counseled literally thousands of people on various ways in which they can properly structure their assets so that their personal wealth is protected in the event that they or their business is sued. Moreover, since most of my clients are entrepreneurs with multiple businesses or commercial endeavors, I've helped them to structure their businesses so that they are separate and distinct from one another. The reason for this is so that if one business is sued, the other businesses can remain protected from a lawsuit against one of the others. The strategies contained in this chapter can help you to do the same thing.

STRATEGY 238: Identify how you might be attractive as a potential defendant and then become as unattractive as possible.

The first, and probably most important, factor considered by plaintiffs when picking a target for a lawsuit is whether there are any "deep pockets" to go after. In the world of frivolous lawsuits, "deep pockets" refers to a potential defendant with sizeable wealth. You may be surprised to discover that you possess the type of wealth that is sizable enough for someone to target. After all, the strategies contained in this book are helping to make that happen and it would be irresponsible for us to help you to create and accumulate wealth only to lose it all through a frivolous lawsuit. While the good news regarding what you are learning in this book is that you are learning how to create and accumulate real wealth, the bad news is that once you have accumulated it, or at least once someone thinks you have, then there is a good possibility that you will be sued at least once over the course of your lifetime. The reason that deep pockets matter to a potential plaintiff is because it means that they believe that you are worth being sued.

Once a plaintiff has made the determination, correctly or incorrectly, that you have accumulated sufficient wealth, the next determination is whether that wealth can be reached. This is the first opportunity for you to really benefit from a proper asset protection strategy. Simply stated, if a plaintiff (and/or his or her attorney) doesn't think that your wealth can be reached if a judgment is obtained through a successful lawsuit, then for their purposes it is as if you have no assets at all and you become a less attractive person to sue.

A third consideration in determining whether a potential defendant is worth being sued is whether or not his or her wealth can be found. It doesn't do a plaintiff any good just to know that a potential defendant has accumulated wealth if they don't know where to look to find that wealth. Obviously, if the potential target has real property in his or her (or its) name, that type of asset can be discovered. What we're really talking about here are other types of assets such as boats, planes, vehicles, stock certificates, jewelry, cash and other types of valuable tangible or moveable assets. If a plaintiff is successful in obtaining a judgment, he or she is sometimes able to force the defendant to disclose the whereabouts of his or her assets, but even then there are no guarantees.

The next consideration for a potential plaintiff in deciding whether you are worth suing is to determine whether or not they think you will settle the case rather than proceed to a trial. Many people who seemingly make a living out of suing people (yes, those types of people do exist), along with their attorneys, prefer settling cases out of court for a guaranteed payout rather than risking their own time and money in hopes that they will win a judgment in their favor from a jury. This is a calculated *offensive* strategy on their part and it requires a calculated *defensive* strategy on your part.

There are several factors which will induce defendants to settle overtly frivolous lawsuits. Probably the biggest reason why defendants will settle a lawsuit in spite of its frivolous nature is because they don't want to spend the money to defend against the suit. Another inducement for settling frivolous lawsuits is not having the time or energy to deal with them. Oftentimes, this is referred to as "nuisance value." Basically, the rationale is that it is worth it to the defendant to settle the lawsuit rather than have to deal with it over a period of months or even years. Another inducement for settling frivolous lawsuits is whether or not they might damage the reputation of the defendant. As you probably know, an individual's or business' reputation can be irreparably tarnished just by the mere allegation of impropriety, regardless of whether the allegation is true. Because of this, many defendants prefer to quietly settle a frivolous lawsuit rather than have their good name dragged through the mud.

STRATEGY 239: Understand the impact of a catastrophic lawsuit to provide motivation for implementing protective measures.

To define the term "catastrophic lawsuit", we need to talk about jury awards for a moment. One out of every six jury awards in the U.S. exceeds the one million dollar level. If that wasn't bad enough, in many states, one out of every four jury awards exceeds one million dollars. Since businesses are more likely to have deep pockets than individuals, businesses are the usual targets of frivolous lawsuits. In the last five years, 7% of all businesses in the United States suffered a lawsuit costing them in excess of five million dollars. The biggest challenge is that once someone successfully sues a company there are swarms of people who come out of the woodworks wanting the same type of financial windfall for themselves. This mentality is what leads to catastrophic lawsuits.

What would happen to your business if it had a total value of $1 Million and it was hit with a jury award totaling $5 Million? Essentially, you've now just lost your business as well as your livelihood. As if that wasn't bad enough, it gets worse. Even after the business loses its $1 Million value there is still $4 Million remaining unpaid on the judgment. If you operated your business as a sole proprietorship, you would be personally responsible for all debts and liabilities of the business. That means that the plaintiff can now seize your personal wealth to satisfy the remainder of the judgment. The effect of this type of catastrophic lawsuit is that it leaves people penniless.

STRATEGY 240: Hold ownership of your business and/ or commercial assets through formal limited liability business entities.

The first line of defense for your business assets is to establish a formal business entity. A business entity is any method of ownership and organization by which a for-profit endeavor is conducted. (Of course, not-for-profit organizations and charities can be held in a business entity, such as a corporation, but that is outside the scope of this book). In our discussion of the different types of business structures, we'll be looking at the following:

- Sole Proprietorships;
- General Partnerships;
- Corporations;
- S corporations;
- Limited Liability Companies; and
- Limited Partnerships.

As you will see, for each of these business structures we'll be discussing what each one is along with its advantages and disadvantages. We'll also touch briefly on how each type of business structure is taxed. However, we'll address the issue of taxes in more depth later on in the book.

STRATEGY 241: *Protect your small business and personal assets by converting your sole proprietorship into a formal business entity.*

The most popular type of business structure by far is the sole proprietorship. One of the reasons for this is that unless a business is specifically formed as a distinct legal entity such as a corporation or limited liability company, it will be a sole proprietorship by default. That means that you are automatically a sole proprietorship unless you take specific steps to become otherwise. Usually, sole proprietorships are small businesses with one owner. Because these businesses may seem simple, many owners must already believe that they don't need a formal business structure. This mistake can cost you and your business thousands of dollars.

Let's first take a look at the advantages to operating a business as a sole proprietorship. One of the biggest advantages is that it is simple and inexpensive to set up and maintain. To operate a sole proprietorship, you do not have to form an entity with the Secretary of State or file any annual reports. Additionally, sole proprietorships are taxed to the owner and reported on his or her personal tax returns. This can be a plus to you, tax-wise, because if your business takes a loss for the year you can file this loss as a deduction on your personal tax return. However, there are specific limitations on this amount.

The simplicity and ease of operating as a sole proprietorship is quite appealing to many small business people. However, I always caution the people that I speak with that the benefits of a sole proprietorship are far outweighed by the disadvantages. With a sole proprietorship, you receive *zero asset protection benefits*. In other words, the owner of a sole proprietorship not only stands to lose any assets of the business in the event of a lawsuit, the owner also is personally liable for all debts and liabilities (not just jury awards) of the business in the event that the business is unable to pay them. If the owner does not have sufficient cash to pay the judgment, then the holder of the judgment can go after the owner's personal assets. This is a tremendous downside to a sole proprietorship. It is enough of a disadvantage that I advise people to steer clear of this type of business structure completely.

STRATEGY 242: Convert your general partnership into a corporation, LLC, or LP to avoid personal liability for the actions of your business partner.

The second most popular type of business structure is the general partnership. A general partnership is basically a sole proprietorship with more than one owner. Just as with a sole proprietorship, if you and a partner are operating a business and you have not filed the paperwork to specifically designate your business as a formal entity, you are conducting business as a general partnership by default. The advantages of operating a general partnership are the same as those for a sole proprietorship.

General partnerships are simple and inexpensive to set up and maintain because nothing has to be filed with the Secretary of State to create the business and no annual filings are required. Additionally, like sole proprietorships, general partnerships are taxed to the individual owners (partners), which in this instance would mean that the partners would file the profits or losses of the business on their personal tax returns, usually in accordance with their respective contributions to the partnership.

The disadvantage of operating a business as a general partnership is the same as for sole proprietorships and in fact it is magnified. This means that any plaintiffs against or creditors of the general partnership can come after the owners, individually, for satisfaction of a debt. To make matters worse, the plaintiff or creditor can elect which owner to pursue. In other words, if the partnership owes a debt it cannot pay, and only one of the partners has any assets, then the creditor can elect to pursue that partner for 100% of the debt, regardless of which partner actually decided to incur the debt.

Because of this, what has occurred is not only does any particular owner of a general partnership not have any asset protection benefits, the risks are actually multiplied by the number of partners there are in the business. In light of these disadvantages, you should never operate any business as a general partnership.

STRATEGY 243: Incorporate your business to receive asset protection benefits.

One popular method for limiting business liability is to incorporate. The reason for this is that a corporation is an entity with a legal existence that is separate and distinct from its owners (shareholders). In layman's terms, it's simply a legal "person" that you create. Because a corporation is a "person," it can do just about anything that a natural person can do such as own property, sell property, conduct a business, extend credit, take out a loan, file a lawsuit, or be sued. Unlike natural persons, a corporation is generally in existence perpetually until either affirmative action is taken to dissolve the corporation or until the corporation is dissolved by operation of law for failure to properly maintain its existence. This would occur by the corporation's failure to file annual reports or to take other statutorily required actions.

Since a corporation is able to incur its own debt and be sued in its own name, this means that unlike the sole proprietorship and general partnership, a corporation can provide you with tremendous asset protection benefits. Since the corporation's debts and liabilities are its own, the corporation itself will be responsible for them, meaning that the corporation will have liability. Because of this, the owners (shareholders), directors, officers, and employees of a corporation are never personally liable for the corporation's debts as long as the corporation is operated properly. This is called the "corporate shield" and is the basis for how a corporation offers asset protection benefits. Furthermore, if the assets of a corporation are insufficient to pay a plaintiff who has won a judgment against it, the plaintiff will have no recourse against the owners of the corporation.

Because of the asset protection benefits, I would definitely prefer a corporation over a sole proprietorship or a general partnership. However, before you stop reading this and run out to form your own corporation, you've got to realize that there are a few downsides. First, to set up a corporation one must file articles of incorporation with the Secretary of State's office in the state where the corporation is to be domiciled. Of course, this requires a fee. Second, the owner of a corporation must keep up with annual filings, hold annual meetings of both the directors and shareholders, and keep up with other formalities related to the existence of the corporation. This is called "corporate maintenance." While these requirements may at times seem like a lot of trouble, they are easily worth the time and effort considering the asset protection benefits you'll receive from operating your business as a corporation.

STRATEGY 244: *Use a properly structured limited partnership to provide you and your business investors with asset protection while you retain exclusive control over the business.*

Another popular option when choosing a legal entity is the limited partnership. Like a corporation, a limited partnership is a legal entity separate and distinct from its owners (the partners). With the general partnership that we discussed earlier, all of the partners have the right to participate in the management of the business, and each partner is personally liable for the debts and liabilities of the partnership. This is not the case with limited partnerships.

Limited partnerships have two types of partners, general partners and limited partners. Only the general partners have the right to manage the company. By contrast, the limited partners have a right to distributions of the partnership but they have no right of control over the partnership. In other words, the limited partners are purely investors in the business. Because of this, limited partnerships are ideal for entrepreneurs who want to attract investors but don't want to hand over the management or decision-making duties.

With respect to taxation, the limited partnership is treated as a pass-through entity in that all profits and losses of the business are passed through to the partners and included on their personal tax returns. Additionally, with a limited partnership the profits or losses can be allocated between the partners however the partners agree, regardless of each partner's contribution to the business. This allows for flexibility when it comes tax time.

STRATEGY 245: Use a corporation as the general partner of your limited partnership so that you can receive full asset protection benefits.

Before you decide that a limited partnership is the answer for all of your business needs, you've got to understand the potential downsides of this structure. As with the corporation, the limited partners to a limited partnership cannot be held responsible for the debts and liabilities of the partnership. For the general partner, however, there are no asset protection benefits, meaning that if the limited partnership is unable to pay a creditor or judgment against the partnership, the general partner can be held personally responsible. Based on what we've just discussed, it seems like you'll be faced with quite a dilemma if you want to be the general partner of a limited partnership. On the one hand, you'll have complete control over the partnership. On the other hand, that control will come at the cost of all asset protection benefits. This is a major dilemma for small business owners.

Fortunately, there is a solution. The general partner does not have to be an individual. It can be another legal entity such as a corporation that is controlled by you. By acting as the general partner through your corporation, you can receive the benefits of control while at the same time knowing that if you are held accountable for the debts and liabilities of the limited partnership you will still be protected thanks to the corporate shield provided by your corporation. This is an outstanding strategy utilized by those looking for a way to receive the best of both worlds when it comes to control and liability protection.

STRATEGY 246: Use limited liability companies to hold investment assets such as rental properties.

Another option that everyone needs to consider for operating their business ventures is the limited liability company (LLC). An LLC is a relatively new type of business entity that fits somewhere between a partnership/sole proprietorship and a corporation. Like owners of general partnerships or sole proprietorships, LLC owners report business profits or losses on their personal income tax returns because the LLC is another type of pass-through entity. But, like corporations, an LLC is also a legal "person" that is separate and distinct from its owners (called "members"). Similar to a corporation, the owners of an LLC own units of ownership rather than shares of stock. Like a corporation, an LLC's debts and obligations are solely its own which provides enormous asset protection benefits.

The downsides of having an LLC are similar to those of a corporation in that they require initial and annual filings with the Secretary of State, along with the requisite fees. There are other formalities which must be maintained on an annual basis, but these formalities are not as much as for a corporation. Many people mistakenly dwell on this downside and choose to opt for simplicity. Remember, the asset protection benefits of an LLC make these required formalities and fees a minor inconvenience.

When it comes to protecting yourself from lawsuits, don't listen to people, including professionals, who tell you that there is no reason to bother with the time and expense of operating your business from within a business entity. They are wrong. Conducting your business with a corporation, limited partnership, or limited liability company, is the best insurance policy you could ever have to protect your personal assets from the claims of plaintiffs and their frivolous lawsuits.

CHAPTER 18

GETTING DOWN TO BUSINESS BY MAXIMIZING LEGAL LOOPHOLES

An economy breathes through its tax loopholes.

Barry Bracewell-Milnes

In an earlier chapter we learned about the ways in which individuals can lower their personal tax liabilities through the use of deductions, exemptions, and other loopholes provided in the Tax Code. As we saw, with just a little knowledge everyone can and should keep more of their hard-earned money in their pockets rather than losing it to taxes. Despite this knowledge, if we were limited to only using these personal deductions, exemptions, and strategies we would still be paying much more than we should in taxes. Personal tax strategies alone are not enough.

Fortunately, there are many more strategies available to us which can help us to reduce our tax bill. The trick is to change how we report our income, and in doing so, change the rules by which we must play. Simply put, we've got to get down to business. What does this mean? It may surprise you to learn that there are two separate, but very unequal, sets of tax rules in the Tax Code: one for individuals and another for businesses. In order for us to save as much money as legally possible, *we have to structure our affairs so that we can be taxed as a business instead of as an individual whenever possible.*

Starting a small business is one of the greatest tax shelters anyone can create. In this chapter we're going to be looking at some of the ways that we can lower our tax bill by being taxed as a business. Toward the end, we'll be discussing particular business entities and how we can maximize our tax savings by operating our business within the right type of entity. Selecting the "right type of entity" takes knowledge of how the different types of entities are taxed.

STRATEGY 247: Understand why you want to be taxed as a business rather than as an individual.

So why is it so much better to be taxed as a business rather than as an individual? The answer is deductions. With individuals, deductions are quite limited and not all taxpayers have the ability to claim the same deductions. With businesses, however, they can deduct any "ordinary and necessary" business expenses. What expenses constitute "ordinary and necessary" can be endless, and so can your ability to save money through the use of business expenses. This is vastly different from the individual tax rules and provides us with opportunities that would not otherwise be available.

The best way to illustrate how to most effectively take advantage of the business tax rules is to take a look at some of the incredible tax strategies available to businesses.

STRATEGY 248: Convert personal assets to business assets.

Amounts spent on personal assets such as furniture, automobiles, computers, and other tools and equipment are not eligible for tax deductions for individuals. However, if you start a legitimate business, and convert these assets to business use, the business use percentage can be deducted. This can be accomplished by leasing or renting the personal assets to the business, which means that you don't necessarily have to go out and buy a bunch of new stuff. This is a tremendous way to immediately free up some additional cash by legally reducing your tax bill.

STRATEGY 249: Take advantage of fringe benefits.

"Fringe benefits" are any type of compensation other than cash that is provided to you by your business. Examples of fringe benefits are health insurance, medical reimbursement plans, educational assistance, child care assistance, or employer-provided vehicles, just to name a few. Chances are, you're probably paying for these expenses yourself right now with after-tax dollars, meaning that you are paying for these expenses out of your own paycheck *after* you've paid taxes on your income. This is something you need to change.

By opening your own business and structuring that business as a C corporation, these expenses can be provided to you. Plus, they can be instant tax deductions for your business. By continuing to pay for these services yourself with after-tax dollars, you are giving up a tax benefit which could help you save hundreds or even thousands of dollars a year. This is money that could be reallocated to pay down debt and/or build up wealth.

STRATEGY 250: Decrease your business' taxable income by shifting income and expenses into the most favorable tax year.

If your business is on a "cash basis" accounting method you can shift income and expenses from one year to another, and as a result, lower your business' taxable income. "Cash basis" accounting means that income and expenses are counted when the cash is actually received (income) or spent (expenses). By contrast, the "accrual basis" of accounting counts income and expenses not when the cash is actually received or spent, but rather, takes into account your business' accounts receivable and accounts payable.

317

When "shifting income," what you are actually doing is deferring income and accelerating expenses, or vice versa, in a combined effort to shift your business' taxable income from the current tax year to the next, or from the next year to the current year if you think your business will be in a higher tax bracket the next year. In order to shift income to the next year, your business should delay cash receipts by delaying billing and accelerate expenses by paying all legitimate business expenses by the end of the year. If it is advantageous to shift income from the next year to the current year, you will want to accelerate cash receipts by sending out your bills as soon as possible and by delaying cash payments for business expenditures.

STRATEGY 251: Offer yourself a retirement plan sponsored by your business.

One of my favorite tax strategies is to offer a retirement plan through your business. By doing this, you can give your business one of the largest deductions available while at the same time working towards turning yourself into a millionaire. In other words, this strategy is a tax-saving *and* wealth-building tool which automatically places it at the top of my list of most effective strategies.

How does this strategy work? Suppose that your business pays you a salary, and you then invest part of your salary into a retirement plan that you've established. Under this arrangement, your business gets a tax deduction for the amount of money it paid you in salary, while you get a tax deduction for the amount of money you invested into the retirement plan. Now consider what would happen if your business sets up a retirement plan for your benefit through a profit sharing arrangement and/or matches you dollar-for-dollar for what you invest. In addition to your business having a deduction for the amount of your salary, it would also have a deduction for the value of its contributions to your retirement plan. This is the type of double duty that I like to see my strategies perform. You can do the same thing with your finances if you can learn to implement these strategies.

STRATEGY 252: *Pay your business' expenses directly from a bank account set up solely for your business.*

All tax-deductible business expenses that are paid directly by your business immediately become tax deductions for your business. However, any tax-deductible business expenditures that you personally pay for can only be considered tax deductions for your business at the point in time that your business reimburses you for those expenditures. Therefore, not only is it easier to take business deductions for expenses when your business actually pays for them, this cuts down on unnecessary accounting as well. The biggest benefit is that this takes care of things for you without you having to remember to reimburse yourself time and again for business expenses that you paid for personally.

STRATEGY 253: *Take a business deduction on your vehicle.*

If you use your automobile for business purposes, you can deduct the actual business related operating costs during the year or deduct the standard IRS mileage allowance of 50.5 cents per mile for 2008. The standard mileage allowance includes all costs except parking and tolls. If you are self employed, you may also deduct the business use percentage of any automobile financing charges. If you are an employee, however, auto financing charges are not deductible.

If you placed your automobile into business service prior to 2008 and have always used the standard mileage allowance, you may continue to use the standard allowance in 2008 or deduct your actual business-related expenses plus straight line depreciation (unless the automobile has been fully depreciated). Once you elect to use actual expenses for any given tax year, you are required to continue using the actual expense method for as long as you use that particular automobile. You can switch from the standard mileage allowance to actual cost, but you cannot switch from actual cost to the standard allowance.

The standard mileage rate also may be used for business trips in a van, pickup, or panel truck as if it were a car. The rate may not be used to deduct the costs of an automobile used for non-business income-producing personal activities. The mileage rate also cannot be used for taxicabs or other vehicles used for hire, such as a fleet operation. Otherwise, you can use the standard mileage rate for up to four vehicles in a business at the same time.

STRATEGY 254: Use the vehicle expense deduction method that gives you the greater deduction.

As a general "rule of thumb," if you use your automobile 50% of the time or less for business use, the standard mileage deduction will be better. If you use the actual expense method, you must keep receipts for all "out of pocket expenses." To make this determination, you really need to know how much you use the vehicle for business versus personal use. Keeping accurate records, such as with a mileage log, can make this much easier and much more accurate.

STRATEGY 255: Deduct all expenses associated with business-related travel.

Whenever you travel on behalf of your business, 100% of the expense qualifies as a business tax deduction. These expenses include transportation, rental cars, lodging, laundry & cleaning, and communication costs associated with the travel. As mentioned in an earlier chapter, many people take advantage of business trips to meetings, seminars, and conventions to make travel to desired locations deductible. While there are rules that must be followed, this can provide you with a substantial discount through the deductibility of these travel expenses.

STRATEGY 256: Deduct meals and entertainment expenses subject to the 50% limitation.

In addition to the costs of traveling for your business, you can also deduct the costs of meals and entertainment expenses subject to a 50% limitation. These expenses relate to the cost of dollars spent to provide food and/or to entertain customers or potential customers. To determine if such dollars qualify for a deduction, the following criteria must be met:

1. The expense was made with the expectation that it generates income.

2. The expense was made while actually discussing business or during activities associated with the discussion of business.

3. The expense was made when business is the main purpose for the meeting.

STRATEGY 257: Take advantage of the depreciation of your business assets to lower your tax bill.

Depreciation is the method that a business owner uses to deduct the cost of tangible (can be seen and felt) property that has a useful life of more than one year. The rules regarding depreciation are detailed in IRS Publication 946. You can access this publication via the internet at www.irs.gov. To take advantage of this strategy, you must first determine the depreciable basis of the property (usually cost or fair market value), the recovery period, the method and convention, and the elected Section 179 cost. The following are the methods of depreciation calculation:

Straight Line. With straight line depreciation, the depreciable basis is divided by the number of years in the recovery period. The annual amount of depreciation remains the same each year.

Example: Bob purchases a computer for $2,000 that is used 100% for business purposes. Since a computer has an IRS assigned recovery period of 5 years, Bob would deduct depreciation expense of $400 ($2,000/5 years) for each year.

200% Declining Balance Method (200DB). The 200% declining balance method is calculated similarly to the straight line method, but with a major twist. Example: Assume the same facts as stated for Bob in the straight line example but Bob elects to use the 200DB method. During the first year, the $2,000 cost of the computer is divided by the 5 year recovery period. The $400 amount is then multiplied by 2 (the 200% method), giving Bob a first year depreciation amount of $800.

Now for the declining balance portion of the formula: In year two, Bob subtracts the first year's depreciation from his cost ($2,000 cost minus $800 depreciation = $ 1,200). The "adjusted" basis of $1,200 is then divided by the 5 year recovery period ($1,500/5 years = $240). The $240 is then multiplied by 2, giving Bob a $480 depreciation deduction in year two. Using this example, it is quite evident as to why this method is also sometimes referred to as "accelerated depreciation." Using straight line, Bob would have deducted $800 ($400 x 2 years) of depreciation. If Bob had elected the 200DB method, he would have deducted $1,280 ($800 + $480).

150% Declining Balance (150DB). This method is calculated the same as 200DB except that instead of multiplying by 2, you would multiply by 1.5. For example: Year one straight line depreciation is $400. For 150DB, you would multiply $400 x 1.5, giving you a first year depreciation deduction of $600. Note: When electing either 200DB or 150DB, you can switch to straight line for the remaining recapture period when straight line gives you a higher deductible amount.

Section 179 (Asset Expensing). Asset expensing can be used for qualified business assets purchased and placed into business service. Assets previously purchased and used for personal use and then converted to business use are not eligible for §179 treatment, nor are any real property or assets that are used in a rental. Asset expensing allows the taxpayer to deduct the business use percentage of the total cost in the year the asset is placed into service. To be eligible, the business use percentage must be at least 51%. Example: Bob purchases his computer for $2,000 and it is used 100% for business use. If he meets all other qualifications, he can "asset expense" the entire cost of the computer in the first year of business use. If the business use percentage of the computer is 60%, $1,200 (60% x $2,000) could be expensed in the year the asset was placed into service. The total cost of §179 property that you can deduct in any one year period increases to $128,000 in 2008.

STRATEGY 258: Use straight line depreciation when appropriate.

You should always use straight line depreciation in the following circumstances:

1. When the business use percentage of tangible property is 50% or less.

2. For all real estate property, whether residential rental or business use.

3. For luxury automobiles used for business, if you elect to use a percentage of actual expenses.

4. For business assets that you think you will have actual usage for a period of time less than the IRS recovery period. For example, if you purchase a computer which has a 5 year life, and you plan to sell that computer and upgrade in two years, you would use straight line.

STRATEGY 259: Use 200DB when you have little or no profits in the year the asset is acquired.

You should use the 200DB depreciation method in years when your business has realized little or no profits. For example: Bob expects little or no profit for his first year of operations and will remain in the 15% tax bracket. However, he expects his income to increase substantially in the next year, placing him in the 28% income tax bracket and subjecting him to an additional 15.3% self-employment tax liability, for a total federal tax rate of 43.3% (28% income tax plus

15.3% self-employment tax.) If Bob elects to asset expense (Section 179) his $2,000 computer in the first year, his tax savings would be $300 ($2,000 deduction x 15% tax bracket = $300).

STRATEGY 260: When necessary, claim your entire depreciation deduction at one time.

Instead of spreading out an asset's depreciation over a number of years, by electing § 179 of the Tax Code you are entitled to take the entire depreciation deduction in the current tax year. Reasons to elect § 179 Asset Expensing deductions are:

1. To avoid the short year depreciation rules.

2. To increase an individual's itemized deductions because of the 7.5% and 2% AGI limits on various deductions (medical expenses and miscellaneous itemized deductions).

3. To increase the earned income credit for Schedule C filers.

4. To help the taxpayer to qualify for a deductible IRA contribution by decreasing AGI.

STRATEGY 261: Avoid making your spouse an employee of your business if possible.

The tax law is very clear that if you want to hire a spouse or a child, you must create a true employer-employee relationship. The spousal employee must be paid a reasonable wage for the services provided, and as with any other employee, should turn in time sheets for the hours actually worked. It is strongly recommended that formal job descriptions be prepared as all business employees (except owners and their children under 18) are subject to payroll taxes. These taxes (Social Security and Medicare) add 15.3% to the cost of wages and must be paid on all employees' incomes up to $97,500. You must pay 2.9% on all earned income over that. Federal unemployment taxes add another 6.2% of the first $7,000 of wages paid to every employee.

If a spouse is on the payroll, you will incur other expenses, such as unemployment and disability taxes, and workers' compensation insurance as well.

Once you become an employer, you must submit quarterly and annual payroll tax returns and issue a Form W-2 at the end of the year. In some states, you also may be required to cover the spousal employee under the appropriate workers' compensation laws. Hiring a spouse will not increase or decrease your income tax liability, but will increase the amount you pay in Social Security taxes which is why I generally advise against it.

STRATEGY 262: Hire your children "tax-free."

Unlike hiring a spouse, hiring your children can save taxes because you do not file a joint tax return with your children. The rules for hiring a spouse also apply to hiring your children. Other rules also apply. The children must be old enough to enter into a true employer-employee agreement (one tax court ruled that the child must be at least 7 years old) the children must actually perform the work, they must be paid a reasonable amount (minimum wage would not be deemed unreasonable), and the children must be paid on a timely basis throughout the year. It is strongly recommended that you prepare formal job descriptions and have the children prepare time sheets. In other words, you should view your child just as you would any non-related employees.

If the child is under age 18 and employed by the parent (not a corporation or a partnership with a non-parental party), the parent can exempt the child from Social Security. Also, a single person claimed as a dependent by another taxpayer can earn up to $5,450 without owing any income tax. Note that this does not mean that you can automatically pay the child that much, the wage must be reasonable. You must also be in full compliance with all federal and state child labor laws. Complete information can be obtained from the U.S. Department of Labor and from your individual State Department of Labor or Employment.

If you meet all the applicable requirements, the wages that you pay your children will be deductible as a business expense. Assume that you are a sole proprietor in the 28% tax bracket and also subject to the 15.3% self employment tax. If you paid your 15 year old child $5,000, you would save $2,165 in taxes. This is a strategy that you will definitely want to explore.

STRATEGY 263: Take advantage of income shifting.

With this strategy, we're going to take the lesson learned from the previous strategy and take it one step further. One of the easiest strategies for using a business to lower taxes, both business and personal taxes, is to shift income from taxpayers in a high tax bracket to taxpayers in a lower tax bracket. In other words, instead of your business paying income to yourself when you may be in a higher tax bracket, pay that same income to another member of your family who may be in a lower tax bracket. By shifting the income, the taxes paid on that income will be lower since the family member is in a lower tax bracket. Additionally, the amount of employment taxes that your business has to pay will be lower as well.

STRATEGY 264: Take advantage of the tax strategies for investment real estate.

Real estate investments fall into two separate categories, your personal residence and investment real estate. This section will address investment real estate. First and foremost, investment real estate is a long-term, illiquid investment. By its very nature, most investors are looking for tax-deferred capital appreciation (the property increases in value, but you owe no taxes until you realize that gain). Current cash flow is also important. Hopefully, you receive more in rents than you pay out in operating expenses and generate a positive cash flow. The benefit with investment real estate is that you are able to shelter that cash flow through the use of depreciation.

Depreciation is the term used for deducting the cost of the property over a specified length of time. Under current law, residential real estate is depreciated over 27.5 years and commercial real estate (shopping centers or office buildings) is depreciated over 39 years. You must allocate your purchase price between the cost of the structure and the cost of the land. The building is depreciable, the land is not.

STRATEGY 265: *When depreciating real estate investments, allocate 80% of the purchase price to the building and 20% to the value of the land.*

Suppose you purchase a single family residence for investment purposes for $100,000. You would allocate 80% ($80,000) of the total purchase price to the depreciable basis of the building and 20% ($20,000) to the non-depreciable basis of the land. Common exceptions to the 80/20 rule would be if you purchased the land and then built the structure. In this case, you would obviously know the cost basis of the land and building. Also, in some jurisdictions, the property tax assessor places a separate value on the land and the improvements thereon. While you cannot, for income tax purposes, use the assessment values, you can use the percentage allocation. Another example would be that if you purchased a condominium, you obviously do not own the land, so the entire cost would be allocated to the structure.

STRATEGY 266: *Write off appliances separately.*

For this strategy, let's take the same $100,000 single family residence in which the building itself will be depreciated over 27.5 years. The contents of the building that are not a physical part of the structure are eligible for accelerated depreciation (200DB) over a much shorter period of time (five years). Assume a $100,000 purchase of an investment property with an 80% allocation to the building and its contents. Assume further that the fair market value of the contents (carpets, appliances, heating and air conditioning units, and hot water heaters) is $1,400. If this $1,400 value is left in the $80,000 depreciable basis, you would have a depreciation expense of approximately $51 per year ($1,400 divided by 27.5 years), requiring 14 years to deduct 50% of the cost of those assets. If you take the extra effort to allocate the $1,400 value of those assets and choose to depreciate them over their allowable cost recovery period of five years and use accelerated depreciation (200DB), your depreciation deduction in the first year would be $560 and in the second year, $336, allowing you to deduct 64% of the cost in only two years. This is referred to as "cost segregation." For more information on utilizing this strategy, contact us at info@artificialwealthtrap.com.

STRATEGY 267: Whenever possible classify individuals who work for your business as independent contractors rather than employees.

A lot of tax professionals advise their clients that they should always classify people who work for them as employees so that they can take advantage of the tax deductible nature of the business' payroll-related expenditures. This is very poor advice. Instead, whenever possible you should classify people who work for you as independent contractors. This way your business will save more money by reducing payroll taxes such as FICA, Medicare taxes, Federal unemployment taxes, and State unemployment taxes. Additionally, you'll save money on insurance premiums, workers compensation, and other expenses that come with having employees.

How do you know when you must classify a worker as an employee rather than an independent contractor? While the law varies in every state, there are some general considerations to follow, such as:

1. Whether your business provides the worker with tools and training.
2. The amount of control your business has over the worker's hours.
3. The amount of supervision your business has over the worker.
4. The length of time during which the services will be performed.

5. Whether the worker is paid by the hour rather than by the job.

6. The degree of permanence of the working relationship.

By no means is this list all-inclusive. If you are unsure about a worker's status, consult with your attorney or tax accountant. This can be a great strategy if your workers qualify. However, as with all tax strategies you should seek professional assistance before you begin implementing this strategy.

STRATEGY 268: Learn how business entities are taxed so that you can select the best type for your small business.

When discussing how to lower your business taxes, the first place to begin is with business entities. In a previous chapter we discussed how business entities can protect you from lawsuits, but they can also provide you with significant tax benefits as well. As you may recall, we discussed the fact that one should never use a sole proprietorship or general partnership to operate a business because they do not offer any asset protection benefits. Accordingly, we will only focus on how corporations, limited partnerships, and limited liability companies are taxed.

STRATEGY 269: Zero out your corporation at the end of the year to avoid double taxation.

The first entity type we will discuss is the corporation. Most people have heard of "C corporations" and "S corporations" but not everyone knows how they are different. First, all corporations are C corporations by default. A C corporation is a taxpayer and it reports its gains or losses on its own tax return. This can be beneficial in some instances but can be a source of complaints as well.

One of the biggest complaints about C corporations is that there is a risk of "double taxation." Since a C corporation is a taxpayer, it pays a tax on its income. If the C corporation realizes a profit and pays dividends to its shareholders, this dividend is also taxed at the shareholder level. Double taxation occurs when the same dollars are taxed once as income to the corporation and again as a dividend to the shareholder. With some simple tax planning, this double taxation can easily be avoided.

First, all payments from the C corporation to its shareholders should be considered "salary" instead of "dividends" whenever possible. (Please note that we are presuming that the C corporation in this illustration is a small, closely-held business where all shareholders are actively involved in the business.) The reason for this is because the salary paid to the C corporation's employees is tax-deductible, thus the value of the salary is not computed in the C corporation's taxable income. Because of this, the amount paid as salary is only taxed once.

This strategy brings up the second way to avoid double taxation, which is to offset all of the C corporation's income with corporate expenses. This is referred to as "zeroing out" the corporation. When this occurs, the C corporation itself will not show a profit at the end of the year, and thus will not owe any income tax. If you are considering a corporation for your business, it's highly recommended that you seek assistance before making this decision. For more information, visit www.secretmillionaire.com.

STRATEGY 270: Structure your corporation as an S corporation to take advantage of "pass-through taxation."

Now that we know the definition of a C corporation, let's talk about the S corporation. In order to create an S corporation, one simply has to file a S corporation Election with the IRS. With an S corporation, the corporation itself is no longer a taxpayer. Rather, the profits and losses of the corporation are taxed at the individual level. This type of taxation is referred to as "pass-through taxation."

Pass-through taxation can be an especially valuable tax tool, especially in the early years of a new business. With many new businesses, because of start-up costs, developing a customer base, etc., the business will show a loss the first year or two of its existence. If the new business is an S corporation, the business losses can be used as a deduction on the individual shareholder's tax return.

STRATEGY 271: Use S corporations to avoid self-employment taxes.

Another great benefit of S corporations is that they can be used to avoid self-employment taxes. Suppose that an S corporation is owned by one person, who is also an employee. With an S corporation, only the salary that is paid to the owner/employee is subject to the self-employment tax. The remaining income of the S corporation can be distributed to the owner/employee and is not subject to the self-employment tax.

Let's look at an example to illustrate this point: Suppose that Jude is the sole shareholder of an S corporation which owns a bicycle shop. Jude works as the manager. In keeping with the industry standard, Jude pays himself $40,000 a year in salary. The bicycle shop makes $100,000 total for the year, and the remaining $60,000 is distributed to Jude from the S corporation. The total employment tax paid is only for the $40,000 paid to Jude as a salary (15.3% of $40,000 paid 1/2 by the S corporation and 1/2 by Jude). The $60,000 distributed to Jude is not subject to employment taxes. If Jude had been operating the bicycle shop as a sole proprietor, however, he would have owed much more in self-employment taxes.

One thing to keep in mind, however, when using this strategy is that the salary paid must be reasonable. In other words, in the above example Jude could not have paid himself a salary of only $5,000 and then distributed the remaining $95,000 free of employment taxes.

STRATEGY 272: *Use a limited partnership as another way to avoid self-employment taxes.*

The next entity type we will discuss is the limited partnership (LP). As you will recall from our earlier chapter, a limited partnership is comprised of two types of partners: general partners and limited partners. The general partner is the only partner with the right to control the partnership. By contrast, the limited partners are investors only and do not have any voice in the management of the entity. Because of these roles, the general partner's income derived from the LP will always be "active income." Active income is income for which services have been performed. This includes wages, tips, salaries, commissions and income from businesses in which there is material participation. With active income, the wage earner will owe self-employment taxes. The income earned by limited partners is passive income since they have no control over the LP. Passive income is generally made up of income received from investment assets.

Like an S corporation, a limited partnership is taxed as a pass-through entity. Additionally, the profits and losses of the partnership can be allocated between the partners however they wish, regardless of the ownership percentages of the partners. This provides us with some great tax planning opportunities.

STRATEGY 273: *Use a limited liability company (LLC) for businesses producing passive income such as rental properties.*

The final business entity we will discuss is the limited liability company, or LLC. Just as limited partnerships were ideal for businesses which produce active income, LLCs are perfect for businesses generating passive income, such as the income realized from rental properties or securities investments.

332

Like the limited partnership, LLCs are taxed as pass-through entities, which again means that the gains and losses of the business are filed on the returns of the LLC's owners (members). LLCs are ideal for passive income-producing businesses for two reasons. First, with an LLC we are able to recoup losses such as depreciation that we would otherwise lose with other entity types. Even in instances where a rental property is generating positive cash flow, an LLC can claim depreciation which can reduce the amount of taxable income or even show a loss. This loss, of course, will be a tax deduction for the individual owners of the LLC. Second, LLCs allow for "free transferability of assets," which is an accounting term meaning that whenever the LLC's owners put money into, or take money out of, the LLC, such transaction will not be considered a taxable event. By contrast, with a corporation, whenever money is put into or taken out of the entity such transaction must be considered a loan or dividend/salary.

In closing, we've discussed a lot of strategies in this chapter. Some of these strategies are quite simple, yet highly valuable. Others, unfortunately, are a bit more complicated. Yet from everything we've discussed, if there is only one strategy in this chapter that you remember, let it be the following:

STRATEGY 274: Always act, and think, like a business.

Whenever you purchase goods or services, make an investment, or act as an entrepreneur you should always be acting and thinking like a business. By following this strategy, you will automatically give yourself the benefit of being taxed like a business instead of like an individual. Remember, the two tax systems are very unequal. People who live paycheck-to-paycheck typically act and think like individuals. Wealthy people act and think as businesses and therefore are taxed as businesses. You need to make this change and begin doing things differently. The difference can mean thousands of dollars to you each and every year.

CHAPTER 19

PRESERVING YOUR ESTATE FOR YOUR FAMILY

*We have long had death and taxes as
the two standards of inevitability.
But there are those who believe that death
is the preferable of the two.*

Erwin N. Griswold

Many individuals mistakenly think that they have to own numerous assets or have a high income or net worth in order to have an "estate." This just isn't true. As long as you are alive, you have some estate planning concerns that will need to be handled upon your death. It's true that the higher your net worth, or income, the more technical your needs may be, but everyone needs to have at least a basic plan. Remember, either you put a plan together for your estate or your state will do it for you. Let me assure you that you will not like their plan.

All too often people worry about lawsuits and income taxes as being the largest threats to their wealth and virtually ignore the threats posed by a lack of estate planning. As a result, their families end up receiving far less than they should and the government ends up with far more than it should. Don't let this happen to you. Follow the strategies contained in this chapter to take care of your estate and your family.

STRATEGY 275: Become familiar with estate planning and formulate a plan for your assets.

Estate planning is a term we've all heard but one that many do not really understand. Essentially, it is the process of setting into place your financial affairs so that things can be efficiently and easily passed on to your heirs and beneficiaries. What many people do not understand is that estate planning can also be considered as planning for their continued prosperity while they are alive as well. Another common misconception that many people have is that they think that simply having a will constitutes an adequate estate plan. As we will discuss in great detail later on in this chapter, if your entire estate plan depends on a will, you really haven't planned at all because a will does not provide your estate with any protection from probate.

STRATEGY 276: Take steps to avoid dying intestate.

If an individual dies without a will he or she is considered to have died "intestate." Basically, the term "intestate" refers to dying without a plan for how one's estate should be settled. In this event, state law will determine the beneficiaries of the estate. A common misconception that many people hold is that when one dies intestate all of his or her assets simply pass on to the state. This is generally not the case. Depending on the laws of intestate succession in a given state, if a person who is married dies intestate, his or her spouse would receive all of the marital or community property. Their spouse would also receive part of their separate property, with the remainder to be distributed to his or her children or grandchildren, parents, sisters, brothers, nieces, nephews or other close relatives. If a person who dies intestate is not married, then his or her assets would be distributed first to their children or grandchildren, if there are any, and then to their then living parents, sisters, brothers, nieces, nephews or other close relatives, in that order.

Certainly, there are a lot of variables about what can happen when one dies intestate, but some things are clear. Through the probate process (which we'll discuss later), the state, not the individual or their family, will get to determine who gets which of the deceased individual's assets. Moreover, the state would determine the guardianship of the decedent's minor children. None of this has to happen so long as you avoid dying intestate by establishing an estate plan.

STRATEGY 277: Avoid probate so that your estate does not lose 10% or more of its value in administrative expenses, legal fees, and court costs.

If a person passes away without a will, with a will, or without an alternate form of estate planning, their estate is going to go through probate. One's "estate" is made up of their total property, both real and personal, which is left at the time of their death. Probate is the legal process used to wind up an individual's legal and financial affairs after their death. Like any legal process, when an estate is probated, a case (called a "probate case") is opened at the courthouse in the county where the person lived. During the probate process the assets and liabilities of the estate are identified and debts, including taxes, are paid from the estate. The remainder of the assets is then distributed to the beneficiaries of the estate as provided by a will. If there was no will, then the probate court distributes the assets in accordance with state law. This would be the law of intestate succession referred to earlier. The probate court, if necessary, will be given the task of choosing guardians for any minor children left behind by a person who dies.

To people unfamiliar with the process, probate may sound like a nice and tidy process for closing the final chapter of one's life, but in reality, the probate process can be a logistical nightmare. Whenever an estate is probated, the headaches for those left behind can seem endless. First, an executor is appointed by the court to be in charge of the estate as it goes through the probate process. If there is a will, the court will usually approve whoever is named in the will as the executor. The executor is monitored and/or must constantly seek approval for their actions from the probate court. The executor is also accountable to all of the heirs and beneficiaries of the estate. Thanks to the complexity of the probate process, you probably wouldn't wish the job of executor upon your worst enemy. Because the role of an executor can be difficult, especially for larger estates, an attorney usually serves in this role. Of course, the executor is entitled to a fee, paid from the estate, for his or her services. If the executor is an attorney, those fees can be substantial.

The second problem with having an estate probated is the amount of time involved. A probate case is a court case just like any other, and like any case, probate cases can take many months or even years to complete. While the estate is in probate, the probate judge must be sought for approval for every action taken with regard to assets. The executor must provide the court with an accounting of all assets in the estate and the court dictates when assets may be used to pay debts and when they can be distributed to heirs and beneficiaries. As you can probably imagine, if a person dies leaving a stay-at-home spouse and small children who depend on their assets for support, the probate process can be especially troubling.

Third, if your estate is probated, all of the assets which are included therein will be a matter of public record. This means that your friends, neighbors, coworkers and anyone else who is curious can find out exactly what assets you are leaving behind. This can be especially problematic if a person dies leaving creditors or if they have chosen not to leave anything to a particular family member. With just a simple phone call to the clerk of the probate court anyone who thinks they should get a piece of your pie can find out what assets you've left behind and they can then file a claim against your estate.

The next challenge with probate is that it is expensive. As we alluded to above, any estate that goes through the probate process can be drained by up to 10% of its overall value. This draining away of your wealth is done by administrative expenses, legal fees, debts, court costs and other types of expenses associated with the probate process. As a result, you can wind up leaving your beneficiaries with much less than what you intended.

Another challenge with probate is that the probate judge, not you, makes the ultimate determination as to the ownership of your remaining assets as well as the guardianship of any minor children. Of course, people usually try to take these decisions out of the hands of the court

338

by executing a will. However, the probate judge can easily overrule your decisions by operation of law or if the will is contested.

And finally, if all of these reasons weren't enough to make you want to avoid probate, consider this: Not only must your estate be probated where you live but also in every other state where you hold property. This means that if you lived in Nevada and your estate contains a piece of real estate in California, your executor will have to open a probate case in California as well. In other words, you've just doubled the harmful effects of probate. As more and more people begin to own properties in more than one state, this becomes a greater issue. The key is to avoid all of these challenges by avoiding the probate process altogether.

STRATEGY 278: Take steps in your estate planning to avoid, or at least reduce, any potential amount of money that your estate will owe in estate taxes.

In terms of preserving wealth, the second threat posed by not having a proper estate plan in place is the estate tax, also referred to as the "death tax." For a definition of the estate tax, no definition is better than the one given by our friends at the Internal Revenue Service:

> *The Estate Tax is a tax on your right to transfer property at your death.*

You read that correctly. The government has put a tax on "your right" to pass on your assets to your family or other beneficiaries after you have died. This means that even though you've already paid taxes on the assets you've accumulated, those same assets are going to be taxed again when you exercise your right to pass them down to your heirs and beneficiaries.

In speaking on this topic and counseling my own clients, I've found that there is a misconception today concerning who is subject to the estate tax. A lot of people mistakenly think that only the super-wealthy will ever have to worry about estate taxes. In reality, nothing could be further from the truth. In 2007 and 2008, the threshold amount for estate taxes is only two million dollars. This means that every dollar over this amount will be subject to the estate tax.

Why do I say "only" two million dollars? Well, hopefully you've paid close attention to the "Accumulate" section of this book and will have accumulated (or be in the process of accumulating) a great deal of wealth by the time you pass away. Yet even for people who leave behind an average-sized estate, reaching this two million dollar threshold is not that difficult because everything you own is included in your estate. Consider the definition of one's "estate" from the IRS:

> *The Gross Estate of the decedent consists of an accounting of everything you own or have certain interests in at the date of death. The fair market value of these items is used, not necessarily what you paid for them or what their values were when you acquired them. The total of all of these items is your "Gross Estate."*

Bear in mind that this gross estate includes all cash, securities, real estate, insurance, annuities, business interests and other assets owned by the decedent when they die. Additionally, assets which you have control over (such as incomplete gifts or assets held in revocable trusts) are also included for estate tax purposes. Furthermore, as noted in the above quote, the value of each asset is not what you paid for it, rather, it is the asset's fair market value at the time of your death. To complicate matters, most married people leave the bulk of their assets to their surviving spouse tax-free because of the unlimited marital deduction. While that is good, it is merely a reprieve because when that surviving spouse dies, their total estate (i.e., the estate of both spouses included) is even more likely to reach the two million dollar threshold.

STRATEGY 279: Keep current on the basic federal estate tax laws and plan accordingly.

So now that we know that the estate tax is a tax upon your right to pass on assets to your heirs and beneficiaries and that it includes everything you own, the question now becomes, how much is it? For the taxable

340

years 2007 and 2008 the minimum estate tax rate is 45%. This means that for an estate valued at $3,000,000, there would be a tax of 45% assessed on $1,000,000 (the amount over the $2,000,000 exclusion), or $450,000 that must be paid to the government. In the year 2009, the minimum threshold for the estate tax rises from $2,000,000 to $3,500,000 with the minimum tax rate staying at 45%. In 2010, the estate tax is repealed entirely.

This sounds like great news until you find out what happens after that. Unfortunately, barring a change in the law, the estate tax goes back into effect with the minimum threshold dropping to $1,000,000 starting in 2011. This will affect many more people and will likely affect you if you apply the strategies in this book for accumulating more wealth. The good news is that we've got strategies for building wealth without ending up losing it all from the devastation of these taxes.

STRATEGY 280: Develop your estate plan around three goals: passing along your estate to your heirs and beneficiaries, avoiding probate, and reducing or eliminating estate taxes.

So far we've learned the definition of estate planning, that you want to keep your estate out of probate, and that you want to avoid or reduce estate taxes as much as possible. We've also learned that a will provides you with zero help in your efforts to stay out of probate. Remember to always focus on three goals with your estate planning:

1. Passing along your estate to your heirs and beneficiaries as efficiently as possible;
2. Avoiding probate; and
3. Reducing, or eliminating, any potential estate taxes.

For the rest of this chapter, we'll be discussing various strategies and tools available for accomplishing these goals.

One of the greatest tools available to smart estate planners is the revocable living trust. This has become a common tool for estate planning but many people are still unfamiliar with the whole concept of a trust. The term itself causes people to conjure up images of the super-wealthy. Yes, the super-wealthy typically do have trusts and so should you. The concept is not overly difficult, it's just different. A trust, no matter what type of trust we're talking about, is simply a contractual agreement. In essence, a trust is merely an agreement where a person (the "trustor", "settlor" or "grantor") gives property to another person (the "trustee") to hold and manage said property for the benefit of someone else ("the beneficiary"). Depending on the type of trust, the trustor, trustee, and beneficiary can be the same person, two persons, or more. All trusts are governed by the terms of the trust agreement and local law.

Generally speaking, trusts come in two types: trusts created during a person's life ("inter vivos") and those created by operation of a will or other document upon the death of the settlor ("testamentary"). Inter vivos trusts are usually revocable, which means that they can be changed or even eliminated during the life of the settlor. By contrast, testamentary trusts are irrevocable, meaning that they cannot be changed. In terms of the creation of a trust, there must be a signed trust agreement and a transfer of property to the trust itself.

The primary type of trust used for estate planning purposes is the revocable living trust. A living trust is typically created by an individual or married couple, which holds and manages all of their personal assets until the time of their death. Once they have passed away, the trustee of the living trust pays off any debts and then distributes the assets within the trust to the beneficiaries. The trustee can also continue to hold assets in the trust for the benefit of a beneficiary who is either a minor or otherwise incapable of conducting their own financial affairs.

STRATEGY 282: Place your estate inside a revocable living trust so that your assets will be distributed to your beneficiaries outside of probate.

First, let's talk about avoiding probate. As mentioned above, the reason why an estate, or an individual asset, goes into probate is because its owner has died. With a living trust, since it actually holds title to an individual's assets, just because the individual has died does not mean that the trust has died. Thus, the estate does not have to be probated, and the individual's assets can pass to their beneficiaries outside of probate.

STRATEGY 283: Properly fund your living trust so that it will operate to provide you with the benefits for which it is intended.

The number one mistake people make when it comes to their living trust is that they fail to fund it. *Funding* refers to the process of changing the title of one's (or a couple's) assets from their own name into the name of their living trust. I can't tell you how many times I've visited with clients who want their living trust updated, only to find that the original trust was never even funded.

Simply stated, if a living trust is not funded it will not operate to keep your estate out of probate. This is true whether an individual drafts their own trust agreement, or if the trust is written by the highest paid attorney in the country. No matter how fancy your trust looks, how well it is drafted, or how much you paid to have it drafted, if your trust isn't funded, it isn't worth the paper it's printed on.

Don't fall into the trap of presuming that whoever drafted your trust also handled the funding. It's highly likely that they included funding instructions in the document that they provided so that you can take care of this part of the process yourself. Regardless of how you take care of it, make sure that it gets handled.

STRATEGY 284: *Distinguish titled assets from non-titled assets and take the appropriate steps for funding your trust.*

There are entire books written on proper funding of living trusts, but for our purposes, I've simplified the process to give you a basic understanding of what needs to be done. In terms of funding, there are basically two types of assets: those that have some sort of "document of ownership," as I call them, and those which do not. An example of an asset which has a document showing ownership is a house, which of course has a deed. By contrast, an example of assets which do not have any sort of document would be your jewelry, china collection, or other personal items. Let's talk about this second category of assets first.

In order to fund your ordinary personal property such as furniture, clothing, dishes, etc., there are two steps. First, you will want to execute (draft and sign) a document known as an "Assignment of Personal Property." If you are doing your trust yourself, you probably have a copy of this document in whatever book you are using, but if not you can find one on the internet. This assignment transfers ownership to your living trust of all of your personal property which does not have any sort of document reflecting ownership.

Secondly, at the end of your trust agreement there is (or should be) a document called "Exhibit A" or "Schedule A." On this document you want to list, as best as possible, all of your personal property which you are transferring into your living trust. In addition to funding your trust, this document also helps your trustee to identify your property after you have passed away. When listing your personal property on Schedule A, you do not necessarily have to list out each individual item. For example, instead of listing every cup or dish in your kitchen it is sufficient to simply list "dishes."

Next, let's discuss how to fund assets which do have some sort of document of ownership into your trust. Again, you're going to need to list each asset on Schedule A, and this time you're going to need to be as specific as possible. If you are listing a piece of real property,

344

you should give the full address of the property and, if possible, the legal description of the property as well. For a vehicle, state the make and model, year, and VIN. For bank accounts, retirement accounts, brokerage accounts, etc., list the name of the account, the location of the account, and the account number.

After listing all of these types of assets on Schedule A, you next need to formally change the document of ownership. If this is a house, you are going to need to execute a *Quitclaim Deed* to transfer ownership out of your name into the name of the living trust. For a car, on the back of the title you will need to assign ownership of the vehicle into your living trust. When it comes to accounts, contact your bank, plan administrator, broker, or other individual to obtain whatever forms are needed to transfer ownership of the account to your living trust. Taking the time to handle these matters will be well worth the effort.

STRATEGY 285: *Execute a properly drafted revocable living trust in order to avoid, or at least reduce, the estate tax.*

The second major benefit to a living trust is that it can allow for the avoidance or reduction of any potential estate taxes. This benefit is only available for married couples who set up a living trust. Unmarried persons are unable to capitalize on this potential benefit. The reason for this lies in the marital deduction which allows married couples to leave an unlimited amount of property to their spouse when they pass away without any estate taxes being owed. This applies only when the surviving spouse is a U.S. citizen.

The challenge with the marital deduction, however, is that now the entire estates of two people are now combined to form one larger estate which is owned by one person. When the surviving spouse passes away, he or she is likely going to be hit with the estate tax. Since the separate estates of two people have been combined to form one larger estate, the odds that the surviving spouse's estate is going to owe federal estate taxes is much greater. Let's go back to my earlier example of a $3 million dollar estate, but this time let's pretend that the estate belongs to a married couple. Each spouse owns $1.5 million of the marital estate. As we know, $1.5 million is less than the $2 million dollar threshold for the estate tax. However, as is usually the case, whenever one spouse dies the other spouse automatically inherits the deceased spouse's assets, and as we've learned, this is tax-free no matter what the amount. Now, the surviving spouse has a $3 million dollar estate, and when he or she passes away, their estate is now going to be hit with a $450,000 federal estate tax, which in this case would amount to a substantial portion of the couple's total assets.

STRATEGY 286: Utilize a marital trust to double your potential estate tax exemption amount.

One great way to minimize the potential impact of the estate tax is to utilize a marital trust. This is where the living trust comes into play to help avoid, or at least lower, the amount of estate taxes owed. The benefit comes from the fact that Congress has allowed for living trusts, at the death of the first spouse to die, to be divided into two, and sometimes three, separate smaller trusts. Instead of one large trust, which is surely to be over the estate tax threshold, married couples are allowed to split the overall estate into smaller parcels (held in separate trusts) so that each of these will be below the estate tax threshold.

For married couples whose total assets fall under $4 million (twice the current estate tax threshold as of 2008), their living trust agreement should contain specific language called an "A-B clause." The way this works is simple. At the time of the death of the first spouse, the couple's total assets are split into two smaller and equal trusts. The surviving spouse's share of the assets would go into a revocable "A Trust" while the deceased spouse's share goes into an irrevocable "B Trust." No estate taxes are paid at the time of the first spouse's death. When the second spouse dies, both the A and B trusts are calculated individually for estate tax purposes.

Let's look at how our A-B clause would help eliminate the estate tax in the case of a $3 million marital estate. We'll presume the same facts as above. However, with a trust containing an A-B clause, the joint marital estate would be divided into two separate $1.5 million dollar trusts when the first spouse dies. When the second spouse dies, each separate trust is below the estate tax threshold, thus no estate taxes are owed. The assets in both trusts are distributed to the beneficiaries of the couple in the same manner as if there were only one trust, but they are able to provide their beneficiaries with $450,000 which otherwise would be lost to estate taxes. This A-B trust is something that all married couples absolutely must consider.

STRATEGY 287: Insert a QTIP provision in your living trust if your marital estate is over four million dollars and in situations where one spouse does not intend to leave all of his or her estate to their spouse.

For estates over $4 million (or twice the current estate tax threshold), their trust should contain a clause called a "QTIP Provision," which is also referred to as an "A-B-C clause." As you might guess, with an A-B-C clause the total marital estate can be divided into a third trust at the time of the death of the first spouse. This third trust will contain the difference between the deceased spouse's half of the total marital estate and the federal estate tax exemption (currently $2 million). It's important to note that this trust is irrevocable. Some experts say that this third trust is unnecessary because it will not offer any additional estate tax savings from what is offered by the A-B clause. This is true. However, this third trust is beneficial in many instances because it provides further protection from the creditors of the living spouse and it helps insure that all of the deceased spouse's share of the marital estate will go to his or her beneficiaries in case the living spouse remarries. This is something that is very important to many of our clients and is something that you will certainly want to consider as well.

STRATEGY 288: Use a charitable remainder trust to get an immediate tax deduction and lower your estate taxes in the future.

Charitable remainder trusts are fast becoming a common tool for individuals with large amounts of wealth. A charitable remainder trust, or CRT, is irrevocable and serves three main purposes:

1. Benefit a charity of your choice.
2. Receive a current year tax deduction.
3. Provide an income stream for you and your spouse for life.

Individuals with large amounts of wealth often realize that they and their children and grandchildren have been sufficiently provided for in terms of lifetime wealth. In searching for potential tax deductions, they come to realize that a large amount of tax dollars can be saved by setting up a CRT. Here's how it works.

First, you donate property (real estate, stocks, bonds, investments, cash, etc.) to a charity through the use of the CRT. The charity will not receive the full benefit of the donated property until some future time, usually when you and your spouse pass away. You, being the tax savvy person that you are, receive an income tax deduction in the year of the donation equal to the fair market value of the transferred property at the time of the donation. Under this format, you and your spouse maintain an income interest in the CRT. This means the income generated by the assets in the trust will be paid to you and your spouse until you die. The amount of your income tax deduction would be reduced by the present value of the income interest retained by you and your spouse. When you and your spouse pass away, the charity would then receive the full benefits generated by the trust assets. This provides you with a great way to benefit a charity while getting some great benefits for yourself.

STRATEGY 289: *Lower your taxable estate by using an irrevocable life insurance trust.*

If you have a great deal of life insurance, you may want to establish an irrevocable life insurance trust (ILIT). The ILIT is established to be the owner of a life insurance policy so that estate taxes are avoided by keeping the payout from the life insurance policy out of the decedents' estate. This may not seem that important, but consider that you may have small life insurance policies from several, often forgotten sources, such as at work, in private policies, through your mortgage, through clubs or memberships in certain associations, etc. It may be a good idea to put the larger one or ones into an ILIT as the smaller ones can quickly add up and could push you over the estate tax exclusion.

ILITs are not overly complex but they must be done properly to avoid any estate tax issues. Seek assistance in establishing and maintaining an ILIT with a reputable professional or firm. If an ILIT is improperly established or maintained, the life insurance policy payout could be revoked or, most likely, included in the decedent's estate and therefore subject to taxes if it sends your estate over the current estate tax exclusion.

STRATEGY 290: *Execute a spendthrift trust to provide for a child who is young, disabled, or irresponsible.*

A spendthrift trust is one of the more popular types of trusts used because of its estate planning and asset protection benefits. Spendthrift trusts are used to protect the interests of trust beneficiaries. A spendthrift trust is called that because it contains a spendthrift provision in the trust document which states that the trust is intended to provide for the health, education and support of the trust beneficiaries. A typical spendthrift provision results in no creditors of the beneficiary being able to attach the beneficiaries' interests in the trust. However, once income is paid to the beneficiary, this now becomes a personal asset of the beneficiary and can be attached by creditors. Spendthrift trusts are commonly set up to provide for the care of beneficiaries who are minors, incompetent, or just plain irresponsible.

When it comes to estate planning, the bottom line is to put a plan in place. As you should know by now, everyone has an estate. Implementing a proper plan for the distribution of your estate can ensure that your family receives what you intend for them to receive without losing it all through unnecessary expenses.

Chapter 20

Protecting Your Wealth
by Protecting Your Health

*Protect your health. Without it you face a serious
handicap for success and happiness.*

Harry F. Banks

When it comes to preserving wealth, our primary objective is to put measures in place that will enable us to keep as much of the money that we've created and accumulated as possible. Part of that process involves identifying the areas and costs that have the capacity to take a large portion of our wealth. One of those areas is health care costs.

So far, we've looked at a number of threats to your wealth and explored strategies for what you can do to preserve your hard-earned assets. With some of these issues, you may have already been aware of the threats such as those posed by lawsuits and taxes. In this chapter, we're going to be discussing an issue that you've probably never thought about as being a threat to your wealth, health care.

---

*STRATEGY 291: Recognize the impact that a serious
health problem could pose to the financial security of
you and your family.*

Previously, we discussed the concept of the "catastrophic lawsuit" and
how one lawsuit can literally wipe out your entire accumulated wealth
to that point along with your ability to earn future wealth. Without a
proper health care strategy to prevent or pay for a catastrophic illness
or injury, your entire wealth could be wiped out just as easily. A
catastrophic illness or injury is any type of illness or injury which has
an enormous physical, social, and/or financial effect on an individual
and their family. In most instances, a catastrophic illness or injury
comes without warning. The management of such an illness or injury
is complex and requires the expertise of a team of health professionals
including physicians, consultants, nurses, therapists, counselors,
and others. A catastrophic illness or injury may come in the form
of a short-term emergency or it could be the beginning of a chronic
long-term condition. Not only is the immense cost of such injuries
potentially catastrophic, but the result of not being able to work can be
devastating as well.

---

*STRATEGY 292: Get a handle on health care costs to
best determine your most cost effective option.*

To truly comprehend the magnitude of the health care crisis, consider
these startling statistics about the cost of health care in the United
States. According to some reports, more than 16% of Americans are
without any kind of health care coverage. In 2002, 23% percent of
U.S. families (18 million households) had high out-of-pocket health
care costs relative to their income. To better understand this statistic,
"high" was defined as 10 percent or more of household income for all
families and 5 percent or more of income for low-income families.
Even worse, things are projected to get much tougher in the coming
years. In the next decade, health care will account for one out of every
five dollars spent in the U.S. Out-of-pocket expenses for health care

352

are expected to rise 5.3% annually, while the costs of health care will increase 6.4%. Clearly, these numbers do not bode well for the future of health care in this country.

Given the high costs of health care both now and in the future, *where* individuals look for their health care coverage is vitally important. Today, approximately 84% of citizens have some form of health insurance. Sixty percent of those persons receive health insurance from their employer. Nine percent of those persons buy individual health insurance policies while twenty-seven percent of those receive insurance through one or more government programs. As noted above, sixteen percent of Americans have no form of health insurance whatsoever, and this figure is expected to increase in the future.

In light of this, with the future of health care and our ability to pay for it uncertain, the dangers posed by a catastrophic illness are greater than ever. As a result, this threat to our wealth is greater now than it has ever been and is only expected to grow worse. Accordingly, we all need to have a comprehensive plan for dealing with the potential threat of catastrophic illnesses. In this chapter, we'll discuss strategies for avoiding catastrophic illnesses and how to survive them financially.

STRATEGY 293: Practice living a healthy lifestyle as your first defense against catastrophic illnesses.

As you've probably gathered from your reading up to this point, I've always been a believer in the wisdom found in colloquial phrases. The statement, "an ounce of prevention is worth a pound of cure," could not be more applicable than when it comes to dealing with health issues. For the purposes of our discussion, a better phrase might be "an ounce of prevention could be worth your entire life savings." Simply stated, by living a healthy lifestyle you tremendously decrease your chances of suffering from a catastrophic illness or even injury.

Certainly, there isn't much you can do about your genetic makeup and any history of family illnesses. However, there is quite a bit that you can do to protect your health and your wallet from many types of diseases which are preventable. In fact, you need to be proactive with your health and think of it as something which you can, to a large extent, control. The fact is that many of the deadliest diseases in our country are largely preventable. These are diseases such as heart disease, cancer, diabetes, and obesity. These diseases and other chronic conditions now account for 70 percent of all deaths in the United States. While this may seem overly simplistic, it's no secret that following good practices can help to maintain a healthy condition on into the future.

STRATEGY 294: Envision yourself living a healthy lifestyle and make a choice to be healthy.

I'm not a doctor, but you certainly do not have to be one to know that there are some common-sense ways to improve your health. Preventable diseases can be avoided simply by making some simple lifestyle and behavioral changes over things which we have control. These changes are things like quitting smoking, eating a healthier diet, exercising, etc. If nothing else, these and other changes in your life can help to eliminate many catastrophic illnesses such as heart disease, cancer, and stroke. You can further help to protect your health by getting regular check-ups and screenings and knowing what your risks are based on your age, sex, and family history. These regular check-ups and screenings can help you to detect any abnormalities quickly so that you can receive treatment before things move to an advanced stage.

Of course, living a healthy lifestyle doesn't absolutely guarantee that you will never get sick. If and when you do get sick, you'll need to have a plan to pay for the cost of medical care. The rest of the strategies in this chapter will focus on ways which you can pay for, and thus financially survive, an illness. No matter how wonderful any plan is, the key is to have it in place before you get sick.

STRATEGY 295: Obtain private health insurance to protect yourself and your family from the financial perils of a catastrophic illness or injury.

Because not all diseases are preventable, and because unforeseen accidents can always be around the corner, private health insurance policies are a popular choice for individuals who do not work for a company that offers a group health policy. In terms of protecting your wealth, health insurance has become one of the most needed resources in American society. As we already discussed, health care costs are rapidly increasing and the ability to pay for health care costs out-of-pocket is becoming harder to afford without insurance, especially in the case of a catastrophic injury or illness. This makes having adequate health insurance essential The emergence of health insurance has revolutionized and completely reshaped the way health care is paid for in this country in less than a century. This shift started with private health insurance so we'll take a look at it first.

STRATEGY 296: Buy private health insurance.

Most people don't know how private health insurance works. Like any insurance policy, the purpose of a private health policy is to reduce the risk of loss associated with the occurrence of certain events, namely sickness or injury. This is accomplished by shifting the financial risk from you to insurance companies. The structure and payment system of insurance companies is based on the probability of these events occurring.

Because most individuals would not be able to pay for the total cost of medical services on their own, insurance allows them to pay a small fraction of the amount of the presumed risk with the thought that if enough people buy into the insurance policy they will have enough capital to bear the cost of the risk in the event of that sickness or injury actually occurring. This works on the principle of the law of large numbers, assuming that the probability is small enough that only a fraction of the total number of policyholders would get sick or injured. Since all policyholders are invested in the plan, there would be enough money to cover the small amount of individuals within the plan who do become ill. The premiums paid to the insurance company would then provide reserves for actual claims of illness. Through this structure, private insurance can be a great strategy for protecting yourself.

Of course, not everyone can qualify for a private insurance plan. Companies which offer private health insurance can pick and choose who they want to insure based on a person's medical history. In fact, they can be amazingly selective. The premiums for private health insurance as well as the co-pays and deductibles are typically going to be higher than what one would pay out-of-pocket if they had a group plan through their employer. Private health insurance companies can also choose not to insure a pre-existing condition. Still, for those who qualify and can afford it, private health insurance policies can be a great source of protection from catastrophic illnesses and injuries.

STRATEGY 297: *Take advantage of a group health policy if offered by your employer.*

By far, the most popular choice of health coverage is through group health insurance policies offered through one's employer. Group health insurance coverage is a policy that is purchased by an employer and is offered to eligible employees of the company (and often to the employees' family members) as a benefit of working for that company. For those who work for such employers, a group health policy is probably one of the most affordable health care plans and to qualify is generally fairly easy.

Depending on the size of the employer who has obtained the group policy, the premiums paid by the individual are often higher than what they would pay for private health insurance premiums. Despite this fact, the benefits of having a group health insurance policy are numerous. Perhaps the biggest benefit is that federal law mandates that no matter what pre-existing health conditions small employer group members may have, no small employer or an individual employee can be turned down by an insurance company for group coverage. This requirement is known in the insurance industry as "guaranteed issue." Additionally, the insurance company must renew the employer's group policy every year, at the employer's discretion, unless there is non-payment of premium, the employer has committed fraud or intentional misrepresentation, or the employer has not complied with the terms of the health insurance contract.

STRATEGY 298: Learn the difference between an HMO, a PPO, and a POS health care plan.

The least expensive, but also the least flexible plans, are health maintenance organizations (HMOs), which require employees to choose a primary care physician from an approved provider list. An HMO is a health care organization created in an effort to lower health care costs for you and whomever is helping you pay for your health care, such as an employer or the government. If you join an HMO, you get to use their services at a very low cost, much less than if you went to the doctor and paid for these services.

A participating provider organization (PPO) is a managed care organization of medical doctors, hospitals, and other health care providers who have contracted with an insurer or a third-party administrator to provide health care at reduced rates to the insurer's or administrator's clients. The idea of a PPO is that the providers will provide the insured members of the group a substantial discount below their regularly-charged rates. PPOs allow employees to see any doctor, but premiums are higher (as are the deductibles) if the doctor isn't in their network.

Finally, a point-of-service (POS) health care plan is a combination of an HMO and a PPO. With a POS, employees choose a doctor who is in the POS network as their primary care physician. The employee may choose to go out-of-network for their preferred medical provider but will have to pay most of the cost themselves. The exception to this rule is when the employee's in-network primary care physician refers them to that specific doctor. In these instances, the health plan will then pick up the tab.

STRATEGY 299: Find out how the various health plans are administered to make the best choice for your individual needs.

The rules for how group health insurance plans are administered vary greatly. Group health insurance guidelines are regulated at the state level, meaning that different laws apply in different states. The laws about how coverage can be issued to large groups are different than those for small groups, and the way that premium rates are determined is also different. Small group policies are generally offered to businesses with fifty or fewer employees and large group policies are for businesses with more employees.

With small groups, federal law mandates that no matter what pre-existing health conditions that small employer group members may have, no small employer or an individual employee can be turned down by an insurance company for group coverage. Additionally, insurance companies which offer group plans to small groups must renew the policy annually, regardless of how many claims are filed by the insured employees. There are exceptions to this where there is non-payment of premium, the employer has committed fraud or intentional misrepresentation, or the employer has not complied with the terms of the health insurance contract. While these are tremendous benefits, there are a few drawbacks to small group policies.

In most states, while employees with pre-existing conditions cannot be turned down for coverage, the insurance company is allowed to look back at an employee's medical history and may decline to cover certain conditions for a specified period of time. This is called the exclusionary, or a pre-existing condition, waiting period. Federal law states that small group health insurance companies may impose no more than a six-month look-back/12-month exclusionary period for pre-existing conditions, but individual states can reduce these time periods. The law also requires health insurance companies to give employees credit against any exclusionary period for pre-existing conditions if they have had prior health insurance coverage within 63 days of obtaining the group coverage from the large employer.

In comparison to smaller group plans, there are some differences when it comes to large group health insurance contracts. Unlike small group contracts, large groups do not have to be offered on a guaranteed-issue basis, so a health insurance company could reject an entire large employer group based on its claim history. Notwithstanding, if an employer has a policy, the insurance company is not able to decline coverage for an individual employee based on his or her medical history. In other words, if a company issues a policy to a large employer, then all of its eligible employees must be issued coverage. The law also requires health insurance companies to give employees credit against any exclusionary period for pre-existing conditions if they have had prior health insurance coverage within 63 days of obtaining the group coverage from the large employer.

STRATEGY 300: Take advantage of federal and state health care programs.

While private health insurance can be beneficial, there are many people who do not qualify for or cannot afford private health insurance. If you are in this category, you should certainly consider applying for one or more of the many government and state-sponsored health care plans. Between the federal and state, there are numerous options available. The Federal government offers Medicare, CHAMPUS (for active military service members), Social Security Disability, and medical care for veterans is offered by the Veteran's Administration (VA). Additionally, Medicaid, which is funded jointly by the federal and state governments, is available for those who qualify. In terms of state-sponsored health care programs, every state offers some sort of workers' compensation insurance as well as a state disability program. There are also dozens of different state-specific plans which provide medical care to children living in the state. For more information on how to qualify for any of these government programs, contact your state's Department of Health or the various federal agencies which offer such programs.

STRATEGY 301: Investigate whether any of the organizations and groups that you belong to offer any health care plans or medical fee discounts.

In many instances, private, civic, fraternal organizations and social clubs may be your best bet for preserving your wealth by addressing holes in your health care strategies. For instance, if you are a member of the AARP (American Association of Retired Persons), they offer a program called "AARP Health Care Options" which offers access to heath insurance, special savings services, and health information. Additionally, many organizations and clubs which do not offer their members health insurance still offer supplemental insurance. This is a type of insurance which can help pay your bills if you are faced with a catastrophic illness and are no longer able to work. Lastly, these organizations and clubs may offer discount cards which can help you save money on prescriptions and eyeglasses. While not technically "insurance," such discount cards can provide some substantial savings on everyday out-of-pocket health care costs. The key to this strategy is to look into things that you already have in place to see if there are benefits included that you may not know about.

STRATEGY 302: Open a health savings account to give yourself a tax deduction on medical expenses, access to lower medical rates, and high deductible insurance coverage.

In the last ten years, one of the most popular alternatives for traditional health care insurance has been Health Savings Accounts (HSAs). HSAs enable you to pay for current health expenses and save for future qualified medical and retiree health expenses on a tax-free basis. With an HSA, you deposit money into a savings account which is then used to pay for any out-of-pocket medical expenses. The money deposited into your account, as well as the earnings, is tax-deferred. The money can then be withdrawn to cover qualified medical expenses tax-free. On top of this, any unused balances roll over from year to year.

360

To qualify for an HSA account, you must be covered by a High Deductible Health Plan (HDHP). For 2008, a HDHP is a health plan with a minimum deductible of $1,100 for self-only coverage and $2,200 for family coverage. The maximum out-of-pocket expenses for allowed costs must be no more than $5,600 for self-only coverage and no more than $11,200 for family. An HDHP generally costs less than what traditional health care coverage costs, so the money that you save on insurance can be put into the HSA. Another great benefit of HSAs is that you own and control the money in your account. How you spend the money in the account is solely at your discretion without interference from any third-party medical providers. You will also decide what types of investments to make with the money in the account in order to make it grow.

Once you have established an HDHP and opened up your HSA, you can then start to deposit money into your account. Single Americans can deposit up to $2,900 annually into their HAS while families can deposit up to $5,800. These savings limits are even higher for older Americans. After making your deposits, you can then use the money in your account to pay for low cost medical expenses or any expenses which are not covered by your HDHP such as cosmetic surgery. After you have met your deductible, the HDHP would then cover all medical expenses so long as they are covered by the policy.

STRATEGY 303: Consider picking up a supplemental insurance policy to protect you from costs not covered by other health care plans or insurance.

Another option that has grown in popularity over the last decade or so is the concept of supplemental insurance. Supplemental insurance policies do not cover ordinary medical expenses, rather, they pick up where traditional insurance policies leave off by paying money directly to the insured. This money can then be used to help pay for ordinary non-medical expenses which the insured can no longer pay for as a result of his or her illness.

STRATEGY 304: *Steer clear of so-called "insurance" services offered by credit card companies which offer to "pay your credit card bill" if you become sick or otherwise disabled.*

A lot of credit card companies offer plans which they call "payment insurance" which purportedly will pay your credit card bill should you become sick or otherwise disabled. These types of "insurance" should be avoided. First, they are not actually "insurance" but usually just delay your payments while you are unable to make them. Secondly, they are not cost-effective. For the same amount of money you can purchase true supplemental insurance which will help you pay all of your bills, rather than just the bill for the credit card company who offers the policy.

STRATEGY 305: *Use supplemental insurance instead of coverage offered through credit cards and other non-insurance company structures.*

There are basically three types of real supplemental insurance policies. The first and most popular is the accident policy. In the event of an accident or death, the policy pays money directly to you or your beneficiaries. Note, however, that only accidents which are specified by the policy are covered. With some policies, accidents resulting from inherently dangerous activities such as lion taming or skydiving would not be covered. Also, the amount of payment usually correlates to the seriousness of the injury.

The second type of supplemental insurance is the hospital indemnity policy. As the name implies, these types of policy pay money to the insured in the event that he or she is hospitalized. Payments with these policies can be made in lump sum or weekly amounts. The third type of supplemental insurance is disease/condition specific policies. These types of policies pay cash to the insured in the event that he or she develops a specific disease such as cancer. In some instances, these policies will pay directly for medical costs as well. These types of policies may be beneficial to individuals with a long family history of certain diseases.

STRATEGY 306: Build your small business by non-traditional means of providing for the health care of your employees.

If you are a small business owner, providing health care for your employees, however you can afford to do so, will benefit your business. With proper health care, your employees will have fewer sick days and will return to work sooner when they are sick. With large corporations, it is easy to negotiate with insurance companies and get excellent health care coverage in return for lower premiums. Yet for small companies, obtaining health insurance for their employees and their families is often a difficult task. On the one hand, obtaining favorable health care benefits is a great way to attract high quality employees which can help the business grow. On the other hand, the costs of such benefits for small businesses can put quite a strain on their budgets.

STRATEGY 307: Have employees purchase private health care policies and reimburse them a portion of the cost of the premiums.

One great health care strategy for small businesses with 5 or fewer employees is to encourage them to purchase private policies and offering to pay for half of their premiums. Another strategy which small businesses can use when searching for the most economical way to provide health care to its employees is to go through a health insurance broker. In some states, you are actually required by state law to use a broker. Even if you are not required to do so, it may be beneficial to use a broker. Brokers are very familiar with the various plans available and can quickly determine which plans fit the needs and budgets of small businesses.

Another great option for small businesses is to offer HSA accounts to their employees. With small business HSA accounts, the business will usually match whatever contributions are made by the employee. This provides a tax benefit to both the business and the employee, and in many cases is cheaper than providing a traditional health insurance policy.

Finally, if you are the owner of a small business you should check with your state's Health Department to find out if they offer any subsidized health insurance programs for small businesses. Many states offer such programs and they are a great way for you to attract quality employees until your business has grown enough to afford a more traditional health care plan.

Having a proper health care strategy is extremely important in preserving your wealth. If you are just starting out in your plans to accumulate wealth, you still should not underestimate the need for such a plan. If you or your family are sick, you can't work. And if you cannot work, you cannot earn income or start to accumulate wealth. Perhaps even more importantly, being healthy can give you quality of life to enjoy whatever financial status you have achieved.

Part VI:

EXECUTE

CHAPTER 21

IMPLEMENTING YOUR ARTIFICIAL WEALTH TRAP E.S.C.A.P.E. PLAN

Pleasure and pain are the only springs of action in man, and always will be.

Claude-Adrien Helvetius

In many ways, this Part of the book is probably the most important. I know that some of you may remember that I've already said that when referring to the ENVISION Part. There, I mentioned that the adoption of the proper mindset was critical in achieving any sort of long-lasting meaningful wealth. That is certainly the case and as you will learn in this Part of the book, that mindset is critical here as well.

What I hope that you have learned over the course of your reading this book to this point is that there are certain strategies that can enable you to build whatever level of wealth that you set for yourself. In spite of the effectiveness of these strategies, not everyone who reads this book will find themselves experiencing financial freedom. The reason for this has nothing to do with the effectiveness of the strategies. The truth is that quite often I find that the strategies work but the people don't.

This statement probably sounds rather harsh but it's true. Most people are simply unwilling to do what it takes to ever become wealthy. They talk about how badly they want to make a change but they never take the time to formulate or stick with a plan for doing so. This chapter is designed to help you to do what it takes to make your financial life

367

better. The key to doing that is to take action. You see, the reason that I say that this is arguably the most important Part of the book is that without action nothing happens.

The strategies that we've covered throughout this book are time-tested and proven. They work and they work extraordinarily well. Unfortunately, most people never truly see how effective these strategies can be in their lives out of a failure to implement them. This chapter will make sure that you don't fall into this trap the way that you may have fallen into the "Artificial Wealth Trap". If you are one of the ones who is facing the challenge of following through with the implementation of your plan or struggling with your commitment or "stick-to-it-iveness," you're not alone.

As you may recall from the Preface where I gave you a little background about myself and my story, years ago I found myself dealing with severe financial challenges. Perhaps the worst part of those challenges was that they occurred after I'd experienced some tremendous success in following many of the strategies contained in this book. I mentioned this then and I'll mention it again right now, what I found was that my difficulties did not result from the strategies not working but from my not working the strategies.

Just like the majority of other people out there who continually deal with the frustration that accompanies financial challenges, I felt the pain. The pain came not only from the money challenges but also from the realization that I had broken a vow to stick to my plan. The guilt and embarrassment associated with this failure was quite painful. Through this pain, however, I found the motivation to get myself back on track and to build things back stronger than they were before. At the time, the pain was something that I hated. I've since learned to embrace that feeling and use it to my advantage. The best part about this is that it is something that you can do as well.

STRATEGY 308: Learn the pleasure vs. pain
motivational continuum and use it to drive you to
achieve your goals.

One of the guiding principles in my life, and one that I've observed quite often in my assessment of others and their motivation for doing things, is the principle of pleasure versus pain as the primary motivating force in determining our actions. Broken down to its core, the principle goes something like this:

People will take action for two reasons and, for the most past, two reasons only. They will act either to receive the pleasure that the action will provide or to avoid the pain that comes from not performing the action.

I learned this concept several years ago and it has become something that I find myself agreeing with more and more all the time. Chances are, you've seen this in your own life if you truly think about it. The example that I use most often in explaining the principle deals with physical fitness. By physical fitness, I mean someone's weight or body condition. The reason that I use this particular example is that it is the one that applies to the most people.

It seems like I talk with people every single day who tell me that they are either on a diet or involved in some sort of exercise program in an effort to adjust their physical fitness level. Basically, they find themselves at a point where they are not content with their current circumstances and want to make some sort of change. They tell me that they want to accomplish the goals that they've set for themselves but continually find themselves unable to stick to a program for making their dreams a reality. Because they know that I spend most of my time helping people to achieve their goals, many of these people will ask me how to go about doing it.

The first thing that I do is to ask them a few questions about why they want what they're working toward. I've grown to be accustomed to hearing responses that are what I would call "vague and ambiguous." Basically, most of the people that I talk with are not truly committed to their plan. I tell these people that the only way that they will accomplish their plan is to turn up the volume on the pleasure and/or pain switches in their life.

STRATEGY 309: *Turn up the volume on your pleasure and/or pain control levels.*

If you're not sure what I mean by "turning up the volume," you're not alone. Most people look at me as if I'm speaking a foreign language when I give them this advice. What I mean by "turning up the volume" is that their motivating forces are currently not great enough to warrant the action necessary to make things happen for them. Unless the pain of their current situation is high enough to cause them to get out of it or the pleasure of getting to their desired point is increased to a high enough level to make them go for it, nothing will happen. This is where most people find themselves.

It's really quite simple. Keeping with our physical fitness analogy, I'll use myself as an example. I am a fairly fit person who is not what anyone would consider overweight but I can assure you that I'm not going to get a call to be on the cover of *Men's Health* magazine anytime soon either. Like anyone else, I find myself thinking every now and then about what it might be like to have the type of body that might get those magazines calling. What I've come to realize is that the volume is not high enough on my "Pleasure" or "Pain" controls to get me to put forth the necessary effort to get to that point. The process that I go through is similar to the one that many people go through, only they don't realize that they're going through it. Here's how it works.

In determining what I'm willing to do, I always ask myself, "what will I gain if I do this?" and "what will I lose if I don't do this?" It's as simple as that. If the answers are not great enough to spur me into action, nothing happens. It's the same way with everyone else.

For me personally, I don't see enough potential upside of having the "buff" body to go through the steps that it would take to get there. On the flipside, there's not enough downside of staying in my current position to motivate me to do what it takes to get out of it. That's the way it works.

If you find yourself in a similar position when it comes to your finances, you need to "turn up the volume levels." You see, I honestly believe that everyone has within them the willpower and discipline to do whatever it is that they truly set their minds to accomplishing. The reason that more people don't accomplish what they set out to accomplish is because they don't truly want it. This may sound harsh but I believe it's true. With rare exceptions, this is the way it is.

STRATEGY 310: Use pleasure or pain to find the courage to act.

Years ago, I remember listening to an outstanding cassette tape by Earl Nightingale. In it, he referred to an award-winning playwright named Archibald McLeish who wrote a play entitled, "The Secret of Happiness." According to Mr. Nightingale, in the play was a quote that made a great impact on his life and has since made a great impact on my life as well. The quote was, *"The secret of happiness is freedom. And the secret to freedom is courage."* If we can muster up the courage to act, we can have just about anything we want in life.

One of my favorite qualities in people is courage. A lot of people don't really understand the whole concept of courage. You may find it surprising to learn that a lot of people who would be considered "heroes" often times don't necessarily have a lot of courage. Let's look at an example. The other day on the news there was a story about a man who was walking down the street and encountered a burning apartment complex. The fire department had not yet arrived and in front of the building was a lady in a wheelchair who was crying for help. It seemed that her elderly sister was still in the apartment, which was quickly filling up with smoke. Without even a moment's hesitation, this man ran inside the apartment and appeared a few seconds later with the elderly sister on his arm.

When the television news trucks arrived, the reporters labeled the man a "hero," and rightly so. One reporter asked him how he had the courage to run into a burning building. The man answered, almost in an embarrassed manner, that he just acted on impulse and that he hadn't really thought about the consequences of his decision until after he had saved the elderly sister. You see, acting on impulse may make someone a hero, but it doesn't necessarily equate to courage. *Courage is about knowing the risks of taking action but taking that action anyway because of the desired results.*

Fortunately for you, in order to escape the "Artificial Wealth Trap" you will not have to run into any burning buildings. What you will need, however, is the courage to act. Whenever I lecture on the topic of taxes I often times find that the reason my audience has always paid more than they should is because of fear, and this fear prevents them from taking action to lower their tax bill. Think about all of the other ways that fear can keep one stuck in the trap: People are afraid to start their own business. People are afraid to get involved in real estate. People are afraid to call their credit card company to work out payment arrangements.

Being afraid may have kept you in the "Artificial Wealth Trap" up to this point, but not anymore, because you do have courage. How? Remember, courage is the ability to act. Your desire to escape the trap and the financial woes you may have been suffering can motivate you. The promises of financial freedom and a better life for your family can motivate you as well. In other words, pain and pleasure can motivate you to act. That motivation is courage.

STRATEGY 311: Overcome setbacks with the "brilliance of resilience."

Along with the courage to act, one of the traits most common in all achievers is resilience. Resilience is more than just never giving up. A lot of people think that resilience means to try something over and over again, the same way each time, and hoping each time that their efforts will lead to different results. That is not resilience, that's insanity. People who follow insanity will fail. People who have true resilience, on the other hand, will flourish.

Instead of doing the same thing over and over again and expecting different results (remember, that's insanity), resilience is always having the same goal but trying different methods until that goal is achieved. In other words, you don't do the same thing and hope for a different result, you focus on one result and achieve it by trying different strategies.

Resilience and using it to E.S.C.A.P.E. from the "Artificial Wealth Trap" involves the realization of two things. First, you are going to have setbacks in achieving your goal of financial freedom. As much as it pains me to tell you this, odds are that you are not going to make a million dollars the first time you start a new business. In fact, you may fail. But if you have resilience, you can recognize where your business plan went wrong and correct those mistakes with your next endeavor.

The second realization that is critical in your resilience if you hope to escape the trap is the knowledge that all things are temporary. What I mean by this is that you should not be complacent "with the devil you know." In other words, things are going to change as you progress along your path to financial freedom. Your job may change, you may have to learn a new skill, or you may even move to a new city. People with resilience are able to handle bends and turns in the road of life. Never being too comfortable with any arrangement, and the realization that change, even good change, can be difficult but bearable, is the hallmark of resilience.

STRATEGY 312: *Avoid the urgency trap by assessing tasks as they emerge.*

To me, one of the greatest impediments in following any strategy is a sense of urgency. Urgency can sometimes be a good thing as it can lead you to action, but all too often urgency can lead to stress, unhappiness, a loss of what is important, a lack of clarity, and ultimately, a sense of failure. Too many times, people become lost in a wilderness of inaction, and mis-action, thanks to urgency and because they confuse urgency with priority. Having priority in following your strategies will lead you safely out of the "Artificial Wealth Trap." Acting out of urgency, on the other hand, will tie you down in a financial quagmire.

Discerning the difference between what is a priority versus what is urgent will be a critical skill that you'll need to develop in order to correctly apply the strategies in this book. By having a true sense of priority, you'll be able to accomplish tasks by working your schedule instead of letting tasks become your schedule.

In developing this sense of priority, you should take the following steps each morning before you take any action:

1. Write a list of the tasks you most want to accomplish.

2. Order these tasks by level of importance, difficulty, and the amount of time needed to accomplish them.

3. Think about how you want your day to progress.

4. Consider how your list of tasks may mesh, or conflict, with others whom you need to work with to finish your tasks.

5. Decide what you will do to provide yourself with respites throughout the day.

6. Follow 1 through 5.

STRATEGY 313: Determine your highest and best use and stick primarily to tasks that utilize it.

The result of differentiating what is urgent versus what is a priority will give you the tools to follow this next strategy, which is to determine what is the highest and best use of your time, your tools, and your efforts. With this strategy, we are again learning a skill that involves balancing. In determining your highest and best use, you'll need to develop a sense for balancing resources versus results. In other words, are the results you are achieving economical given the amount of resources you are expending? Always remember that our economic objective is to achieve maximum results with minimal efforts.

Finding out if you are spending the right amount of effort for the right amount of results means being able to put a premium on your resources. In short, you need to decide how your time, your effort, and your resources can best be put to work, and then allow those decisions to maximize the results.

STRATEGY 314: Create a rewards system to provide yourself some incentive.

Throughout every day you should find ways to provide yourself with breaks. This concept of taking breaks is from the more universal strategy of creating a rewards system to provide yourself with incentives. I don't know if you are a dog person, but most dog trainers say that the best reinforcement for positive behavior is a reward. Similarly, in following your E.S.C.A.P.E. Plan from the "Artificial Wealth Trap," rewards are important because they will increase the likelihood of your continuing to work your plans.

Let's look at an example of this by thinking back to our strategies on saving money for retirement. As you may recall, at no time did I tell you to never take your kids on a vacation, eat out at a restaurant, or buy flowers for your wife. What I did tell you, however, was that you could save for retirement without putting yourself in the poorhouse or depriving yourself of all of the joys of life. Just as you plan your retirement and your goals for how to get there, so too should you plan your short-term rewards whenever you achieve those goals. Sure, it will be a great reward when you are able to retire comfortably, but by giving yourself some small rewards along the way you will tremendously increase your chances of getting there.

STRATEGY 315: Map things out and measure your milestones.

In several of the chapters in this book, I've mentioned that becoming proficient in developing a plan can help you in succeeding at certain strategies. If you didn't take my advice before, now is a good time to do so. Like devising a reward system for when you accomplish goals, you should also devise a plan, or better stated, a road map, for rewarding yourself as you reach various milestones, for your journey to financial freedom. A great way to do this is with a spreadsheet, but using a flowchart or any other design that is easy for you to understand is fine too.

Whatever format you use, the goal for your "milestone map" is to allow you to:

1. chart the goals which you must achieve to progress out of the trap,

2. the time it takes you to achieve each goal, and

3. where you are in the process.

By keeping this map accurate, you can take pride in your accomplishments to date and keep your focus on which goals you must achieve next.

STRATEGY 316: *Avoid the trap of trying to do too many things at once by keeping it simple.*

Whenever I'm counseling clients or speaking before large groups, I often find that sometimes the best way to explain things is through sports analogies. Whether it's baseball, basketball, football, or any other sport, sometimes a team will be down by a large margin and start to panic. For example, in basketball the team who is behind may try hoisting up three-point shots one after another in an attempt to make up lost ground. But as is often the case, these teams find themselves falling into a larger and larger deficit. Instead of focusing on one play at a time, they will try to gain back all of their losses with one shot. Of course, there is not a 20-point shot in basketball. Similarly, in your journey out of the "Artificial Wealth Trap," there is no one strategy you can follow to lead you from the poorhouse to the penthouse overnight. The sooner you realize this, the sooner you can begin down the road to financial freedom.

Still, we're all human, and trying to do too much is something we've all been guilty of at one time or another. You may be behind on your bills today. It is only natural to want to do everything you can to rectify your financial situation. However, by trying to do too many things at once, instead of progress you may become overcome with stress, worry, failure, and ultimately, stuck in the same old rut. The way to keep this from happening is to focus on one thing at a time.

STRATEGY 317: Make small changes that can yield big payoffs.

Instead of trying to do too much at one time, you must begin by following one strategy at a time. While you may think that, at such a rate, you'll never get out of your financial mess, I've got some good news for you. What you will find is that if you focus on the small changes you can make in your life, both personal and business, they can be the ones that have the greatest impact. It's been said that 80% of what we accomplish can be achieved in just 20% of our time, and I've certainly found that this is true. The way to make this happen is to focus on one thing at a time, but identify which simple steps can lead to big payoffs.

A great example of this rule can be seen in the chapter on retirement planning. Remember how we said that by eliminating small expenses such as that daily cup of coffee we can begin to build our fortune. Of course, this is possible thanks to the miracle of compounding interest. Yet in order to tap into this power, it only took cutting out one cup of coffee a day. I promise you that as you go about implementing other strategies in this book you will find that small changes in behavior can lead to great shifts in your future.

Over the course of this book, I've laid out for you the E.S.C.A.P.E. plan for getting out of your present financial situation and realizing your dreams of financial freedom. Even with all of these strategies, the reality is that you're not going to find yourself rich beyond your wildest dreams one day, one week, one year, or maybe even one decade after you read this book. Obviously, everyone who reads this book is starting out with a different education, status in life, work history, age, and life experiences, all of which makes our own journey to financial freedom unique. Yet by following the strategies in this book, the following promises will come true in your life:

1. You will enjoy your life;
2. You will take control of your finances;
3. You will thrive in work and play in retirement;
4. You will pass on these lessons to your children; and
5. You will E.S.C.A.P.E. the "Artificial Wealth Trap."

EPILOGUE

*It marks a big step in a man's development when he comes to realize
that other men can be called in to help him do a better job
than he can do alone.*

Andrew Carnegie

This book is about building up your own personal knowledge of how
to best handle your finances. As your knowledge increases, you will
find that your confidence continues to build as well. With your newly
found confidence you will also find yourself eliminating two of the
most common reasons that many people find themselves ill-equipped
to tackle their financial matters. Those two reasons are fear and risk.
Each of these reasons is overcome with knowledge and experience.

It's been said that the School of Hard Knocks is the best teacher in
the world. Unfortunately, it's also the most expensive. Consider
this book as your scholarship for that school where you are able to
get the benefits without having to personally pay the painfully high
tuition. You can begin your journey to wealth by capitalizing on my
experience as well as the experience of all those who I've learned
from as well. Once you begin applying the knowledge you gain from
this book, you will build your own experience without the necessity of
paying that high cost.

We live in a world that offers us some pretty incredible opportunities.
Those opportunities become more available to us as we increase the
amount of our resources. To do this, you've got to position yourself to
get the maximum results. As I learned from a very successful person
years ago, the Constitution guarantees us equality of opportunity, but
no one guarantees equality of results. It's up to you to go out there and
create the world that you want for yourself.

You can build any type of life that you set out to build. Even better,
you can do it no matter what type of economic environment that the
country experiences as a whole. In times of inflation, recession,
economic uncertainty, or worse, there are always those people who

thrive financially. You can be that type of person. The most successful people in life see opportunities where others see only difficulties.

In my life, I've had the opportunity to work with a lot of amazingly successful people. I've also worked with many people who just never made their lives into much of anything. I've had the privilege of seeing people at the starts of their career when they were just beginning the wealth process and I've worked with people as they were winding down their careers and lives in general. Regardless of their circumstances, I've learned some phenomenal lessons from them all. Every one of these people had something to teach me. Some of the lessons that I learned were things that I sought to emulate and employ in my life. Other lessons served as reminders of what to avoid. These people have taught me the good that money can do and also the havoc that it can cause.

The greatest lesson that I've learned in my life is this: *we do indeed become what we think about.* Since we can control what we think about, we can control what we become. This is the message that I have spent my life trying to help people understand.

I've worked with countless people over the years and I hope to continually work with more and more people for the rest of my days. Helping others to realize their dreams is what gives me the greatest happiness in the world. The best part of it all is that it merely requires my sharing the gift of knowledge that I've been given by others who sought to help me. It's a circle of giving that I hope you will continue on in your life as you share it with your friends, family, and those closest to you.

I truly wish you all the happiness and success that this life has to offer. Remember, we're all given the gift of life. It's what we make of it that determines what type of gift that we give back in return. Make the best of yours.

My best for your success-

383

385

CPSIA information can be obtained
at www.ICGtesting.com
Printed in the USA
LVHW010704160620
658144LV00001B/106